942.38   HAWKINS, D   AVALON & SEDGEMOOR

AVALON AND SEDGEMOOR

AVALON AND SEDGEMOOR

Desmond Hawkins

TABB HOUSE

Published by Tabb House Ltd,
7 Church Street,
Padstow,
Cornwall,
PL28 8BG, 1989

First published by David and Charles, 1973
Second edition by Alan Sutton, 1982

Printed by the Short Run Press, Exeter, Devon

CONTENTS

LIST OF ILLUSTRATIONS

Woodcuts *(Clarks Ltd)*

FOREWORD

My interest in the Somerset Levels began in 1946. At that time I had recently joined the BBC's West Region as a producer of radio documentaries and I found an attractive subject in the story of a river which was not shown on the current Ordnance Survey map — the Huntspill river. Exploration of the war-time circumstances in which the river was created introduced me to E.L. Kelting, the Engineer of the Somerset Rivers Board (subsequently incorporated in the Wessex Water Authority). Besides being one of the major architects of the modern Somerset landscape, Louis Kelting was a man of wide ranging and extremely knowledgeable interests in many aspects of the life of the county, and I could not have found a better or kinder mentor. He first kindled my enthusiasm for the peat moors of Avalon and the wide expanse of Sedgemoor.

Other radio programmes followed, particularly on the traditional rural life of Somerset, and through them I came to know another remarkable man, Harold Meade of Athelney. Cider-maker, withy grower, elver catcher, bee-keeper and landlord of the most extraordinary pub I ever entered, Harold epitomised the whole traditional character and folklore of the Sedgemoor countryside. For many hours I sat at his feet and learned the inward nature of the quiet floodlands.

To these two men of Somerset and to many others — farmers, basket-makers, naturalists, cheese-makers, peat-cutters and archaeologists — I owe a debt for teaching me so much about their part of England: a debt that I tried to repay in 1954 when I wrote *Sedgemoor and Avalon*. Now, more than a generation later, I have been taking a fresh look at the radically transformed country that I first knew in its immediately post-war fashion. The alterations are manifold and sometimes startling. Seen in the perspective of over a quarter of a century they emphasise the speed with which English life — particularly rural life — is changing. And yet I have at times been surprised to find how strongly the character of the countryside and its people still comes through the forms and styles of the contemporary world. The feeling of continuity is strong; and to my delight I could still find that tranquility and harmonious stillness which give to the innermost stretches of the moors their special atmosphere.

In this new book I have tried to relate the modern scene to its long and fascinating history. I am again indebted to the many Somerset people who have borne patiently with my questions, shown me their skills and enriched me with their conversation: to name them all individually would be too great an undertaking. But I must record my deep sense of obligation to those on whose specialised knowledge I have been permitted to draw, notably Sir Harry Godwin, FRS, whose extensive study of the prehistoric landscape of the Vale of Avalon is a classic work in its own field; Professor Michael Williams whose outstanding book *The Draining of the Somerset Levels* supersedes everything previously written on the subject; Mr J. Morley of The Nature Conservancy; Mr R. R. Williams and Mr K. G. Stott of the Long Ashton Research Station; Mr J. Stuckey of the Taunton Cider Co; John Burton and Michael Kendall of the BBC Natural History Unit; Mr W.C. George of Edmund Taylor (Teazle) Ltd of Huddersfield and Mr Alfred Male of Fivehead; Mr Roland Duckett of Wedmore; Mr Vernon Smart of C. & J. Clark Ltd; Mr Geoffrey Rowson of Showerings Ltd; the librarians at the University of Southampton, the BBC at Bristol, and the Dorset County Service at Dorchester and Verwood; Mr Leonard Gill, the Fisheries Officer of the Somerset River Authority; and the authors whose books, on many aspects of Somerset life, are listed in the bibliography.

I am obliged to Basil Blackwell & Mott Ltd for some lines from John Philips's poem, *Cyder*; and to Pitkin Pictorials Ltd for permission to quote from Dr Ralegh Radford's *Glastonbury Abbey*. I also acknowledge the consent of Routledge & Kegan Paul Ltd to my reprinting some lines by William Diaper.

My grateful thanks are due to the photographers whose studies of the moorland scene help the reader to sense the atmosphere of Avalon and Sedgemoor more fully and clearly than my struggling words can convey. Their contributions are detailed in full in the list of illustrations.

And finally I must record my gratitude to Teresa Donovan for the care and skill with which she typed and retyped my manuscript in its various stages.

D.H.

'Tours of this kind, tho' but moderately written,
if taken thro' a considerable tract of country,
must contain sufficient matter of instruction
and amusement, to exercise the powers of the
mind, by the most pleasing exertions.'

S. Shaw: *A Tour to the West of England in 1788*

To my children
who discovered Avalon and Sedgemoor with me,
and who will always – I hope – find pleasure
in exploring their own country.

CHAPTER ONE

LANDSCAPE AND CHARACTER

Very few English counties can show so wide a variety of scene as Somerset. The area around Midsomer Norton and Radstock, stamped indelibly with the characteristics of its coal-mining history, is a far cry from the wild uplands of Exmoor: and between these two extremes lie the Quantocks and the hills of Mendip, the central moors and marshes of Avalon and Sedgemoor, the narrow graceful range of the Poldens, the rich farmland of Taunton Dene, and the Brendon Hills. The northern boundary is the low coastline of the Bristol Channel. Southwards a broken hilly landscape builds up to the downs of the Dorset border. Every few miles the scenery changes its character and offers fresh attractions.

With such prodigality it is perhaps understandable that some parts of the county should be overlooked or undervalued. Nine people out of ten have customarily made their first and probably their last acquaintance with the Somerset Levels by journeying along the road from Bristol to Bridgwater; and their total impression is likely to have been a negative one, of a dull, flat and featureless bit of country — a kind of visual silence between the noble chords of Mendip and Quantock. And if the A38 reveals little of interest, still less can the motorway offer as any incentive to pause and explore. In twenty miles, by either route, the only memorable feature is Brent Knoll, an isolated hill rearing up so abruptly that it seems artificial. At no point does the near presence of the sea make itself felt. The rivers over which the traveller passes are uninspiring. The only town, Highbridge, is singularly unimpressive. One looks with growing disillusion for the characteristic church towers of Somerset, for a well-set farmhouse, for a group of trees, indeed for anything to break the monotonous nullity of the scene. And one looks in vain.

Yet all the time just beyond the tips of one's senses, just out of immediate reach, there is some of the most fascinating ground in all England — a countryside of subtle texture and numinous power, a landscape charged with distinctive beauties and legends and mysteries that feed the imagination as few other English scenes can do. Turn aside into the Vale of Avalon and wherever one stands on the peat levels — the 'immense turbary' that Stradling surveyed from his Priory at Chilton Polden — there is no escape from the presence of Glastonbury Tor. At Glastonbury Joseph of Arimathea is reputed to have built the first Christian church in England, on the Isle of Avalon where King Arthur was buried. These so-called 'islands' among the flooded marshes had a special value, in times of war and plunder, as secret places where monks and hermits could worship undisturbed and warrior kings could hide. Across the Polden ridge on the edge of Sedgemoor, at Athelney, King Alfred waited for the day to come when he would destroy the heathen invader; something which Arthur had failed to do. And on Sedgemoor itself, many centuries later, Monmouth's Rebellion ended in the last battle to be fought on English soil.

This is one of those evocative places where the older patterns of history and legend still reveal themselves in the lineaments of the present. But it is not merely the echoes of past glories that make this a landscape of unique character. Physically it stands apart. Walking from South Brent to Pawlett in 1799 Richard Warner observed that 'this part of Somersetshire exhibits the province of Holland in miniature'. It is indeed foreign to any conventional idea of a typical West Country scene. The willow-fringed rhines enclosing the green rectangles of the grazing lands; the sombre chocolate-brown masses of peat; the wetland flowers, kingcup and wild iris and sweet gale; the colourful bundles of withies drying by the roadside; the fields of teazles in the Isle Valley; all these combine to create a countryside that fascinates by its strangeness and unfamiliarity. For any closeness of similiarity one must look to the Fens of East Anglia.

The key element of course is water. The nature of central Somerset is conditioned to a very high degree by the single physical fact that it is as aptly designed for holding water as a saucer. On three sides it is surrounded by hills, and on the fourth by the coastal strip that has been raised by deposition to a level which offers a precarious natural barrier to the sea. It is indeed a dried-out lagoon, marshy and waterlogged in places, subject to the formation of pools in wet weather, and still liable to inundation if the man-made defences were not constantly maintained. Its ancient pristine atmosphere coexists with the sea walls and sluices and pumping stations of more recent days. Indeed a great deal of its charm and interest is due to its paradoxical character in being at once more wild and primitive and yet more artificial than almost any other part of England.

The interaction of human control and elemental nature is here continuous and plain to see. The embanked rivers and elevated roadways tell the same story as the peaty levels and the poverty of trees — a story of the eternal seeping of water into a plain that lies too low to shrug off its surplus. This one governing characteristic has in part preserved a type of landscape which was once common in this country but is now rarely seen; and in sharp contrast it still challenges us to tackle problems in the bridling of natural forces which elsewhere seldom arise. In central Somerset the main issue down the centuries has been to establish and assure the conditions in which human beings could live there. Time and again in its history there has been a swift irruption of flood-water, inundating villages and destroying life and property.

Those who lived on the moors came to terms with the constant threat of flooding. They were prepared to move essential furniture upstairs when the need arose, and many of them kept a small boat lying handy. Nowadays the successful defence works and drainage schemes of the Somerset River Authority have dispelled the old 'siege mentality' but the area is still rich in anecdotes of departures made via the bedroom window; and almost a note of pride can be detected in the comment 'that settle's been through two floods, and yet 'tis as good as ever it was'. In such country you easily become sensitive to every rise and fall in the level of the land. A lift of only a few feet means an 'island', a change of soil, a change of vegetation. A slight decline carries you from ploughland to the wide unbroken green of the moor. When you are sometimes barely a dozen feet above sea level, every foot of altitude counts.

The general plan of the area is easy to grasp. Along the north-eastern border the limestone ridge of Mendip rises like a wall, running inland from the Bristol Channel to Wells and Shepton Mallet. As Mendip tails off, the line of the Fosse Way marks the eastern boundary. To the south lies the oolitic upland of the Dorset Downs, and westward the area is finally locked by the Blackdown Hills, the Brendons and the Quantocks. The moorland basin of central Somerset which lies within these bounds is divided by the Polden Hills and for convenience these two divisions may usefully be designated 'Sedgemoor' and 'Avalon'. Avalon in this sense is the group of moors between Mendip and the Poldens; Sedgemoor is the area south and west of the Poldens.

Neither title is strictly accurate, but they have the virtue of a familiar ring and some historical and traditional validity. Avalon is the more fanciful, for there is probably no very sound reason for identifying that Celtic paradise with Glastonbury. But custom has it thus, and the Ordnance Survey map declares Glastonbury to be situated on the Isle of Avalon. Consequently the low land from Glastonbury Tor to the coast, which geographically is the valley of the river Brue, is often called the Vale of Avalon: and properly so because it is Glastonbury Tor which dominates the whole landscape. The little conical hill with the tower on top, the fabulous Avalon of myth and legend, is the one commanding landmark here; and it is the name which can best represent the land that runs from the skirts of Mendip to the Polden villages. Brent Marsh was the older name, before modern romantics got to work on the identification with Avalon; but Brent Marsh lacks poetry, and in any case Brent Knoll and the Brent villages stand apart nowadays from the peat moors. Today the 'marsh' looks to Glastonbury-Avalon and not to Brent, and I take Avalon as its broadly descriptive name.

Sedgemoor has a sturdier accuracy. There are in point of fact a King's Sedgemoor, a Queen's Sedgemoor and a West Sedgemoor. There may be other Sedgemoors too, for the moors of Somerset are all but uncountable. But if any one of them is to typify all beyond the western scarp of the Poldens is must be that plain and unadorned Sedgemoor which is a household word for the battlefield where the Duke of Monmouth failed in his bid for the English throne. Sedgemoor — a word as literal and realistic as Avalon is fanciful — is the commonly accepted collective name for the marshy levels south-west of the Poldens. Some of its components, such as Aller Moor and Curry Moor, proclaim their individuality — but it has no serious competitor.

The humble range of the Polden Hills, running between Sedgemoor and Avalon, looks surprisingly lofty from the absence of any competing feature. At no point do the Poldens rise to more than about 300ft, but they command remarkably widespread views on both sides and achieve an almost majestic effect with the utmost economy. They are the backbone of the moors, running evenly from the neighbourhood of Glastonbury to the outskirts of Bridgwater. No major road crosses over them. They seal off Sedgemoor from Avalon in a remarkably decisive way, like a neutral corridor belonging to neither side and preserving a distinctive character of its own.

The general structure of the land shows the shaping influence of sea and river. The limestone fold of the Mendip Hills plunges far below the present level of the moors, and borings in search of limestone bearing coal deposits similar to those at Radstock and Pensford have gone down to over 2,000ft without result. What some borings have revealed is not coal or oil — or gold — but a great bed of salt, laid down when the whole area was submerged beneath the sea. Some fifty years ago salt was worked commercially at Puriton, in what were locally know as the 'Treacle Mines', when a salt-bed was located at 650ft below the surface. The Treacle Mines were indeed quite a local industry for a time, but they closed down in the 1920s when water drunk by cattle from the King's Sedgemoor Drain was found to be tainted by the effluent from the salt-washing. Borings also disclose areas of marine sand under the alluvium and peat of the surface, and some of these sand beds are as much as 12ft thick.

A more distinctive deposit than salt and sand is the blue lias which filled the valleys and which provides the characteristic building-stone of central Somerset. Blue lias and the peat which formed on top of it are the noticeable elements in this landscape. From Somerton to Stoke-under-Ham is little more than half a dozen miles but the cold blue stone of Somerton might be a continent away from the most golden and warm of the oolites, which is quarried at Ham Hill. The Liassic clays present a soft and yielding landscape, in contrast with the surrounding hills. And the rivers which flow down from the bordering hills of Wiltshire and Dorset have found only minor obstacles in their way. When the sea retreated, the Brue, the Axe and the Parret, with their tributaries, scoured away the softer rocks of the plain and isolated the tougher cores of lias and marl which now form the islands of Wedmore, Brent Knoll, Burrow Mump and many another. Glastonbury Tor itself is a stubborn remnant of Middle and Upper Lias.

But though the rivers scoured away anything yielding that lay in their courses, they also carried down into the moors the alluvial soil which washes out from the hills where they spring. To the moorland farmer these muddy floods of alluvium-bearing waters were the much-prized 'thick water' which fertilised his land and gave to Somerset the reputation of having some of the best-grazing land in all England. In the nineteenth century the lowland farmers developed a technique of 'warping' their land by deliberately flooding it with silt-bearing water that was kept on the land for long enough to deposit the silt and then drained off.

To understand the very mixed opinions that are expressed about flooding one must grasp this important distinction between 'thick' water and its opposite. Rainwater is not 'thick' since it carries nothing within itself. A flood caused by rain brings to the land only surplus water, which is the one commodity of which there is no shortage. But river-borne floods carry the fertile top soil scoured away from the uplands; and that soil, allowed to settle as a surface deposit, is as good as a dressing of manure. Floods therefore are not quite simply a good thing or a bad thing. It is an altogether subtler matter than that. The two factors that count are the deposit the flood leaves, and the amount of inconvenience to the farmer, and damage to the land, which the depth of water and the duration of the flood may cause. Nothing is more welcome than a flood of thick water which comes after autumn grazing has finished and is gone before the farmer's spring operations begin — provided, of course, that it does not get up to his mantelpiece over Christmas.

The historical result of the actions of sea and river has been to carve out the hard-cored islands and ridges, and to build up an alluvial belt of slightly higher ground along the coast to an average width of about five miles. This coastal belt helps to keep the sea out, but it also finally land-locks the boggy moors, set as they are in a horseshoe of surrounding hills. Consequently the volume of water that drains into the central basin is too great for the natural courses of the rivers to carry away.

In a more rugged terrain, with a gradient inclining sufficiently towards the sea, the tendency would be for the water to cut new channels or deepen the existing ones; but the Brue, the Parret, the Axe and the Tone find it much easier to sprawl sideways. They are down almost to sea level when the coast is still fifteen or twenty miles away, so there is no natural impulse to hurry on forwards. And their banks have none of the stern geological obduracy which disciplines better-behaved rivers. Left to themselves, the Somerset rivers would follow their natural inclination to unbutton and expand in a spreading obesity of water. Centuries of human endeavour have therefore been directed to 'corset' the rivers with stiffened embankments and to provide them artificially with the tidy habits that by nature they so conspicuously lack.

Before men began to transform the area, by systematic drainage and by the erection of barriers, Sedgemoor and Avalon must have been a waste of marsh-land and saltings, where they were not positively submerged. Below Glastonbury, in the vicinity of Meare, there was a large pool which did indeed survive until the beginning of the eighteenth century. In Henry VIII's reign the size of Meare Pool was estimated as a mile and a half in breadth and five miles in circuit. Leland, writing about 1535, substantially confirms that estimate — taking it at winter high water. And he adds that the perimeter of the pool never shrank to less than two miles and a half. Much of it was drained about 1630 and an unsuccessful attempt was made to grow flax on the re-claimed land. What was left of Meare Pool was probably drained in Queen Anne's reign: about 1712 it disappeared from the map of Somerset. In its time it had contained a great abundance of 'pykes, tenchards, roches and jeles' and had also supported forty pairs of swans, belonging to Glastonbury Abbey; and other swans — belonging to wealthy landowners in the vicinity — were kept here and on the adjoining pools.

There is no doubt that permanent lakes and meres of this kind were extensive, and it is frequently said that at some earlier time the sea used to stretch right up to Glastonbury. There is no difficulty in believing that, if you go back far enough, since the Tor itself is the result of marine deposition and must have been submerged. But it is assumed that, long after the fundamental geological constitution was settled, the sea swirled about Brent Knoll and the Isle of Wedmore and stretched in an otherwise unbroken expanse to a coastal settlement at Glastonbury. It is, of course, historically true that sea floods often reached Glastonbury. They did so as late as 1811, and the whole Vale of Avalon was inundated to a depth of 12ft in 1607. On the other hand the records of human settlement in the lowlands point to there being for long a sort of watery no-man's-land rather than a positive area of the sea. It must be remembered that the Somerset coast has one of the highest tides in the world, and the sea would therefore overrun much more than it could occupy. To the hunters and fishermen of the Stone Age the Somerset marshlands must have been a favourable territory, and their relics point to the occupation of sandy spots and dunes which verged on salt-water lagoons.

Any attempt to establish a date for the foundation of the present coastline must be largely a matter of conjecture. The editor of the Ordnance Survey map of Neolithic Wessex specifically refuses to make such an attempt. Submerged forests off the Somerset coast indicate that the level of the land was at some time higher than it is now, but the broad story of human settlement unfolds here in an amphibious world of shallow lakes and stagnant marshes, invaded from time to time by the sea, and offering a limited foothold on certain well-defined islands and along elevated ridges and natural causeways. Web-footed country in fact!

There can be no doubt that the marsh was a valuable feeding-ground for primitive man. In addition to fish it offered venison, wildfowl of many kinds, wild boar and more exotic things like pelicans, which seem to have been quite abundant. With the development of farming techniques and the setting up of primitive homesteads the tendency was to colonise the foothills which bordered on the marshes. Anyone who today visits Somerton may look on it with some surprise as the ancient county town, for it is no longer a centre of anything in particular. But Somerton had its hour of glory — its many hours — under Saxon and Roman and Celt. The vicinity of Somerton, lying between the unbroken forest and the productive but diluvian marshes, was a very

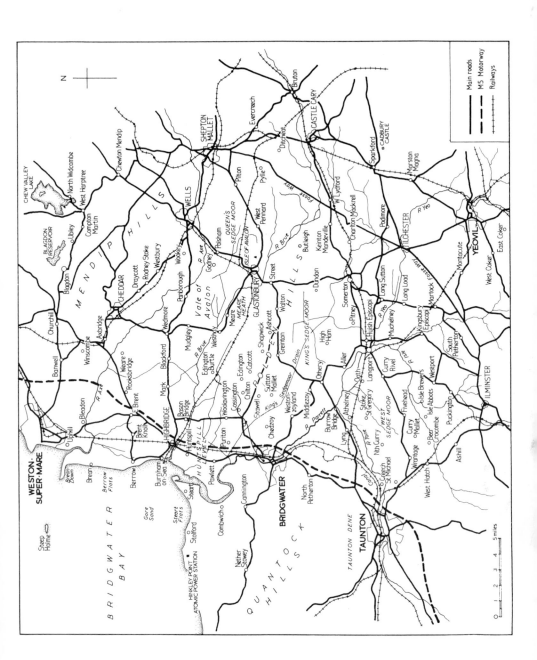

desirable neighbourhood for our remote ancestors. The soil was light enough to cultivate and it was well drained. When the Romans reached Somerset they found a well-established tradition of civilised life in the foothills that envelop the inland termination of the Polden ridge, forming a rough arc from High Ham to Glastonbury Tor, with Somerton as the centre.

The most remarkable of these British communities were the lake villages at Godney and Meare, in the Glastonbury area; and here the evidence suggests that the Romans were not attracted to continue the native tradition. But elsewhere the Roman way of life was grafted on to the British pattern with strikingly strong continuity, in some instances superimposing a new Roman building on the foundations of an earlier British one. Round Somerton and Ilchester and Langport, on the higher ground that lies between the Parret and the Brue, the Romans or Romanised Britons found good building sites for their homesteads. And they in their turn followed earlier dwellers who had discovered here the conditions they needed. At Littleton, for example, a Roman house sufficiently prosperous to have a mosaic floor was built on the site of an earlier and more austere Roman dwelling, which in its turn overlay two earlier levels of British building.

On the other side of the Brue the lake villages of Meare and Godney flourished from about 250 BC on the verge of what was then probably a large lake and later became Meare Pool. Where so much of early Glastonbury history remains conjectural it is comforting to see the copious and varied evidence of life in the lake villages. When in 1892 a young archaeologist, Arthur Bulleid, picked up some fragments of pottery and bits of bone and charcoal from a group of molehills between Glastonbury and Godney he was on the verge of one of the most extraordinary archaeological discoveries ever made in this country. In collaboration with H. St George Gray he unearthed two complete villages which, from the fact that they were buried in peat, were wonderfully preserved. After visiting the Lake Collections in the museums at Glastonbury and Taunton it is easy to feel as closely acquainted with the habits and daily life of these Iron Age folk as of one's next-door neighbours. And easy too to recognise that Roman accounts of the native British were about as inaccurate as most battlefront journalism — for there was nothing of the uncouth savage about these highly skilled and sensitive craftsmen of the Glastonbury moors. Some of their metal-work was superb — notably, of course, the famous Glastonbury bowl — but no less impressive is the simpler triumph of so transforming a piece of bone by delicate shaping and incised decoration that one loses all sense of its ever having been what, in fact, it originally was, just a bit of animal bone.

The fate which overtook the lake villages is uncertain. Dr Bulleid suggested that the lake may have begun to dwindle and so have lost its defensive value. Whatever the reason, their history seems to have ended without violence shortly before the Romans arrived, but their use of the marshlands for fishing and hunting would undoubtedly have been continued by the newcomers. It is indeed possible that the Romans were the first to consider a deliberate exploitation of the area by building sea walls. Previously the natural conditions of flood and swamp must have been accepted by the inhabitants, but the engineering skill of Rome might be expected to respond to such a challenge. The siting of a Roman villa at Yatton has been held to point to the erection of some kind of sea defence in order to make the place habitable. Perhaps it will never be possible with absolute certainty to determine who first attempted to control the flow of water in and out of the marshland basin, but the birth of that idea — whenever it may have happened — marks the beginning of the modern landscape.

CHAPTER TWO

LAND AND WATER

Our hunting and fishing ancestors would have remained content to accept the bogs and marshes as they found them. With the farmers it was a different matter. The islands were suitable in varying degrees for settlement and cultivation, and much of the waste lands that were submerged in winter dried out as useful summer grazing. The characteristic termination of place names in 'ey' or 'y' or 'oy' indicates a settlement on an island: Godney, Othery and Middlezoy, for example. The depasturing of domestic animals in large and increasing numbers was probably the most important spur to change the condition of the moors, as the 'islanders' and the occupants of the surrounding foothills tried to reclaim waste land, to bring it into individual ownership and to improve the quality of its herbage.

Little is known of Roman influence on the lowlands but it can not have amounted to much. The Fosse Way, keeping to the higher ground as it travelled to the south west, appears to mark a sort of Roman boundary. The Somerset villas clustered round the main road, and to this day the Fosse Way seems to mark a natural margin. The Romans would have hunted and fished on the levels and availed themselves of summer grazing for their animals as opportunity offered, but they made here no investment of skill and labour of the kind that elsewhere marked their particular way of life. They had their lead mines on Mendip and their port at Sea Mills (in what is now the city of Bristol) but south of Mendip they looked seawards from their farmsteads along the Fosse Way with no great enthusiasm. One may assume that they knew the ancient route along the spine of the Poldens to the ford over the river Parret at Combwich, but they made little use of it.

It is to the Saxons, and more particularly to their great monastic foundations, that one must look for the first innovations and determined policies that gradually transformed this landscape. What religious life persisted in Glastonbury through the Dark Ages remains a mystery. Its earliest church may have been cared for by hermits and monks and 'holy men' of one sort or another. And as British resistance succumbed to the new invaders the body of Arthur may have been brought to the sacred burial-place on the Isle of Avalon. From the last days of the Iron Age villages in the marshes near Glastonbury to the beginnings of a Saxon administration in the area about the middle of the seventh century the evidence is all too scanty.

But about the year 705 the Saxon King Ine rebuilt the original church. In 878 King Alfred founded Athelney Abbey. Muchelney followed in 933 (though it could claim an earlier origin in the small monastic settlement that was founded there in the middle of the eight century). For a time, under the onslaught of the Danes, monastic life in Britain nearly collapsed but the determination of Alfred and the inspiring zeal of St Dunstan were victorious. The Normans, when they came, were invaders with a difference: they were the first Christians to invade a Christian England and their effect on the monasteries was to strengthen them. Thanks to Saxon and Norman piety two thirds of the medieval lowlands were ecclesiastical possessions, administered by the abbots of Glastonbury, Muchelney and Athelney, and the Bishop, Dean and Chapter of Wells. They were the large and progressive landowners who came to grips with the real problems of land-management in the moors.

In essence the problem was two-fold: to keep the sea from breaking in, and to make the river outlets capable of conveying the flow from the upland watershed without spilling it. The first called for massive walls and embankments. The second required the power to widen and deepen existing waterways, to excavate new ones, and — ultimately — to lift water by pumping from a lower level to a higher. It has taken maybe the best part of 1,000 years to find the answers, or most of them. And the lessons have usually been learnt the hard way.

The history of the floods is a long and dramatic story. At some remote time, during the Pliocene period and afterwards, the sea level fell by at least 50ft to 60ft, and there is some evidence to suggest that it may have fallen as much as 200ft. Vegetation preserved in the peat indicates that the land thus became higher and drier than it is now. Forest remains have been found at a depth of 18ft at Athelney, and on Mark Moor oak and yew are found at a depth of 4ft to 6ft. Lower levels of peat yield similar evidence of a vegetation foreign to the present marshy conditions. It was a subsequent rise in sea level which waterlogged the Somerset lowlands and produced the characteristic landscape of historical times. The submerged forests which can still be seen in places on the Somerset foreshore were originally overwhelmed by this invasion of the sea.

The pioneer of pollen analysis, Sir Harry Godwin, whose field work concentrated on the evidence of the peat moors, suggests that this marine invasion reached its climax long before the arrival of Neolithic Man. Eight thousand years BC there would have been forests of birch and pine covering the hills and valleys; and it was in about 6000 BC that the sea level rose, the valleys were flooded and a flat salt marsh spread far inland. Subsequently the lowest levels of peat began to form.

This encroachment of the sea would naturally lead to the silting up of the area and the formation of marshy delta country with shallow saltwater lagoons. The extent of the deposits is well shown at Crandon Bridge, where a depth of as much as 3m of silt lies on top of the peat, and no doubt this slow banking-up of the land gave a gradual definition to the coastal frontier. But the rivers must have sprawled to a great width of indeterminate bog, and any higher than usual sea tide flooded inland without hindrance.

In a subsequent drier and warmer period the typical landscape was of large bogs covered with ling, cotton grass and sphagnum moss. Where the peaty surface dried out some form of habitation was possible. And when the climate worsened again, making movement difficult, the people of the late Bronze Age laid down timber trackways in the areas of Meare, Westhay and Shapwick. The Meare Heath trackway, over a mile in length, ran from the 'island' of Meare to Ashcott. It was made up of large, horizontal timbers, about 2m long, laid in pairs about ½m apart, with vertical piles morticed into the main timbers. Stringers of twisted wood and bundles of brushwood made up the surface.

Conditions had improved when the Iron Age people built their so-called Lake Villages and the next evidence of flooding comes in the middle of the first century AD when the villages were abandoned. Around the year 200 the sea broke in again, depositing clay along the coastal strip and in the river valleys. There is some evidence that the village site at Meare was reoccupied in the fourth century for a time before further flooding deposited clay on top of the last signs of human occupation: the last, that is, before the ending of Roman rule and the eventual resettlement of the marsh-encompassed islands by the Saxons.

The devotion felt by King Ine for Glastonbury and by Alfred for Athelney is proof enough of the importance the Saxons attached to lowland Somerset. From them we get the first word pictures of this countryside in its primitive wildness. Asser, the companion and biographer of King Alfred, records that in the ninth century Athelney was inaccessible except by boat. The island itself was densely covered with thickets of alder which sheltered deer and other game; and the usable area of dry land was barely two acres. The movement of men and materials between the islands obviously made extensive use of the rivers, pools and floods. In the eighth century Bleadney was reckoned to be a port, which suggests that the Axe valley was used for navigation up to the gap which separates the island of Wedmore from the little Mendip spur that runs out from Wells.

Incontrovertible evidence of Saxon measures to control flooding is lacking but the extent of Saxon settlement suggests an intensification of farming on and around the islands to a degree that could scarcely have been unaccompanied by some primitive attempts to cut a drainage channel or to strengthen a river bank. The old chroniclers indicate that Alfred's men could construct a causeway when necessary in the Athelney area, and the distinction between a causeway and a flood wall is sometimes a fine one. It has also been argued that St Dunstan made the first moves to strengthen the banks of the river Brue at Glastonbury. But it is not until the Normans began their careful documen-

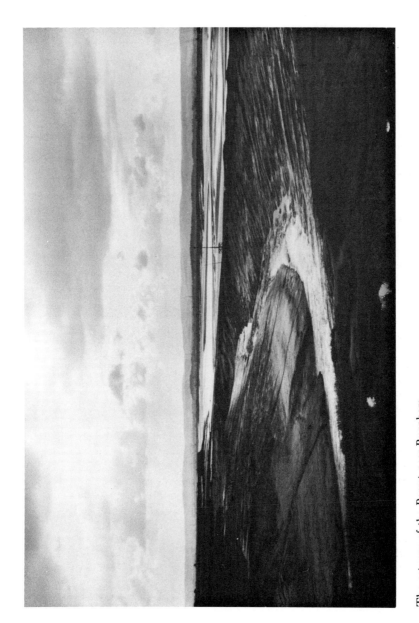

The estuary of the Parret near Burnham

Sedgemoor — 'To see the moors there is no better vantage-point than Red Hill'

Winter flooding seen from Burrow Mump, a common sight in the 1950s

tation of the ecclesiastical estates that precise and detailed accounts appear of the reclamation of flood lands and the building of protective walls. In 1129 the Abbot of Glastonbury, making a journey down the Axe valley, inspected some arable land at Lympsham and was pleased to see corn ready for harvest, 'coloured red and gold, murmuring sweetly in the gentle breezes'. This was land which earlier had been classified as worthless but now it was encircled and surrounded on one side by a sea wall.

Another interesting example of medieval improvement is to be found in the island of 'Sowy', as it used to be called. This is the ridge of slightly higher ground that is occupied by the villages of Othery, Middlezoy and Westonzoyland. It is fertile land and would have been brought into cultivation by the Saxons; rather less than 2,000 acres could be regarded as free from flooding, and when these were fully used the only way of expansion was to look to the moorland waste that bordered the island. Additional pasture could be gained by enclosing and reclaiming suitable land of this kind. A survey of 1234 shows that 722 acres of meadow had already been reclaimed in this way in earlier years. What is more, their condition was secure enough for forty houses to have been newly built on them. In the next six years a further 200 acres were reclaimed on the outskirts of Sowy, and the rent-money flowing into Glastonbury was mounting substantially.

Given the desire to expand on this scale, the need to tackle the menace of flooding became increasingly urgent. There was nothing to stop the Parret from overflowing in its monotonously familiar way, particularly when a strong incoming sea-tide met a heavy flow coming downstream. Accordingly the movement to enclose and reclaim moorland in the thirteenth century was accompanied by unprecedented activity in the construction of embankments. Southlake Moor at the southern end of Sowy was virtually surrounded by a wall. North of Earlake Moor, the Lake Wall ran from Sowy to the banks of the Parret and kept out flood water dispersing from King's Sedgemoor. As a result substantial crops of barley, beans, peas and oats were growing in Southlake Moor and Earlake Moor in 1311. From Sowy to Langport the Parret was embanked to protect Aller Moor. And to improve communications Sowy was linked to the Polden Hills by a causeway known as the Greylake Fosse, and to High Ham by another causeway called Beer Wall. In the valley of the Parret's tributary, the river Tone, reclamation work during the thirteenth century was undertaken mainly by the Dean of Wells and the Abbot of Athelney. In 1374-5 the Abbot of Athelney and other landowners joined forces in a particularly ambitious project, the diversion of the river Tone in order to improve its capacity to carry floodwater.

North of the Poldens a similar story could be told of intense activity during the thirteenth and fourteenth centuries to improve the waterways and reclaim land that was normally subject to flooding. In the Glastonbury area and along the Brue valley watercourses were diverted, straightened, embanked, deepened or widened and generally improved as part of a complex plan in which it is sometimes difficult to decide whether better navigation or more efficient drainage was the dominant motive for a particular work. Wells and Glastonbury each had berthing and loading facilities for sea-going ships on the Axe, and the cutting of the Mark Yeo (or Pillrow Cut) to connect the river Brue to the Axe must have been an important innovation for Glastonbury — important for its shipping but important also in terms of more effective drainage. In 1235 Glastonbury had a waterborne route to Mark (at the western end of the Wedmore 'island') and the cut onwards from Mark to the Axe was probably completed later in that century: it was certainly in use early in the fourteenth century.

The checking of floods and the improvement of navigation were not the only motives for the great changes that the ecclesiastical landlords wrought on the landscape in the thirteenth and fourteenth century. The desire to improve grazing led to the first steps in what we are apt to think of as a much later historical process — the enclosure of common land. The Statute of Merton, 1235, permitted a landowner to occupy and enclose the 'wastes' in which commoner's rights were exercised provided he left enough pasture for his free tenants. There is every reason to suppose that the Somerset moors were over-grazed, not only because of an increase in the number of animals belonging to commoners but also because of illegal grazing and of the custom which allowed some commoners to bring in extra beasts temporarily from the upland farms and in this way to sell grazing rights to people who were not entitled to them.

To improve the quality of the pasture and of the livestock land-reclamation required more than protection from flooding: it was necessary to set up boundaries and to exclude unwanted beasts. Enclosure and individual owner-ship began to replace the traditional free-for-all. Throughout the period there is a rumbling ground-bass of dispute at all levels from Abbot and Bishop to the lowest and most impudent of squatters. Titles of ownership are debated, concessions and compensations offered, bargains finally struck with good will or ill. Occasionally, as tempers rise, excommunications are threatened, fights take place, banks are broken down and fisheries damaged. Nevertheless one can but admire the determination and boldness of these men of medieval England in their challenge to the elemental forces of a hostile environment. The floodwaters they were attempting to master were like a wild beast that devours the crops, a giant that throws down houses and embankments. For the men of the moors water has always had an almost animal reality: they may be beleaguered by it, ruined by it, even killed by it.

In the thirteenth and fourteenth centuries a great step forward was taken. And then the impetus began to flag, checked perhaps by the decimation of the Black Death and the civil chaos of the Wars of the Roses, and certainly halted by the dissolution and destruction of the monasteries in the 1530s. The gains were real enough but so were the problems that remained untouched. The great plain of King's Sedgemoor was a waste that flooded regularly. The peat lands of the Vale of Avalon slept undisturbed. The rivers frequently over-flowed. Worst of all the sea defences were inadequate. For all the misery and damage that river flooding could bring, it was nevertheless the sea that — until modern times — presented the really frightening menace. To make matters worse, the fourteenth and fifteenth centuries saw a widespread subsidence of coastal land (which was not confined to Somerset) and this made the defences of the low-lying coastal area fronting Bridgwater Bay the more vulnerable.

The normal rise and fall of the tide in the Bristol Channel is the second highest in the world — a range of about 35ft between the highest tides and the lowest. A 19ft tide at Bridgwater Bridge has been estimated as 24ft above Ordnance datum, and plenty of the surrounding land is lower than that. A breach of the sea walls can let the tide inland for miles. From early times the proprietors of coastal lands were compelled by law to maintain sea walls at appropriate places, and if the wall was broken they had to replace it. In 1485 the monks of St Swithun at Bleadon gave up their 'knife-money' to rebuild the sea wall, so there had evidently been an inundation shortly before. At an even earlier date — certainly before 1425 — Cannington Priory lost a manor and various tenements as a result of a sea flood. Until the Reformation the great religious houses of Somerset were active in the organisation of coastal defences, and it is ironical — to say the least — that after the Dissolution of the Monasteries the stones of some of their buildings were used for repairing the sea walls. In the reign of Edward VI the people of Yatton enquired about the prospect of buying a chapel which stood in the churchyard, so that they could use the stones to raise a sluice 'against the rage of the sea'. For the same purpose they sold the church's silver cross.

There is no knowing how much stone from the abbeys of Glastonbury, Athelney and Muchelney may have gone to strengthen the flood defences, but the whole system seems to have been gradually weakened by the removal of firm monastic control. Or perhaps the disaster that came sixty years later was just bad luck. Whatever the explanation, on 20 January 1607 the wall gave way near Burnham and the sea poured in, to a depth of 10 or 12ft, flooding an area 5 miles wide and extending 20 miles inland. Thirty villages were submerged, including Brean, which was 'swallowed up', losing 7 houses out of 9. Twenty-six of the inhabitants of Brean perished, 11 were drowned at Uphill, and 28 at Huntspill. A Berrow milkmaid, 'round about beset' by the waters, was marooned on a bank for 24 hours with swarms of rats and mice and voles around her. Swimming oxen looked like whales, and rabbits jumped on the backs of sheep and perched there until both sheep and rabbit drowned to-gether. On one large estate the horses were brought into the mansion and stood in the hall with water up to their bellies, until the floods abated. A sinister aspect of the tragedy was that seafaring men came in boats, not to rescue but to loot.

The size and swiftness of the flood seems to have taken the people by surprise. A contemporary account describes the first onset as 'huge and mighty hilles of water, tombling one over another, in such sort, as if the greatest mountaines in the world had overwhelmed the lowe valeyes or marshy grounds. Sometimes it so dazzled the eyes of spectators that they imagined it had been some fogge or miste, coming with great swiftness towards them.' For ten days the church at Kingston Seymour was 1½m deep in flood water; a chiselled mark in the church shows the maximum flood level as nearly 8m above sea level. At the height of the flood Glastonbury was surrounded by sea water, and extreme measures were needed to deal with the calamity. Under the threat of what further tides might add to the damage, a force of 500 men were put to work to repair the wall at Burnham. Such was the sense of emergency that even the justices helped 'not with their eyes only but with their hands'. In face of a peril of such magnitude there was evidently no place for the niceties of social rank.

For about a century there was no further visitation on this scale though the extent of normal winter flooding was greater than we perhaps realise. However, no major disaster occurred until the great storm of 1703. This was a national calamity, for London suffered a million pounds worth of damage and the Royal Navy lost a dozen ships and 1,500 men. Somerset felt the full force of the storm. A falling chimney at Wells killed Bishop Kidder and his wife, and the sou'wester whipped up a tide that rose 4ft above the height of the coastal walls. An elderly woman was drowned as the sea swept in breast-high, and the floods spread six miles inland. One curious effect of the high tide, noted by Defoe, was that several vessels were driven ashore and grounded in the meadows. Apparently they were borne in near the salt works at Burnham and carried for at least 100yd before settling on some pastureland, where they remained as a most incongruous spectacle after the sea had withdrawn.

And so the sorry chronicle of flooding goes on. When Defoe referred to the road from Bristol to Bridgwater (know in his day as 'The Lower Way') he warned that it was sometimes impassable 'being subject to Floods and dangerous Inundations'. This danger persisted into the present century, for as late as 1902 the sea broke through and covered the road. But by degrees the danger of a large-scale incursion by the sea has been overcome. Over the centuries earth walls have given place to stone, and stone to concrete, until today it can be claimed that no single tide would have the power to breach the ten miles of major walls and the hundreds of miles of tidal embankments. If repair work were not attended to promptly a succession of exceptional tides might still do some damage but it seems safe to prophesy that we shall not again see Glastonbury surrounded on three sides by salt water, as it was as comparatively recently as 1811.

Modern flooding has in the main been river flooding. Unusually heavy rainfall in the 1870s and 1880s brought widespread floods. Even in summer an exceptionally heavy fall of rain could have disastrous consequences. Twenty hours of rain, depositing 24cm in the upper reaches of the Brue, caused the river to burst its banks in 1917: the swollen waters carried away the hay crop at Meare and Shapwick. The most disastrous inundation of the present century followed a break in the south bank of the river Tone in 1929, when 10,000 acres of land were submerged from November to February and the villages of Athelney, Curload and Stathe had to be evacuated.

At Athelney the village street nestles against the river bank, which at this point is roughly level with the bedroom windows. I remember once parking my caravan for a time in an orchard adjoining the bank, and climbing up the slope to look down on the caravan roof from the towing-path. It was curiously eerie to be so aware of the presence of the river and yet not to see it, unless one deliberately mounted the bank. And there was little incentive to go up and watch the muddy water drifting past, with nothing but an occasional fragment of refuse — a carton or a cabbage stalk — to break the dull grey monotony of the lumbering tide. Across the river were flat fields and the main Taunton road and the inadequate Alfred monument on a swell of rising ground; and at one's feet the oozy, slimy banks of the Tone and the muddy water. Not an attractive scene, and one ignored it. But the river was always there, always present in one's thoughts, behind its high bank.

And in 1929 the Tone burst the bank. As the dark flood came spilling through, the solitary humble street of Athelney heard the age-old cry of the Somerset lowlands — 'The bank's gone.' Men already weary with fighting the rising tide hurried past the scattered line of cottages, calling their traditional warning to the inhabitants — 'The bank's gone.' Whether it was the twentieth century or the fourteenth made no great difference. The water was spreading across the road and into the moor, easing itself outwards, deepening inch by inch, bringing a sheeted anonymity to gardens, jabbing its fingers under doors and over steps, sidling inquisitively into parlours and kitchens.

The bank had gone — and the people followed the customs of their ancestors, tidying up and making ready for the siege of water. One of them could remember something of the kind in the 1880s when rabbits took to the trees and men rowed round to capture them. Another had heard his grandfather tell how he brought his barge up-river to a breach in the bank and then steered it clean across the moor to join the river again, higher up. So, in 1929, the cider apples were methodically loaded and hauled to the station, to be railed away to other cider makers out of the district. And furniture of the more perishable and portable sort was heaved upstairs to safety. And in due course, but not so suddenly as to cause any panic, the water lapped comfortably and quietly round the mantelpiece, and the boat was moored to the bedroom windowsill.

The tenacity of the moorland people is something to marvel at. A lot of them, I imagine, ought not to be there at all. Many of the little homesteads that lie in the narrow strip between road and river bank seem to have grown up when no one was looking — on waste patches and bits of common land, built perhaps from a cargo of bricks that was going cheaply off a passing barge. The great brickfields of Bridgwater were near enough, and there was prosperity along the river banks in the heyday of the barge trade. Many of these cottages were cider houses; you can still see occasionally the name of an inn on the back of a house, facing the river, for the business side of the premises was not the side that faced the road. The water was the old trunk route, and at such places the many barges stopped for refreshment.

But however they came to be there, no fear of flood shifted these people. And the moorland farmers were equally tenacious. The story of one farmer on Curry Moor is typical: in 1929 the only dry ground in sight was the high arch of the bridge that spans the river outside his gates, so he promptly fenced it in and converted it into a corral for his beasts. The cattle were enclosed at one end of the bridge, and the horses at the other. The bridge, incidentally, came to be described — and not without justice — as the best manured bridge in Somerset. For five weeks his beasts lived there, fed out of the two halves of a cider cask which he salvaged and sawed in two. Dealing with the milk presented no real difficulty. His mother-in-law made fifty pounds of butter each week on the roof of an outbuilding and sent it away to market by boat.

To such people the hazards of flooding are part of the natural pattern of events. Another man, a smallholder in the area of Huntspill, described the uses to which his boat was put in the daily routine of farming before the Huntspill Level was drained. The water sometimes rose a foot or two within a few hours, so that after seeing his beasts comfortably grazing in the morning he would have to put out in his boat to fetch them in later in the afternoon through two or three feet of water. Crops had sometimes to be fetched in the same way, and he rowed out to cut submerged cabbages with a staff-hook. On the homeward journey the water under the railway bridge was so high that he had to lie in the bottom of the boat and press his hands against the arch, forcing the boat down until it was almost shipping water.

An even more striking instance of human adaptation to this amphibian style of living occurs in an eighteenth-century manuscript which refers to a special type of cradle, designed to float if floodwater entered the house while the baby was left unattended. This cradle was said to have been introduced into lowland Somerset after the great flood of 1703, and in its buoyant security many a child of Sedgemoor and Avalon must have earned the right to claim to have been literally 'cradled in the floods'.

CHAPTER THREE

THE RIVERS

The rivers of central Somerset are difficult to love, which is a pity, because so often the sparkling coherent vitality of a river can give unity and charm to an otherwise undistinguished landscape. And Somerset is reasonably blessed in this respect in the other regions of the county. The Exe in its youth, to the westward, and even the modest Chew flowing north from the Mendips are gay and lively streams which add grace to every mile they traverse. But the Brue and the Parret are duller metal. To Coleridge the Parret looked 'as filthy as if the "Parrots" of the House of Commons had been washing their conscience therein'. And the only superiority that can be claimed for the Brue is that it does not lend itself quite so readily to that sort of pun.

Springing from the Upper Greensand near Alfred's Tower at Stourton, the Brue drains a watershed which was estimated in 1872 as 136,850 acres. The same Parliamentary report estimates the watershed of the Parret and its tributaries as 362,860 acres. Swollen with upland waters from the surrounding horseshoe of hills, the two rivers wind uneasily across the low moors with little natural incentive to follow an orderly course. The Parret falls at the almost imperceptible gradient of only 1ft per mile from Langport to Burrow Bridge, and 1½ft from there to Bridgwater. The Brue is already below high-tide level by the time it reaches Godney Moor: its downward gradient over its last 8 miles is something less than impetuous at 8½ in per mile.

The rivers of Sedgemoor and Avalon, then, are neither grand nor beautiful. Perhaps it would be fair enough to call them drains and leave it at that. Like almost all English rivers they suffer from the utilitarian contempt which regards them as heaven-sent receptacles for every sort of rubbish: though we have our medieval precedents for such ill-use. There is a stone barn at Muchelney which was first constructed as the Abbey lavatory, and here the good monks forestalled the modern flush-closet by diverting a stream beneath the privy cubicles; the stream no longer flows beneath the barn, but you can still see the arches and fragments of the cubicle walls.

However, Brue and Parret are drains in a larger sense than that, and theirs has been a dominant role in the development of this countryside: a double role, moreover, since they are both friend and foe, by turn and turn about. They are the vital arteries in that system of subtle interplay between river, sluice and rhine which draws surplus water off the moors and feeds it in again when it is needed. The silt they bring down has been the perennial source of fertility, and they were the trade routes of the area to a very large extent before the improvement of road-making and the invention of the railway destroyed their economic importance. The rise and fall of Langport and the changing fortunes of Bridgwater are stories that the waters of the Parret might well recount as they meander seawards.

But how to control the volume of those waters in time of flood is a key problem. Improved drainage in the lowlands, though it gets the water away more quickly, tends to be counteracted by improved drainage in the uplands which sends water down the rivers just as much more quickly. It used to take thirty-six hours for water to come down from the uplands; now it arrives in six. From the time of the first commissioners of Sea-Walls and Sewers to the modern River Board the disposal of water from this spongy saucer has been a difficult and thankless task. And the moody mischief of these two Calibans — Brue and Parret — has time and again thrown down the works of hopeful men and reasserted the old rule of chaos.

The Parret rises in Dorset, at South Perrot, and crosses the Somerset border at North Perrot. Its length is thirty-six miles against the Brue's twenty-nine. Feeding the Parret are several important tributaries — the Tone, the Isle and the Yeo. The lower reaches of the Parret are tidal almost to Langport and, along the Tone, up to Hook Bridge. An additional tributary was the river Cary which used to flow into the Parret at Burrow Bridge: late in the eighteenth century the Cary was diverted into a new channel across King's Sedgemoor. Travellers whose journeys took them into the Parret valley have left us some vivid pictures of the sprawling morass of floodwater that developed in autumn and winter as the level of the river rose above its banks. In 1633 Thomas Gerard noted that some of the moors beside the Parret were 'so covered with water you would rather deem them sea than land'. Another report of that period describes the moors between Langport and Aller as being covered for most of the year 'by the waves'. People living on the higher ground beside Aller moor had to go by boat to church. And if someone died when the floods were out, the corpse had to be put in a boat and ferried to a suitable place for burial.

Langport, where Yeo and Parret meet, has always suffered badly. According to D. M. Ross, in his *History of Langport*, there was an attempt in the reign of Richard I to secure land in Langport beside the Parret by means of an embankment. Associated with this work is the name of Sir Robert De Odburville, a name which becomes more interesting to modern eyes if it is spelt d'Urberville. A century later there was much activity along the north bank of the Parret below Langport; conditions in Aller Moor and North Moor were improved by the digging of new rhines and the river itself was embanked.

But neither bank nor rhine could counter the Parret's ineffectual nature as a drain. As late as 1894 the boats were afloat again in Langport's Bow Street and in 1910 the railway track through Langport was impassable.

The lack of a steep enough gradient is notoriously one of the Parret's shortcomings. Less obvious but no less serious is the inadequacy of its estuary. A sharply decisive outfall into the sea would redeem some of the shortcomings in the upper reaches, but from Bridgwater to Steart Point the Parret wanders circuitously in a muddy silt-laden meandering progress that is all too plainly dominated by the vagaries of the Bristol Channel. When the sea-tide flows up the Severn it is squeezed and contracted by the narrowing funnel of the land to such a degree that the water is forced up turbulently into waves. With the big spring tides this wave-formation can build up to become the massive crest of water known as the Severn Bore. At the time of the equinoxes in spring and autumn the added force of strong south-westerly winds can produce a Bore 2m high. The Parret, though more modest in scale than the Severn, is subject to the same conditions: the tide that flows into the Severn estuary throws off a smaller Bore which runs up the Parret. Richard Warner, who was ferried across the Parret at Combwich in early September 1799, gives us this entertaining account of what he saw:

> As I had been informed that the Parret was remarkable for the impetuosity with which the tide enters its mouth, I waited about an hour and a half, till the commencement of the flood, in order to observe the phenomenon. Its approach is announced by a distant roaring sound, which gradually increases upon the ear, until the cause itself appears; a volume of water, like one vast wave, sometimes rising to the height of four feet (though when I saw it, not more than two) rushing on with irresistible violence, and covering instantaneously the steep banks, which had been left dry by the recess of the tide. It is called a *Boar*, in allusion, I presume, to the formidable sounds which this indomitable animal emits . . . It has been known, when strengthened by a spring-tide, to have overturned large boats in its furious course.

This turbulence of sea-tides in the winding estuary leads to the deposition of great quantities of silt. A report prepared in 1898 indicated that as much as 12ft of silt could be deposited in a year on the 'slime-batches' at Bridgwater. These slime-batches were platforms of brick rubble dumped on the banks of the Parret and they provided the basis for a very strange and profitable industry. The filthy appearance of the oozy slime makes it difficult to believe that it was used extensively by the Victorians for cleaning, but such is the case. It is a paradox which inspired a local poet of the period, E. H. Burrington, to honour the river with this amusing 'Apostrophe to the Parret':

> Upon the soft brown pillow of thy shore,
> No shells lie scattered, such as childish hands
> Delight to gather, yet thy sandy store
> Is richer than the gems of Cashmere's lands,
> So prettily described by Thomas Moore.

Parret, thou art Old Ocean's lawful daughter,
And to her breast thou rushest down with glee!
I cannot praise the blueness of thy water, —
Less blue than Baltic waves or Aegean sea;
But thou flowest ever beautifully thick,
Leaving thy filthy slime to make Bath brick!

Bath brick, well known to our grandmothers, was a popular scouring agent until it was superseded by the powders of the present day. The slime was moulded into 'bricks' and dried in the sun. Manufacture began in the 1820s and production eventually reached an annual level of 24 million bricks. Some were exported to Western Europe and North America, the price in 1860 being 40s per 1,000. In spite of its name Bath brick was made in Bridgwater and not in Bath. Some writers have suggested that it was sold in bulk from the city of Bath, but the simple truth appears to be that it was a Mr Bath who invented the brick and gave it his name. Just what precisely were the properties of the particular stretch of 'filthy slime' which furnished the brick, I do not know; but it was freely deposited with each tide, and the slime above and below the fruitful patch was on the one hand too coarse and on the other too fine. With the passing of Mr Bath and his ingenious industry it might be thought that the river mud would revert to the humble status of just mud. But it still had its value. The men of the brickyards used it to seal the 'wickets' of their kilns.

Some historians regard the Parret as an ancient frontier, which divided the invading Saxons from the British kingdom of Dyvnaint or Dumnonia. Certainly Saxon progress across Somerset was slow, for they took 133 years to advance from the Bristol Avon to the Blackdowns. Cenwealh reached the Parret in 658, after his victory at the Pens (which is considered to have been Penselwood), but no permanent crossing of the river is recorded until Centwine's advance twenty-four years later. There were fords at Combwich and Langport, and perhaps a crossing of some kind at Bridgwater, but with the added obstacle of the surrounding marshes the Parret must have been a formidable barrier. However, its significance as a frontier would lie not so much in its stability as a defended military line as in its demarcation of the zone where militant Saxon invasion and Celtic withdrawal petered out. If we may assume that Dyvnaint achieved a stalemate along the Parret and thereafter dwindled, first into vassalage and then into ultimate absorption and incorporation in the Saxon kingdom, we can well believe that the older nation retained a great deal more of its native character on the western side of the river.

Some authorities have argued that differences of physique and dialect still persist into modern times between the people east and west of the Parret, and as additional evidence Melville Ross, in his *History of Langport*, comments on the ecclesiastical division of the town so late as 1911 when Langport Eastover was still included in the Archdeaconry of Wells, and Langport Westover in that of Taunton. Bridgwater incidentally has this same demarcation of Eastover and Westover. Consistent differences of physique would be difficult to investigate in this age of rootless mobility, and it is dangerous enough to dogmatise about dialects. But no one can fail to recognise a radical division in speech between West Somerset and the old core of Wessex on the chalk and limestone. With local variations there is a broad similarity of dialect ranging from the Wallop villages in Hampshire to the Mendips and the ancient forest of Selwood. It is slow, deep-throated, with a characteristically burred 'r'. Around the Somerset-Dorset border you still frequently hear the aspirated 'r' of the Saxon: hrain, hrunning — 'Garden could do wi' a drop o'hrain.' But the Quantock voice marks a clear transition, and on Exmoor you have unmistakably the higher lilted cadences and fluted 'u' sound which one associates with the Devonian. The Parret may or may not be the precise frontier, but Bridgwater certainly looks eastward and not westward for its affiliations of speech, while Taunton as surely faces the opposite way — in spite of its Saxon foundation.

The importance of the rivers for the supply of food has perhaps become difficult to credit, for we mostly regard freshwater fish as being virtually inedible. But it was not always so. In 1379 the Bishop of Wells was anxious to make it know that 'inasmuch as certain persons unknown have taken many fish in the River commonly called Tone within the manor of North Curry, to the prejudice of the Chapter of Wells to whom it belongs, to the peril of their own Souls, and to the encouragement of evil-doers, we command you as to all and singular daring persons of this kind, also those affording them assistance, that they incur the just sentence of the greater excommunication'. River fish were an important element in the diet of our forefathers, but the most important source of food in the Somerset rivers is the eel, which has retained its place in the esteem of Somerset folk from the earliest recorded times to the present day. Some idea of the scale of consumption at Glastonbury Abbey is shown by a twelfth-century record of the fishing-station at Martinsey (or Marchey as it is now called) which supplied the monks with 2,000 eels a year, taken from the river Axe. And Martinsey was only one of the Abbey's fishing-stations. The waters of the Brue must have yielded a big additional quota.

On the other side of the Poldens Langport peck-eels were apparently famous in Tudor and Stuart times. Gerard, writing in 1630 or thereabouts, noted that Langport market on a Saturday was full of 'peckeles as they call them, because they take them in those waters by pecking an eale speare on them where they lie in their beds'. The eel-spear, made by some local blacksmith, is still used for 'pecking' eels in the Vale of Avalon, to my certain knowlege; and doubtless in Sedgemoor too, though I have not chanced to come across one there. Another method, used in Gerard's day, has quite definitely gone out of fashion. This is the use of cormorants, in a sort of submarine falconry. A noose slipped round the cormorant's neck prevented the bird from swallowing and obliged it to disgorge its catch after each successful sortie. This method of fishing is still employed in Asia, but it is a forgotten art in Somerset. At any rate I can find no trace of it, in practice or in human memory, but perhaps some enterprising eccentric may care to make a pet of a cormorant and revive an ingenious style of eel-hunting.

The current popular technique, apart from trapping, is 'rayballing'. The equipment is primitive in its simplicity, and a child can master it with ease. All you need is the willingness and the corresponding dexterity to threat a quantity of earthworms on a line. You then loop up the worms to make a ball, and tie the other end of the line to a pole or rod of comfortable size. The tackle is now ready, and the only other thing that is needed is a receptacle to drop the eels into — preferably something that floats, like a galvanised iron bath. The whole point of the operation is that the eels can be relied on to seize the ball of worms underwater and to hang on while the triumphant rayballer lifts them above the surface of the water; but the passage through the air to the receptacle needs to be as brief and smooth as possible, or the eels let go too soon — too soon, that is, from one point of view — and fall back into the water. The first essential is a steady hand. The second is a temperament free from gusts of jerky excitement at the critical moment. Given these things, the eels fly through the air with the greatest of ease and land in the right place. Turbid water after a thunderstorm is said to provide the best conditions for rayballing — or 'clotting' as it is sometimes called — and finer technical points of this kind are earnestly discussed in the lowland pubs and cider houses, where rayballing has as much the status of a country sport as ferreting has in drier parishes.

All honour, then, to the eel — but much more still to its off-spring, the elver. The eel is good staple food: the elver is a delicacy. When the elvers reach the Somerset rivers, in March they are in size and shape 'like a bodkin' — to quote one of the ladies of Langport. Enormous numbers of elvers run up the rivers on the big spring tides, staying out in mid stream while the tide runs, and coming closer to the banks to avoid the ebb when the tide turns. This gives the opportunity to the local people who catch them at night with nets made of cheesecloth on withy benders. A flashlamp or a hurricane lamp is held behind the net to attract the elvers.

An interesting account of the Elizabethan way with elvers is given by Camden. Although he is referring to the Bristol Avon, his words apply equally well to the elvers in the Parret. 'These', he writes, 'with small nets they skim up in great numbers, and by a particular way of ordering them make them scour off their skins. Being thus stripped and looking very white, they make them up into little cakes, which they fry and so eat them.' The modern method of cooking is very similar to Camden's. The elvers are first put into hot water, which removes the slippery slime. The formula is five pints of boiling water to one of cold; if entirely boiling water were used it would remove the flesh as well. After this preparatory cleansing, which is probably what Camden meant by 'scour off their skins', the elvers are ready to be cooked when required. They are first simmered gently just below boiling point for a few minutes, then strained and fried with beaten egg yolks. Or they may be made into a soup. The taste is very delicate.

Elvers are sometimes offered for sale in the district. Thirty years ago the price in Langport for live elvers was threepence or fourpence a basin. Today it would be many times as much, if one were lucky enough to find a seller. More

The Mill, High Ham, Langport (owned by the National Trust)

The River Parret between Langport and Muchelney

The Parret Bore running through Bridgwater — 'It has been known to have overturned large boats in its furious course' *Richard Warner, 1799*

King's Sedgmoor Drain, from Greylake Bridge

probably any surplus to personal requirements would go for export as there is now a keen market for live elvers to stock eel-farms in Europe and Japan. Primarily, though, they are caught for personal use or to be given to a neighbour or acquaintance as a piacular offering. 'Old Jack usually brings me a basin of elvers about now', is something I have heard said, 'I wonder what's happened to him lately.' And there will be a faint uneasiness until Jack turns up one day with the annual tribute, and a good time is had by all.

At the other end of the scale from the tiny elver is the salmon which, as in the Severn, is caught in the Parret by means of the trumpet-shaped traps known as 'putchers'. These traps are made of the local withies and are mounted in ranks. By progressively narrowing they eventually hold the salmon rigidly tail-first against the flow of the tide and, in effect, drown it. They must be cleared after each tide, if the catch is not to fall prey to the gulls and crows. This can be hard work twice a day and poorly rewarding if there is not a good run of salmon. Today putchers are illegal except on authorised sites which are the subject of ancient rights. Dip-nets are also used when turbid water drives the fish to the surface. The tip of the back-fin and the tail-fin are the sign that the dip-netter watches for. The reported catch nowadays is no more than twenty-five to thirty fish a year but poaching would account for an unknown number in addition. In 1956 the year's reported total was as high as 552 salmon. The older fishermen speak nostalgically of the thirties when salmon weighing twenty to thirty pounds were common. A fish taken in putchers in 1951 weighed forty-one pounds — a weight which has not been surpassed in twenty seasons since then.

The Brue has a much less interesting history and character than the Parret. Even its name lacks conviction. Before the eighteenth century it was sometimes known as the Brent river, and in 1638 its lower reaches were called the Fishlake river. Its course too is uncertain. The leading authority on the watercourses of the Somerset Levels, Dr Michael Williams, suggests that before the thirteenth century the Brue probably flowed northward from Glastonbury, past the eastern side of the Wedmore island and up the Axe valley. The fortunes of Brue and Axe are certainly inter-related in an interesting way because — if they were separated near Glastonbury — they were partially reunited downstream by the Pillrow Cut, which linked the two rivers round the western flank of the 'island' of Wedmore. The modern course of the Brue was established when Meare Pool existed and the river flowed out of it. Neither the Brue nor the Axe is tidal. Their outfalls are sealed with 'clyses' or sluices which hold back the sea. The Brue was controlled in this way before 1485, the Axe in 1806.

Nowadays it is difficult to believe that the Axe could ever have carried a significant sea-going traffic but it certainly did so when Glastonbury was at the height of its medieval glory. In a country-side so dominated by water, and in many areas so impassable on land, the fullest use must always have been made of the rivers, the lakes, the lagoons, indeed of any water deep enough to float a boat. There is no knowing who were the first primitive craftsmen to make a boat and put out in it on the Somerset floods and water-ways, but the peat has preserved one or two early examples. A dug-out canoe, about five metres long and in good condition, was found near the Glastonbury Lake Village and is now in the Taunton Museum. Another, 'formed from an immense oak', was described by a local antiquary in 1839. It was known in the district as 'Squire Phippen's big ship' and was broken up by the neighbouring cottagers for fuel.

When the great monastic houses began to reclaim and drain the land they also started to improve and develop the rivers; and they did so with three or four different purposes in mind. To the medieval planners and engineers each river was a drain, an essential source of food, a highway for the transport of goods and people, and a source of motive power for their mills. Not surprisingly these different uses sometimes led to vehement conflicts between rival interests. Anything which obstructed the flow of water and caused flooding angered the farmers whose land was affected; and if it also impeded shipping it enraged another section of the community. Ham Mill on the Tone, for example, which belonged to Athelney Abbey, was for long the subject of litigation because the mill was held to obstruct navigation and cause flooding.

In terms of waterborne traffic the most important innovation made by the monks of Glastonbury was the Pillrow Cut. It is difficult to decide the proportional values that the creators of the Cut assessed for it as a drainage work and, by contrast, as a shipping channel. The fact that it drew off a large volume of water from the Brue and diverted it into the lower Axe must have improved the drainage of the Brue valley. Nevertheless its prime importance appears to be that it gave Glastonbury an excellent access-route to the open sea. The estuary of the Brue, opening through Highbridge to the treacherous sandy flats around Steart Island, must always have been unsuitable for shipping. Glastonbury therefore looked to the mouth of the Axe, at the Uphill end of Weston Bay and sheltered by the promontory of Brean Down. Here the Abbey found its port of entry. The Pillrow Cut struck out northwards from the main channel of the Brue, crossed Mark Moor and made its junction with the Axe near Rooks Bridge. At Rooks bridge were a mill, built by Abbot Walter de Monyngton, and port facilities for loading and unloading the boats that came alongside the wharves to put goods ashore or to tranship their cargoes into smaller vessels that plied upstream from Rooks Mill to Meare Pool and Glastonbury itself. And as well as its sea-going traffic the little port at Rooks Bridge must have found plenty of activity in the bustle of transport between the Abbey and its coastal estates at Brent and Berrow.

The value of such a sea-route is made startlingly clear by what happened in about 1500, when the Abbey masons were completing the church of St John's. The seats for the church were to come to Glastonbury from Bristol, an overland journey of about twenty-five miles across the Mendips. Presumably, however, this route was too difficult, for the seats were shipped at Bristol in two large boats 'from the Back near Temple Friars' and transported down the Avon and round the coast to the mouth of the Axe. At Rooks Mill, some miles up the river, the cargo was transhipped into barges which had come down from Meare, and thus conveyed up to Glastonbury — though some part of the seating was carted from the Bristol ships when they unloaded at Rooks Mill, so there was no insuperable difficulty about moving it without boats. Clearly the sea-route from Bristol to Glastonbury was the more sensible and practical way of carrying goods in 1500.

Such ideas are extremely difficult for us today to grasp, but we must contrive to envisage Glastonbury as an important seafaring centre in medieval England. Axwater was one of the three main ports of Somerset in the fifteenth century, the others being Minehead and Combwich, and it was the Abbey at Glastonbury which dominated Axwater and gave it its significance. The Abbot claimed the rights of 'wreck of sea' from Berrow to Brean Down and appears to have had his own system of customs and excise. In the reign of Richard II, at the end of the fourteenth century, there was a dispute with the Crown over some salt that was brought up the river Axe by a merchant named Roger Brymmore on board the *Mary de Dertemuth*. The Abbot was accused of buying this salt at his own price and not at the King's price — which sounds like another way of saying that he was dodging the Customs. The matter came to trial and the Abbot's procurator, Thomas Barton, successfully resisted the charge. He was able to prove that the Abbey had owned the river from time immemorial and possessed the right to levy its own dues on all kinds of merchandise.

Certainly the use of the Axe for Glastonbury's shipping was already well established, because in the previous century the Abbot had been accused of breaking several fisheries with his boats in the Axe. The cutting of the Pillrow river extended and to a large extent perfected a system of waterborne transport which the monks had progressively developed from the earliest times. The Abbot himself was accustomed to visit his estates by boat, and it is pleasant to imagine the great man in all his dignity riding down the Brue in some kind of state-barge to pay an official visit to the Abbey lands at East Brent. He might stay for a few days at High Hall, one of his outlying residences in the village of Mark, and then proceed along the Pillrow river, accompanied by his cook, his huntsman and his dogs.

On such expeditions, business and pleasure were combined. There would be time for some hunting as well as the round of interviews with the Abbey's tenants. And on the way down, the Abbot would doubtless pass barges plying upstream to Glastonbury with foodstuffs and building materials and the various merchandise that his officials needed for the conduct of the community's life and work. A thriving and colourful picture, that fades in the light of the present day and leaves no reflection on the empty waters of the river Brue. At Rooks Bridge a few houses scattered about a crossroads communicate nothing of the past. All that remains of the Pillrow is a weedy rhine beside a narrow and insignificant roadway. It would be hard to find a more inarticulate or unassuming scene anywhere in the county. No trace of High Hall survives, and the great lake of Meare has vanished as if it had never been. Only the Brue itself persists, turbid and inscrutable, the forgotten highway of Glastonbury's shipping.

CHAPTER FOUR

RECLAIMING THE LEVELS

The Mark Yeo was the first major artificial waterway on the Somerset Levels. Historically therefore it can be described as the prototype of the eighteenth-century King's Sedgemoor Drain and the twentieth-century Huntspill river. What they have in common is the determination of Somerset men to improve Nature's unhelpful design. But when one examines them separately they are interestingly different in their combination of motives; and their stories are strikingly characteristic of the periods to which they belong.

The Mark Yeo was an expansion of communications: to the men of Glastonbury Abbey it probably had the sort of significance that a new motor-way has for us. King's Sedgemoor Drain was an essential part of a larger money-making scheme to enclose and reclaim the moor. The Stuart Kings, always in financial straits, saw in the scheme the prospect of a quick profit. So, a century later, did the noble landlords who were pressed to settle their gambling debts by one means or another, and saw a hope of salvation in an Enclosure project. The neglected wastes of Sedgemoor inspired more than 100 years of cupidity and sharp practice before the great Drain was finally cut and the thousands of improved acres parcelled out to their new and fortunate owners.

By contrast the Huntspill river, in the earlier stages of its planning, had the misfortune to arouse, not greed, but parsimony. Modern anxiety to avoid displeasing taxpayers and ratepayers, combined with the supine and dilatory process of public administration, delayed the Huntspill river for a century, until wartime necessity brought it into being. The manufacture of munitions spoke a more eloquent and urgent language than the needs of land-drainage.

King's Sedgemoor, lying between the Poldens to the north and Sowy and High Ham to the south was too big a problem for the medieval engineers to tackle. They made the Greylake Fosse across it, as a causeway, but they were resigned to the fact that it was regularly subject to flooding. At times there was an unbroken sheet of water stretching across King's Sedgemoor and extending over Somerton Moor to the very doors of the houses in Somerton. Up to 1600 about one third of the floodable land in central Somerset had been reclaimed, assuming a total of 65–70,000 acres of land at risk. In this connection it is interesting to note that the great flood of 1872–3 covered almost 70,000 acres; this figure therefore represents with probable accuracy the land which was low enough to be submerged in an exceptionally wet winter. The early improvers concentrated their efforts on the clay lands of the coastal belt and the alluvial deposits that skirted the 'islands'. What still remained untouched when the Stuarts began their reign was the great moorland wastes north and south of the Poldens. And the most tempting and challenging was King's Sedgemoor where 12,000 acres of pasture were only fit for cattle during two or three months of the year.

The first move was made by James I in 1618. Since the whole of the moor had belonged to Glastonbury Abbey until the Dissolution of the Monasteries James claimed that it had then become the property of the Crown and he therefore had a legal right to drain it and to enclose land. The royal title to the land was questioned by some but the Attorney-General disposed of their objections. Then rumours were spread about that the drainage was not to be done for the King but for a private person. To put an end to these doubts and uncertainties James demanded that all the local lords, tenants and owners 'should subscribe their names to their assents or dissents'. This seems to have silenced local opposition. The neighbouring manorial lords had grazing rights to be considered, and so had the lesser commoners, but these were matters for negotiation and compensation.

Inevitably James lacked the capital to finance a major drainage scheme so he had to turn to speculators and developers who were prepared to advance money in return for allotments of land. The King's slice of the drained and enclosed land was to be 4,000 acres, one third of the whole area. The local landowners were to have most of the remainder, with the King's 'agents' — the developers — having a promise of 300 acres to spur them on. Opposition from the commoners delayed the scheme and was to become a recurring obstacle to the metropolitan speculators. Seven years passed inconclusively after James's first move to reclaim the moor and then, in 1625, he died without having achieved anything.

In the hands of Charles I the affair turned into a sort of political comedy, with King, landowners, agents, commoners and investors intriguing and manoeuvring and pulling in all directions. From time to time the financial underworld threw up such humorous characters as 'John Battalion, alias Shotbolt' and Mr Waldron, 'a man very criminal and defamed'. The Stuart Kings were not the wisest selectors of men when they chose their aides and financial helpers. The character of Sir Giles Overreach in Philip Massinger's play *A New Way to Pay Old Debts* was a topical satire indeed when it first appeared in 1633. This rapacious plotter of enclosures and other stratagems to extort money was a portrait of Sir Giles Mompesson, who made use of his family connection with James I's favourite, the Duke of Buckingham, to become a commissioner for the issue of certain licences and thereby to amass a fortune by oppression and fraud. James also made Mompesson surveyor of the profits of the New River Company (the forerunner of London's Metropolitan Water Board) with an annual income of £200 to be paid out of the profits. Mompesson's unscrupulous conduct became so blatant that the House of Commons started an inquiry: in due course he was disgraced, deprived of his knighthood and exiled. One of his associates was the 'very criminal' Mr Waldron.

The time came, in 1632, when Charles I lost all hope of making any money out of the drainage of King's Sedgemoor and decided to sell out. It may have been a sensible move because the opponents of enclosure at that time could be distinctly rebellious. When the King did have a success, in the drainage and enclosure of Alder Moor, there was something like a riot in Glastonbury and Crown officials were besieged there by an angry mob; subsequently walls were thrown down and rhines filled in. The buyer of the King's interest in Sedgemoor was a London merchant named Kirby, an interesting but shadowy character who paid a lump sum of £12,000 plus an annual rent of £100. Jeffrey Kirby seems to have had a positive approach to the drainage of the moor. He already owned an estate in Sutton Marsh, Lincolnshire, and was associated with Cornelius Vermuyden the celebrated engineer who drained the Fens.

What precisely was the business relationship between them is difficult to determine but one suspects that Kirby was acting as a front-man so that Vermuyden's presence could be concealed from those who would resist a 'Fenland' project south of the Poldens. However this new turn of events produced nothing in the way of action before Kirby died and the Civil War broke out. Not until 1655 was there any further attempt to do anything, and then Vermuyden petitioned Cromwell for a new commission to 'go on with so good a work'. A Bill eventually came before Parliament but the opposition of the smaller men, the tenants and freeholders, was powerful enough to frustrate it. And now, like others before him, it was Vermuyden's turn to shrug his shoulders, cut his losses, and sell. The contribution that this most famous of drainage engineers might have made to the Somerset landscape remains an enigma. He leaves the story as he entered it, without disclosing his plans.

After the Restoration there were new attempts to revive public interest in the drainage of King's Sedgemoor but they languished in what was now a familiar and almost stereotyped way. Parliament was invited to empower commissioners to sound local opinion and take the preliminary steps towards some degree of a consensus among the interested parties. The smaller men who, by force of numbers, amounted to a massive public opinion that could not be lightly disregarded, offered their customary opposition: on balance they apparently preferred to retain the limited usefulness of the moor as it was, rather than risk losing all their claims in the legal wrangling and sharp practice that were likely to accompany a major enclosure scheme. The commissioners wavered and procrastinated until their power expired with nothing decided. And so, for another 100 years, the great moor was left undisturbed. The winter rains flooded it, sheep were often rotted in the boggy conditions and in summertime the pasture was liable to be overgrazed as more and more beasts were turned out, legally and illegally.

What gradually began to change public attitudes was the general movement for the reform of agriculture. The latter part of the eighteenth century saw radical new initiatives in farming, with the dissemination of scientific knowledge through newly founded agricultural societies like the Bath & West (founded in 1777). The raising of standards by more up-to-date methods took on something of the nature of a crusade. When Arthur Young saw King's Sedgemoor in 1771 he described it as 'a sea' in winter and made the significant comment 'What a disgrace to the whole Nation it is.' This passion to bring even the most unpromising land into a state of highly efficient production was one that local landowners might have been expected to share, and yet in the same year as Arthur Young's visit a meeting was convened in Bridgwater to organise opposition to a bill 'for draining, dividing and inclosing King's Sedgemoor'. The chairman at this meeting was Sir Charles Kemyes Tynte, a local manorial lord and a Member of Parliament who might have been expected to support the bill. Indeed he remarked in his speech (as reported in the *Western Gazette*) that 'it had been represented to him that the inclosure of the Moor would tend greatly to the benefit of the Lords of the Manors adjacent'. Nevertheless he was evidently suspicious of the promoters of the bill who had apparently circulated a rumour that he had signed a document in support of it. And this 'he did himself the honour to assure them it was absolutely false'.

The suspicions of men like Tynte did not lack justification. In the more disreputable and financially desperate circles of London society there still persisted a wild dream of the instant fortune that lay beneath those stagnant waters south of the Poldens. The seedy 'agents' of Charles I's day were small-timers compared with the eminent rogues of the eighteenth century. Now it was men like Lord Bolingbroke and the Earl of Ilchester's son and heir, Lord Stavordale, who turned to Sedgemoor for a method of staving off and settling their gambling debts. A prominent creditor was Lord Carlisle; and fortunately he preserved the letters in which George Selwyn kept him informed about his chances of being repaid, as a result of the King's Sedgemoor Scheme on which Bolingbroke and Stavordale now pinned their hopes.

In November 1775 a petition was presented to the House of Commons and leave was given to bring in a bill prepared by a Mr Coxe and Bolingbroke's brother, Mr St John. George Selwyn was chairman of the Commons committee appointed to handle the matter and there is no doubt where his sympathies lay. He wanted to see his friend 'Bully' in funds again and he wanted Lord Carlisle to recover the money Bolingbroke owed him. In a letter to Carlisle Selwyn wrote — 'Bully has a scheme of enclosure, which, if it succeeds, will free him from all his difficulties. It is to come into our House immediately. I can not help wishing to see him once more on his legs.' He also reported to Carlisle that Stavordale was 'deeply engaged in this Sedgemoor Bill' and stood to gain £2,000 a year by it. Doubtless an important consideration was the fact that the

Ilchesters were lords of the manor of Somerton and would therefore have rights in Sedgemoor; Bolingbroke similarly owned land in the area.

As Selwyn settled down to the apparently undemanding task of piloting the Bill through his committee he evidently thought that, as he wrote to Carlisle, 'it was a matter of form only'. He was certainly unprepared for the opposition that confronted him. 'I had no sooner begun to read the preamble to the Bill, but I found myself in a nest of hornets.' Later he wrote 'This Bill will not go down so glibly as Bully hoped it would.' The opposition meanwhile won the support of influential figures like Lord North and on 12 December 1775, the Bill was defeated. Selwyn himself was alert enough to realise that a last minute effort might have mustered just sufficient support to scrape through but the promotors of the Bill were too complacent to take the trouble. And so 'this phantom of £30,000 clear in Bully's pocket vanishes'.

The key to the vigour of the opposition is revealed in Selwyn's analysis of what went wrong. 'They sent one Bill into the country for the assent of the people interested, and brought me another, differing in twenty particulars, to carry through the Committee, without once mentioning to me that the two Bills differed.' One can sympathise with poor Selwyn when he adds tartly, 'This they thought was cunning, and I believe a happy composition of Bully's cunning and John's idea of his own parts.'

In the light of this sort of fraud it becomes easier to understand Charles Kemyes Tynte's indignant disclaimer at the Bridgwater meeting four years earlier. Local feeling against enclosure was at times violent: in 1775 a man working on a survey of King's Sedgemoor was 'threatened with his life' and a hogshead of cider was offered as a reward for catching him. But by degrees calmer and more rational voices began to make themselves heard. Arthur Young's estimate that drainage would improve the value of Sedgemoor from 18d an acre to £1 or 25s was not to be lightly ignored. And there were local men, much respected in the farming community, whose fervent advocacy of new ideas and methods undoubtedly influenced public opinion.

One was John Billingsley, who farmed at Sutton Mallet; another was a Burnham grazier, Richard Locke. Both these men were capable journalists and they pressed their arguments in pamphlets and in the columns of the Journal that the Bath & West Agricultural Society had started to issue. Like Arthur Young they regarded the poor condition of the moors as a gross neglect of national resources. They had no patience with the suspicious and reactionary attitude of the humble commoners who liked their inefficient easygoing way of life and asked no more than the right to keep a few cattle, a pig or two and some geese. To the 'improvers' there was something downright immoral in such behaviour. Billingsley's scornful pen portrait of a commoner rises to a final pitch of indignation with the words — 'At length the sale of a half-fed cow, or hog, furnishes the means of adding intemperance to idleness.'

Ranged against such fecklessness was the pressure of men whose energy and capital needed space to expand. In his study of Richard Locke, Michael Williams draws attention to the dramatic rise in the prosperity of the coastal graziers during the eighteenth century. In 1750 only one man in Burnham was reputed to be worth £1,000. Before the end of the century fifty were worth £10,000 or more; and ten were worth £100,000. By sheer force of example Locke had a crushing answer to the 'owners of geese' who burnt his effigy as a token of their resistance to the gospel of drainage and enclosure. But theirs was now a losing battle.

When the Rev S. Shaw passed through Somerset in 1788 he clearly echoed the opinion of informed observers when he wrote of the flooded moors as 'a discredit to so fine a county' and indicated that an immediate enclosure was 'now likely to take place'. He recalled the disastrous attempt of 1775 and added an ironical footnote to Bolingbroke's discomfiture by reporting that, after the defeat of his scheme, Bolingbroke sold his 400 acres for 'the inadequate sum of £500' — inadequate indeed in comparison with the dream of £30,000; and 'what a bargain' Mr Shaw remarked, with enclosure coming at any moment.

It was in fact just three years later, in 1791, that Parliament at last passed an Act for the draining of King's Sedgemoor and so brought to an end nearly two centuries of argument and conflict. The plan was to divert the river Cary away from the Parret and into a new channel cut straight across King's Sedgemoor to an outfall secured with a 'clyse' at Dunball on the estuary of the Parret below Bridgwater. From Henley Corner, where the diversion of the Cary began, to Dunball the new channel was twelve miles in length and the cost of the project was about £31,600. Of the 4.063 claims to some part in the share-out of the moor 1,796 were allowed.

But if King's Sedgemoor provided the biggest and most protracted controversy it was by no means the only one that came to a head at the end of the eighteenth century as a result of the vigorous campaign waged by the 'improvers'. With one victory achieved attention now turned north of the Poldens, to the valleys of the Brue and the Axe. And as if to add emphasis to the declared needs of the area the sea broke through the coastal defence wall at Huntspill and filled the Vale of Avalon with salt water that the Brue drainage system was unable to absorb. The reformers were now in full cry and the elements continued to argue their case for them. In September 1799 the Rev Richard Warner walked over Crannel Moor — 'Crankhill Moor' as he called it — from Glastonbury to Wookey, and then over Cheddar Moor. Later in the month, on his return journey from Devonshire he intended to follow the same course but was compelled to go round through Wells because 'the whole country was inundated, and one wide sheet of water spreads itself over the flats'. And so it remained for five months in the Axe valley during that winter.

By the turn of the century Parliament was ready to take the necessary action. At a cost of £60,000 the Brue Drainage Act of 1801 produced new rhines and an orderly pattern of enclosure: the cost was recovered by selling part of the land affected, the remainder of the land being allocated to those who could prove commoner's rights. A similar Act of 1802 dealt with the Axe valley. The introduction of floodgates at Bleadon put an end to navigation up the Axe, and the maritime history of Glastonbury's port at Rooks Bridge and Wells's at

Rackley was thus formally closed although of course both had long since decayed. Uphill, at the mouth of the Axe, retained a seaborne trade for a time. In 1829 its coalwharf could accommodate vessels of up to eighty tons.

The transformation which took place in the latter part of George III's reign is greater than we may perhaps realise. For example, the willow-fringed rhine — so typical of this countryside and seemingly of such long tradition — was absent as late as the 1790s from the moors between Burrow Bridge and Curry Rivel. Collinson says specifically of these moors that in his time they were not 'divided by ditches, planted on each side with willows, like those about Glastonbury'. And a print of the same period, showing the view across Sedgemoor to the Burton Pynsent monument, has no trace of a willow in it. The landscape as we now know it was first patterned by the boundary marks of the new enclosures. In Hay Moor and Curry Moor this began in 1797; in West Sedgemoor not until 1816. And Billingsley, in his practical and economic way, noted down the cost of making a rhine — anything from 1s 2d to 2s for a length, known as a 'rope' which measured 20ft. And he added that such a rhine would be 8ft wide across the top, 4ft wide at the bottom and 5ft deep. Not all rhines are still 8ft wide; some of them perhaps have not been scoured out as they ought to be, but it takes a pretty good leap to get across most of them.

CHAPTER FIVE

CANALS, RAILWAYS AND MUNITIONS

Perhaps the most important achievement of Locke, Billingsley and their supporters was that for the first time the problems of the Levels were examined in terms of a complete river system. This was certainly the case with the Axe and the Brue, and it could be argued that the King's Sedgemoor scheme was quite largely a reformation of the river Cary. One might have expected therefore that the nineteenth century, with new sources of power and increased engineering skills, would soon make good any defects in the detail of what were fundamentally good approaches to the remaining problems.

In the event nothing could be further from the truth. There was a total failure to produce large enough administrative units with adequate means of finance to control a whole catchment area, and there was plain neglect of the sort of maintenance that is essential in the pervasive wateriness of this country where sluice-gates rot, channels silt up and banks slip and slide down into the rhines at the first sign of neglect. In an astonishing comment Dr Williams says, 'The drainage situation in 1900 was no better, and possibly worse in some localities, than it was a hundred years before.' Even the heavy rainfalls and consequent large-scale floods of the 1870s and 80s' were answered by little more than official reports and administrative hand wringing.

What may perhaps offset these inglorious years was the nineteenth-century preoccupation with another kind of waterway and with questions of industrial communications rather than agricultural drainage.

Expanding trade and the application of new economics to farming led to a demand for better transport. Traffic on the rivers was handicapped by the high rise and fall of the tidal reaches, and by other inconveniences, so canals became the enthusiasm of the day. As early as 1795 a canal between Bristol and Taunton was being discussed and work was actually commenced after the passing of an Act in 1811. Billingsley, himself an active supporter of the scheme, has left this comment:

It was intended to commence at Pill near Bristol, and to communicate with the Grand Western at Taunton. The Bristol and Western Canal, as it was called, might have been carried near 50 miles without a lock, and for the most part through a strongly clay soil. It would, in conjunction with the Grand Western Canal, have delivered coal to the inhabitants of the county of Devon at nearly half the present price; and yet all these benefits were frustrated by a certain nobleman, merely because he conceived he had not been treated by the ostensible promoters of it with becoming deference and respect.

Some part of the canal was cut, however, and came into use. The stretch from Taunton to Bridgwater was begun in 1824 and opened in 1827. There followed a ferocious battle with the Conservators of the river Tone, who first of all secured heavy compensation and then proceeded to fight a price-war in the tolls levied on shipping. In the end the canal company had to buy them out, and eventually the annual income from tolls reached £7,000.

Meanwhile even greater plans were brewing. In 1810 Rennie made a first survey for a ship canal, capable of carrying vessels of 120 tons burthen from the Bristol Channel to the English Channel, via Bridgwater, Ilminster, Chard and Axminster to Seaton. Described at the time, and not without reason, as 'one of the grandest schemes ever projected in this country', the canal was designed to save the long and often dangerous haul around Land's End. In 1825 an Act was passed, with the appointment of Telford as engineer, for a modified and yet more ambitious version — capable now of carrying vessels of up to 200 tons, at an estimated cost of construction of £70,000 per mile. And it was confidently prophesied that Taunton would become 'a second Liverpool'.

How quickly dreams can fade! The grand project was never executed of course, and the railways finally killed it, though from time to time the proposal has been renewed and still finds an occasional supporter. A less ambitious project, providing a southward branch from the Bridgwater & Taunton Canal to Chard, met with more success. Though it was never profitable, it opened in 1842 and operated for a time. An engineering curiosity with its four inclined planes and three tunnels, it was closed in 1866 and has now largely disappeared, though here and there you will find traces of it still surviving. Near Lillesdon and Wrantage the ruined watercourse is still an impressive sight. The channel is clearly defined, and the remains of a powerful stone aqueduct point the way to the tunnel which penetrates through Crimson Hill for a mile and emerges at Beer Crocombe.

The crossing over the road at Wrantage has been dismantled and the walls of the aqueduct, built of large blocks of lias stone, have been incorporated into farm buildings. The watercourse of the canal is now lined with willows and covered by a grassy sward dotted with trees and shrubs. The stonework at the entrance of the tunnel was in surprisingly good condition when I last saw it, but the interior has collapsed and become impassable. A line of square socket holes in the wall on either side may be been used to give a grip to the poles with which the barges were propelled through the tunnel.

Compared with these disasters the other Somerset canal schemes had a happier history, at least for a while. In 1795 the Ilchester Canal Company began to develop the valley of the Parret above Langport. Before 1795 craft had come up the Parret to below Langport on the tide. In that year an Act empowered the Ilchester & Langport Navigation Company to develop the valley of the Parret above Langport by building a navigation which would carry vessels by way of the Portlake rhine and Long Load to Ilchester. The projected works never reached completion, however, and in 1836 a new company came into existence which did more for Langport's waterborne commerce. This was the Parret Navigation Company, which operated until 1878: it improved the navigation and built locks up to Thorney, and it created a little port on the Ilminster road at Westport by cutting a branch canal to meet the Parret's tributary, the river Isle, shortly before it joins the main stream in its passage past Muchelney to Langport. Incidentally it was a man trained in the canal trade of Langport — Walter Bagehot — who became Disraeli's adviser in the greatest of all our canal projects, the buying of the British interest in the Suez Canal.

Another canal which stopped short of the wilder flights of fantasy and enjoyed a period of modest success was the Glastonbury Canal which, for a generation, revived Glastonbury's old connection with the sea. The canal made use of the South Drain through the Brue valley and linked with the lower reach of the Brue to join the sea by a tidal lock at Highbridge. Work started on it in 1829 and the canal was opened on 15 August 1833. It improved the drainage of the Brue valley and seemed to be a dual-purpose asset, channeling the waters of Avalon into a good mercantile use and expelling any surplus. But the effectiveness of the canal began to deteriorate when waterlogged peat swelled up in the bed of the waterway and obstructed traffic. There were growing difficulties too with accumulations of silt at Highbridge.

The canal was already in decline when the shadow of the new rival, the railway, began to fall on it. In 1841 the first trains on Brunel's Bristol and Exeter Railway, an extension of the broad-gauge Great Western from Paddington, ran through Highbridge from Bristol to Bridgwater. Freight drawn by steam locomotives passed over the river Brue and the freight-barges on the canal, in the first visible display of the power that was so swiftly to conquer the waterways. In 1848 the Glastonbury Canal was bought by the Bristol and Exeter Railway Company for £7,000 with a promise that the canal would be maintained in good order and worked in connection with the railway.

The promise may or may not have been sincere but it was certainly short-lived. A railway following the same route as the canal and extending to Wells and Bruton had been canvassed locally during the 1840s. At a meeting at Bridgwater in 1851, chaired by George Warry of Shapwick, the Somerset Central Railway Company was launched, with the intention of constructing and operating a line from Highbridge to Glastonbury. An Act authorising the new company to proceed was given the royal assent on 17 June 1852, and work began on the twelve miles of track. The Bristol and Exeter adopted a 'big brother' attitude to the new company and helped it in various ways, including the sale to it of the Glastonbury Canal for shares to the value of £8,000 in the Somerset Central. Six years after it first passed into the hands of the railway-men the proviso that the canal would be kept in good order came to an abrupt end. In July 1854 the canal was closed.

In the following month the first train ran from Highbridge to Glastonbury, taking 35 minutes over the journey and the stop at Shapwick to collect 'some of the natives', as George Warry described his neighbours. From the station at Glastonbury there was a triumphal march through the town to celebrate the inauguration of the new service. 'Railway and Civilisation' was the slogan on one of the banners, and it leaves one in no doubt of the almost evangelical fervour of the railway's champions. They were conscious of having written a new chapter in the history of the peat moors.

In retrospect what seems particularly significant about the Somerset Central is the composition of its board of directors, which showed that new industrial elements were entering the old closed world of landowner and farmer. Much of the driving force in the management of the railway came from James Clark who, like his brother Cyrus, was a founding director. And in these brothers one can discern the shift of power from agriculture to industry. Cyrus had started a business in Street in 1825 as a fell-monger, a skin-dresser and — more particularly — a maker of sheepskin rugs. His brother James joined him in 1833 and took the marketing of the sheep's by-products a stage further with his introduction of wool-lined slippers. Together they founded the dynasty of the great footwear company that bears their name and today provides one of the dominant forms of employment in central Somerset. In the 1850s they championed the railway as the new and modern mode of transport for an England that was already becoming increasingly industrialised even in apparently rural areas.

In 1857 the railway was extended to Burnham, making a promising connection with a newly built landing-slip there. A trading link with South Wales was an important aim for the railway. A regular steamship service with Cardiff was inaugurated and survived until 1888 in spite of the unsuitability of Burnham as a shipping terminal. There were plans to improve matters by altering the course of the Brue and constructing a harbour but they came to nothing. Burnham Pier continued to be used as an occasional landing-place for pleasure boats like the Campbell steamers until about 1910, but mud and tide were too strong for Burnham to overcome and it was Highbridge which proved to be more successful as a rail-head port.

However Burnham had its hour of glory when the Somerset Central amalgamated with the Dorset Central in 1863. The men of the famous 'Slow and Dirty' line dreamed the same dream that had haunted the canal-builders — a through connection from the Bristol Channel to the English Channel, linking the expanding industries of South Wales with the European mainland. In 1865 the Somerset and Dorset Railway opened a combined rail and steamship service from Burnham to Cherbourg via Poole Harbour. With the Cardiff-Burnham service already established a new era in travel must have seemed to dawn as the slumbering peat moors trembled and vibrated under the cosmo-politan traffic of shuttling Welshmen and Frenchmen. Alas, the dream was swift to fade. After only two years the service from Poole to Cherbourg was withdrawn.

Highbridge, by contrast, had quite a long run as a cargo port, particularly in the handling of rails from the Welsh steel works which were shipped from Newport for use on the Somerset & Dorset tracks, and later on the London & South Western Railway. As the railway workshops were also at Highbridge the town owed much of its prosperity in Victorian and Edwardian days to the Somerset & Dorset. Equally it was to suffer grievously when the railways began to economise, to prune and to contract. The workshops at Highbridge closed in 1930. Three years later the railway company disposed of its shipping interests. Two cargo boats, the *Julia* and the *Radstock*, were sold; and for the little port of Highbridge the end was in sight although other sorts of shipping used it occasionally until about 1950.

The politics of Somerset's railways were involved and often treacherous. Consider the fate of the Somerset Central. Built under the guardianship of the Bristol & Exeter, it shared Brunel's broad gauge of 7ft. But the broad gauge was dropped and, after amalgamation with the Dorset Central, the combined Somerset & Dorset pursued an independent course. However the completion of the *Bath Extension* in 1874 brought it to the verge of bankruptcy and it was bought by a narrow-gauge partnership of the Midland and the London & South Western (the GWR's arch enemy). It was incidentally down the Somerset & Dorset from Bath to Templecombe that the first through freight trains ran from the Midlands to the South West — many of them taking Burton beer and spelling doom to local breweries. After the opening of the *Bath Extension*, the Somerset & Dorset's main line was always regarded as Bath–Bournemouth, and the original Somerset Central out of Highbridge became a quiet branch serving the peat land and carrying a few cross-country passengers, though a creamery was later opened at Bason Bridge and an occasional milk train still trundles for the first few miles alongside the deserted canal.

Another Bristol & Exeter branch was that from Durston to Yeovil, through Athelney. The branch itself fell victim to the Beeching axe, but in 1906 part of it had been rebuilt as a link in the new Great Western short-cut to the west via Castle Cary. As David St John Thomas says in his history of West country railways:

> 1906 was too late for a railway drastically to alter the economy of a rural area — not that the erstwhile section of the Yeovil branch had made much difference to the willow-growing district even during the last century. The scenery and way of life in this flat country have changed less than anywhere else in the West, except moorland above the 1,000ft contour. Except when the occasional express thunders across, carrying passengers for destinations which to the local inhabitants are mere names, there hangs an almost uncanny silence and stillness . . . For the most part the expresses come at intervals of two hours in each direction; they have as little to do with the area as the aeroplanes overhead.

The heady dreams of the men who built the canals and the railroad perhaps helped to distract attention from the more fundamental failure of the drainage system on which the wellbeing of town, village and farm ultimately depended. The economic depression of agriculture in the 1870s and '80s, precipitated by cheap imports and the introduction of frozen-meat, had an additionally enervating effect on the finance and administrative vigour available locally. In the decade of the 1870s the value of the finest grazing land in the neighbourhood of Pawlett fell by 50 per cent. For any undertaking that required to levy a local rate this was a time for retrenchment and tightly reined ambition. Those who bore technical responsibilities for flood-control might know well enough what most needed to be done but they could expect scant encouragement and very little practical support.

The only meaningful stimulus to action came from the sheer force of Nature's elemental hostility — from the great floods of 1917 and 1919 that yet again inundated 70,000 acres. Even more eloquent were the events of 11 November 1929, when the river Tone burst its banks at Athelney and caused a vast flood which persisted for three months and left hundreds of people homeless. Action on a major scale was clearly imperative. In the following year Parliament passed a Land Drainage Act which created the Somerset Rivers Catchment Board as the single authority in charge of all the rivers concerned and with wide enough financial and administrative powers to get to grips with the cardinal problems. Even so an ingrained infirmity of purpose and a nervous dependance on the time-wasting procedures of surveys, reports, discussions, re-examinations and all-embracing plans saw the thirties drifting away with disappointingly little to show as a positive achievement. The legal framework was now satisfactory but two innovations were needed to profit from it. One was a new conception of the status and role of the Board's Engineer, giving him executive authority. The other was the mood of public urgency that too often needs a national crisis to arouse it. These were to be the parting gifts of the thirties and together they quickly became involved in a remarkable enterprise which heralded the modern transformation of the moors by writing a new river on the map of Somerset, the Huntspill river.

The story of its creation is worth telling. Though it was made in a hurry, it was not planned in a hurry. Something quite like it was outlined as a proposal in Billingsley's survey of 1797, and we may infer that succeeding generations of Commissioners and Boards were increasingly concerned with the making of some form of new cut south of the Brue. Outline plans were certainly ready long before 1939. What was not forthcoming was the will to finance a substantial public work of this kind. As is so often the case, it took a war to put the thing in motion.

Over the immediate circumstances there plays an engaging irony. At Puriton an immensely secret factory was to be built, for the production of a new type of explosive. And the process of manufacture demanded the assured supply of 3½ million gallons of water per day, winter and summer. Now that is, by any standards, a lot of water — particularly in a dry summer at Puriton which in 1940 had no remarkable sources of supply. Charged with the duty of providing it at all costs, the Somerset Rivers Catchment Board produced again the plan which in peacetime had been thought about so often, and in next to no time the Huntspill river had begun to cut across the moors. A new channel, five miles long from the Parret estuary to Gold Corner, was to connect with the South Drain; with sluices at each end it would become a sort of elongated reservoir, impounding water when necessary. Powerful excavating equipment, reserved for work of high priority, was made available for what seemed to be an unimportant drainage scheme; and so well was the secret of its real purpose kept that one indignant Army unit attempted to commandeer it.

An interesting sidelight is thrown on the nature of the moors by the excavators' experience in digging to the depth they had proposed in their original plan. A channel 24ft deep would carry the water to the sea by force of gravity, so the first cuttings were made at this depth. The excavated spoil, of brown clay mixed with peat and followed by a lower stratum of soft blue clay, was thrown up to form a large bank on either side of the new river. But the weight of the spoil broke the supporting crust and forced up mounds of soft clay through the floor of the newly dug channel.

Scientific analysis of the subsoil indicated that the greatest depth possible for the new river was only 16ft — not enough to carry away all the low-lying floods inland. The only solution was to pump the water up from the lower drains into the new river. And so, at Gold Corner, on the open moor between Woolavington and Edington Burtle, there arose a smart new building which sometimes startled the occasional passer-by by emitting a powerful grunt. Visitors were scarcely encouraged, but those who managed to look inside were able to see the smooth immaculate engines that made no trouble about shifting 250 million gallons inside 24 hours whenever the need arose. And when the need did not arise they slumbered and exhaled an occasional deep sigh scented with diesel oil, while an attendant engineer groomed them to that pitch of metallic sleekness and glossiness that only engineers know how to achieve.

So the Puriton factory got its water, and the need for an alternative emergency source led to improvements in the King's Sedgemoor Drain as well. Since then new works have followed one upon another with great rapidity. The big diesel pumps have given way to automatic electric ones. Concrete and elaborate earth-moving machinery have made the sea walls and river banks virtually impregnable. As for the Huntspill river, its banks have been grassed for many years now and two generations of anglers have accumulated already a store of memories and anecdotes of the good fish in its waters. From the transient emergency of wartime it has passed into the permanence of the moorland scene. Its appearance mellows year by year and men already forget how it came to be there, while they talk nowof the great new motorway of the seventies. Each generation adds something and modifies something else in this age-old struggle to civilise the moors.

CHAPTER SIX

BRIDGWATER

The two principal towns of the Somerset Levels, Glastonbury in the Vale of Avalon and Bridgwater on the Parret estuary, could scarcely provide a stronger contrast. While Glastonbury seems to be permeated through and through with the legends and history of many centuries, Bridgwater has the practical matter of fact manner of a place where today is the most important day in the lives of the people who bustle about in its streets. Its very name appears to be a simple good humoured pun on its only claim to fame: it provides a bridge over the water-barrier of the Parret. And it is indeed true that, to a considerable degree, the bridge and the water are the town. The Parret is the natural frontier between Saxon Wessex and the wild west of Quantock and Exmoor. One has to cross it somewhere and Bridgwater holds the key.

But the pun has no proper validity, for the ancient settlement, the *burh*, went at the Conquest to Walter of Douai, and it has taken time for our tongues to corrupt Burgh Walter. Having knocked the 'l' out of Walter we forgo the 'e' of Bridge as a sort of *quid pro quo*. However, the instinct was right: Walter is dead and forgotten but the waters of the Parret are decisively present and a bridging town is what the situation requires. Between Burrow Bridge and the sea Bridgwater has for centuries offered the only crossing-place for traffic passing between Bristol and Devon.

Before 1958 it offered a single bridge only for road traffic and it had earned national fame of an unwelcome kind as a formidable and unyielding bottle-neck, until the A38 bypassed the centre of the town and turned away over a new bridge. The M5 motorway brings yet another crossing of the Parret and still further reduces the importance of the original bridge, though its long and varied history offers something of a challenge to its modern supplanters. In its first recorded form it was described by Leland as 'a right auncient stronge and high bridge of stone of three arches', and so it remained until 1795. Its successor was an iron bridge – 'a newly constructed iron bridge of curious mechanism' is how Henry Skrine described it in 1801. Southey was more emphatic, dismissing it as 'a miserable iron bridge'. He was probably right because it lasted for only eighty years or so and was replaced in 1883 by the present bridge, a wider and stronger affair with corner pillars of Ham Hill stone.

To concentrate on Bridgwater as a bridge-town, however, is to do the place an injustice. It is not merely a traffic-channel to be passed through en route to happier scenes, to the seaward heathy splendour of the Quantocks, to the holiday landscapes of Devon and Cornwall. To get the best out of any town one must make it one's destination — if only temporarily — and put it into some sort of context. The essential thing about Bridgwater is that it is a brick-town — historically one of the foremost manufacturing centres of brick and tiles in the west of England. In the 1850s there were sixteen brick-and-tile works operating within two miles of the town bridge and a further seven in the outlying rural areas, basing their prosperity on the much-prized Bridgwater clay. The mass-production of cement tiles and machine-made bricks started a decline which by 1970 had turned the years of prosperity into a fading memory. But the character of the town, its visual presence, is an enduring memorial to the old industry.

The most rewarding way to approach Bridgwater is from the south, across the moors, in the way the Parret approaches it — through the stone country of square church towers. Back across the moors, and beyond them, the blue lias stone is the dominant building material, variegated here and there with the warmer Ham Hill stone and its cousin of Doulting. The stone villages and small towns inland, with their peerless churches, are the pride and glory of the county; but the sheer abundance, the ubiquitous rearing grey masses of the lias in particular, begin sometimes to oppress the imagination. At such a moment the rose-coloured tower and delicately drawn spire of St Mary's, Bridgwater, pencilling up to what seems a miraculous height, comes like a revelation of new possibilities. And the Georgian brickwork of Castle Street, warm and gracious to the eye, offers an oasis to anyone who earlier in the day has passed through the blue stone severity of Somerton.

Erected by the Duke of Chandos, Castle Street has been justly described as 'one of the most typically Georgian streets outside Bath'. But you may pass through Bridgwater many times without discovering it, for it lies to one side of the busy press of modern activity. That is no reason, though, to disparage the present. Much of the appeal of Bridgwater lies in its continuous vitality, its resilience in all the changing circumstances of its history. There can hardly ever have been a time when this quite modest town was not vigorously at grips with its destiny; and that sense of enduring virility colours its present character. Glastonbury, by contrast, has collapsed under the weight of its enormous past. It has never quite coped with life since the Abbey died.

Bridgwater, however, is in its way more fortunate. It has had no over-whelming season of greatness. Its fortunes have had their ups and downs. Sometimes it has backed the wrong horse to a disastrous extent, and has then had to recover, to readapt, to make a fresh start. When you come across traces of its past they are not detached, as trophies on a mantelpiece isolated for admiration, but more in the nature of those graven lines and softening shadows which deepen the expressiveness of a still lively countenance. There is not much, of hope and of despair, that has not been lived out — generation after generation — in this unpretentious town.

After the Conquest it was in favour. In 1180 it became the property of Lord William Briwere or Brewer, who contrived to be popular with four kings — Henry II, Richard I, John and Henry III. A remarkable man was Lord William evidently, and it is pleasant to find his name still written somewhere on the county — in the village of Isle Brewers, beyond Langport. From King John he got a charter for Bridgwater as a free borough in 1200, and he got permission to build a castle. He also founded an Augustinian Hospital of St John — and the present St John Street is named after it. His castle was completed in 1210, and some authorities credit him with another great addition to the town — the first stone bridge over the Parret. Gerard dates the old bridge from the time of Richard I, which gives credit to Brewer, but on the other hand the Bridgwater official guide book — and an excellent little book it is — says that Sir John Trivet built it in 1395.

It looks at first sight as if there might be a confusion between Richard I and Richard II, as another reference to the bridge describes it as being 'new' in 1379; but Collinson clouds the issue by asserting that Brewer began the bridge in the reign of John and Trivet completed it in the reign of Edward I. Perhaps one may hazard a guess that Brewer built or began to build a bridge as a necessary adjunct to his castle, and that Trivet renovated and reconstructed it in its later form, with three pointed Gothic arches, a small chapel at one end and the arms of Sir John Trivet cut in the parapet. And in this form it survived until 1795, when the ironfounders of Coalbrookdale stepped in with their more modern affair of 'curious mechanism'.

One other building of the thirteenth century is worth mentioning. Lord William Brewer's son founded a Grey Friars Priory in 1230. He had need to build it well because in 1276 Bridgwater suffered an earthquake, and indeed has continued to quake at intervals. There were earth tremors here in 1682; and on 22 May 1839, the village of Chilton Polden a few miles away suffered so violent a concussion that, in the words of one eyewitness, 'everything was gingling'.

The early prosperity of Bridgwater must have been greatly helped by the Flemish weavers who came to Somerset in the 1330s to develop the woollen trade. 'Bridgwaters' — like 'Tauntons' and 'Dunsters' — became known as a special type of fabric, and the town's Cloth Fair at midsummer was a famous occasion in the trading calendar. Probably it was the prosperity of the weavers which nourished the building of the present parish church. In spite of the Black Death, or perhaps as an act of thanksgiving by the survivors, work was begun on 28 June 1367, with red sand-stone from Wembdon and stone for the spire from the quarries at Ham Hill. A Bristol contractor, Nicholas Waleys, erected the spire — 175ft high — and put in a bill for the job amounting to £143 13s 5½d. That odd halfpenny gives one confidence that he had overlooked

Glastonbury Tor and the Vale of Avalon — 'Wherever you are on the moors your eye turns to the Tor as if it had some magnetic power'

Pollard willows beside a rhine on Stan Moor

The Chard Canal, Crimson Hill Tunnel

The nuclear power station at Hinkley Point

nothing, and yet had kept the price as low as possible. Another sort of man might have made it a round sixpence. Or he might even have been like that astonishing bishop who came to Bridgwater in 1851 to consecrate a new cemetery, and afterwards sent in a bill for £50 for his services.

Apart from its nobly proportioned steeple, the church of St Mary the Virgin has two other striking features. The first is the painting which hangs over the high altar. The other is the rich display of carved woodwork. In some churches it is the proportion of the fabric which is everything; in others it may be the stone carving or the stained glass or the monuments; in St Mary's it is the art of the woodworker that stays in one's memory. And two restorations, in 1697 and 1937, have seemingly done more good than harm. It looks as if some local tradition of high craftsmanship runs through the centuries and is still flourishing. The pulpit is of the early fifteenth century. The Jacobean age is represented in a superbly carved screen. The roof is Victorian, and in its way very fine too. And even newer, but still in the same noble tradition, are the modern screens carved in Bridgwater by the brothers Culliford. Probably the tradition stems from Glastonbury, for you will find magnificent screens in many other churches of Avalon and Sedgemoor — at High Ham and Weston-zoyland and in Glastonbury itself. The monastic craftsmen set up standards of workmanship which their successors have maintained. Even so, in this county of superb carvings, St Mary's, Bridgwater is remarkable for its ample and sustained use of woodwork as its dominant theme. It commands your attention from the moment you cross the threshold.

The altar picture is too well known to need more than a passing reference. It has been ascribed to Murillo, to Tiepolo and to a dozen others. How it came to be in the West Country is a question nearly as obscure as the identity of the artist who painted it. Lord Anne Poulett picked it up in Plymouth in the reign of George III, and it is said to have come into Plymouth as booty captured on the high seas. But who it was who lost it to the sea dogs of Devon, and where it should have been delivered, are mysteries that remain unsolved. Perhaps you see a mystery also in an English peer with a girl's Christian name, but that at least can be explained. Poulett was honoured by having Queen Anne as godmother, and an unfortunate error of sex was not permitted to hinder him from receiving the royal name. Lord Anne Poulett, then, gave the picture to Bridgwater; thither came Sir Joshua Reynolds several times to study it, breaking his journey between London and Plymouth for the purpose; and there it remains, an object of delight and possibly of wonderment to the parishioners of St Mary's.

The completion of the great church seems to mark a high tide in the affairs of the town, which at that time had the power to elect two Members of Parliament. In the following century trade must have gone awry, for in 1468 the town was in such great ruin and decay by want of repair that the merchants no longer came with their ships. The bridge in particular seems to have been in a poor state: to provide for mending it and fortifying it, Edward IV granted a toll on every cart and plough crossing the bridge. The reference to ploughs may be misleading. Until the nineteenth century Somerset folk used the word 'plough' to describe a kind of cart, and referred to the farm implement by its old Saxon name, sul. Thomas Hardy used this ancient word in his story *Interlopers at the Knap*, where a man complained of the burden he carried with the words 'These straps plough my shoulders like a zull'. In the 1880s John Price of Long Ashton said that fifty years previously a plough was always called a 'zul' or 'zulow', and 'plough' meant a waggon; so perhaps Edward IV's toll was levied simply on any wheeled vehicle. The King may well have decided that the town's affairs were not being run properly, because at the same time he gave Bridgwater a mayor and corporation.

One constant task was to preserve the channel of the Parret and maintain its soft and slippery banks, and there are frequent payments recorded for digging away the ooze and providing thorns to bind the mud of the banks firmly so as to resist the swirling water. Sixteenth-century invasion alarms led to some modest fortification of the coast, but Sir Walter Raleigh wisely pointed out, in a report on national defence, that Bridgwater was a port 'into which small barques cannot arrive without precise observation of tide'. No Spaniard attempted the tricky navigation of the Parret, but the failure of the Armada brought no benefit to the town. In 1596 the shipping trade had so decreased that only one barque of any account belonged to the town.

Prosperity returned later. When Defoe visited Bridgwater he found it a populous trading town, well built, and with many families of good fashion dwelling in it, besides merchants. In 1720 upwards of forty sail belonged to the town and ships of 100 tons were often entering. Coal was imported from Swansea and Defoe noted that the cargoes from Bristol included iron, wine, hemp, flax, tar, lead, oil and dyestuffs. By 1750 the port's customs dues were worth £3,000 a year. A hundred years later 4,000 ships traded annually in and out of Bridgwater and emigrants to the United States of America could sail direct. Some of the vessels passing up and down the Parret were built in Bridgwater.

So much for trade: in other spheres Bridgwater's fortunes were more dramatically chequered. In the religious warfare of the seventeenth century the town backed the losing side twice in one lifetime. In the Civil War the castle became a Royalist stronghold and was considered so strong that the King's supporters sent valuables in from far and wide to be stored there. However, in 1645 the Roundheads forced the Parret at Langport and invested Bridgwater. In the siege that followed the nearest the Royalists came to making history was when Fairfax and Cromwell went out in a boat to reconnoitre near Dunwear and were almost capsized by the Bore. Before the castle surrendered most of Eastover was burnt down, and the only pleasant memory that survives is of the Governor's wife — a bold and defiant lady who became so indignant at the suggestion of a surrender that she snatched up a pistol and sent her personal reply in the form of a bullet intended for Cromwell's head. However, she was no more successful than the Bore had been, and was soon obliged to follow the example of her more submissive husband. The Roundhead troops did well out of the affair, as they received five shillings each from the sale of the booty taken from the castle.

Quite otherwise was the experience of a Mr Harvey who had bought the castle along with the manor of Bridgwater in 1630. Mr Harvey had leased the castle to the King's Governor for a rent of £40 a year, which probably seemed to be good business at the time. I do not know if he managed to collect his rent in 1645, nor whether he had put anything into the lease about dilapidations. But the stark and sorry truth was that his property had been knocked about by Roundhead and by Cavalier impartially, so Henry Harvey sat down after the siege and prepared a most detailed and indignant bill for damages incurred. And doubtless he wasted a lot of time, poor man, in trying to find someone to pay it. He certainly got scant sympathy so far as the castle was concerned, because orders were promptly given to dismantle it. In ruin and decay it lived on for many years, and some traces of the walls remained until 1810. All that now survives is a part of the water-gate.

Yet in spite of destruction and defeat, Bridgwater has its cause for pride in the years of Roundhead supremacy, for it was a Bridgwater man among the Puritan leaders whose fame and reputation are today most highly esteemed. Robert Blake, one of the greatest of British admirals, was a Bridgwater man — born in the town in 1599 and baptised at St Mary's. His resolute defence of Taunton was very different from the feeble Royalist command of his native town, and it was probably in closer sympathy with the people of Sedgemoor. The Protestant faith was strong among them, and it was in the cause of that faith that they rose, forty years later, against the restored monarchy. Into the town rode the Duke of Monmouth, to make it his last headquarters. And for the second time within men's memory Bridgwater had backed the losing side. Had Blake been alive to take command, perhaps the massacre of Sedgemoor might have been averted. After all it was very soon afterwards that William III came to achieve with little difficulty what Monmouth had failed to do. But meanwhile Bridgwater suffered under the savage vengeance of the Bloody Assize.

Are these things worth remembering as you pass through Bridgwater, past the multiple shops and among the jostling crowds on the narrow pavements that make this town increasingly like any other? Has history such as this any but a sentimental meaning? Blake on his pedestal points helpfully to the bus stop, in case you may have overlooked it. If you study the tide you can see the Bore that nearly drowned Cromwell. You may find the road that Monmouth's men trod on their way to the battle, if anyone you meet can remember which it is! And St Mary's may invite you to step aside for a few minutes and speculate about times past. But in the main life here goes on with small regard for anything it leaves behind.

That is the essence of Bridgwater's story. There is in the place an ebullience of spirit which makes and discards and remakes. As one industry fails a new one is started. Lassitude gives place to energy, and corruption follows endeavour. The weaving industry expired a century and a half ago; in 1821 only one clothier was left. The traffic of the port has gone. The last ship built locally, the *Irene*, was launched in 1907. The town's docks, becoming derelict in the 1960s, finally surrendered to the specialised needs and styles of modern transport. The winding narrowing estuary of the Parret is unsuitable for modern shipping, which has followed the modern tendency to look for cargo handling facilities further down river. And road transport has proved too competitive for many sorts of goods. With the town's docks closed, the wharf at Dunball is the only one handling general cargo. Eighty per cent of all Parret shipping goes to the specialised Walpole Wharf in the form of petrol and oil from a Swansea refinery to the adjoining 'tank-farms'.

But what is particularly interesting is the development still further down river, at Combwich, of facilities for landing heavy equipment required by the nuclear power stations at Hinkley Point. This is a short-term arrangement but one wonders if Combwich may find other uses as the cargo handling centre for Bridgwater's future needs. The village has a long history as a crossing-place for early pilgrims and for travellers who used the ferry which linked Combwich to Pawlett Hams until the nineteenth century: this latest chapter is certainly an unexpected addition.

Bridgwater Market has suffered a similar decline. At one time it was famous for its cheese. A Cheddar-type of cheese made at Huntspill and South and East Brent was sold under the name of Bridgwater cheese, but the trade was lost to nearby Highbridge. So today, to offset these losses, Bridgwater turns increasingly to new light industries, making shoes and cellophane and anything else that will keep its 27,000 people busy and prosperous. Cellophane provides one third of the town's manufacturing jobs, besides creating the peculiar smell which has become one of the distinctive features that visitors to the town most vividly recall.

And there are less material ups and downs to record. In 1785 the mayor and a group of citizens initiated the first petition to Parliament for the abolition of the slave trade. In 1844 George Williams founded, in Bridgwater, the Young Men's Christian Association — the YMCA. And between those dates the town won such a reputation for political bribery that it was eventually disfranchised. In 1835 Mr Broadwood, the piano manufacturer, offered £40 for a vote — and was outbid by his opponent in the election, Mr Leader, who was prepared to give £50. 'Mr Broadwood's piano-fortes were eclipsed', so the saying went, 'by Mr Leader's piano-fifties.' In such conditions a victory at Bridgwater was apt to cost the lucky candidate some thousands of pounds.

Some of the ways in which bribes were paid are admirable in their ingenuity if in nothing else. One voter sold a parrot to a candidate for 100 guineas. A blacksmith charged fifty guineas for shoeing a horse. And there were secret meetings with a mysterious stranger known as 'The Man in the Moon' who distributed 'samples of tea'. Excellent samples, because they consisted of rolls of money. Perhaps the voters of Bridgwater took the view that all politicians, when elected, dip a hand into the citizen's purse, and that it was therefore a wise precaution to lay hold of some of their money beforehand. But the Bribery

Report of 1868 saw the matter differently, and Bridgwater lost its representation in Parliament until — after a decent interval had elapsed — it was restored in 1885.

Things are quieter now and more seemly — except perhaps on the Thursday nearest to 5 November. That night is set aside for Bridgwater 'squibbing', and the shops will be boarded up, and Blake's statue encased in wood, and people will come in their thousands from all over the county to see the carnival and watch the fireworks. The traditional Bridgwater squib, so large that it might justly be described as the father and mother of all squibs, was always made in the town, though no one seems to know how the custom arose. Perhaps it is Protestant zeal which set Bridgwater on a level rivalled only perhaps by Lewes in devotion to the memory of the foiling of Guy Fawkes, though it becomes somewhat ironical when one recalls how the town fared under the Stuarts. Perhaps after all they are indicating what Guy Fawkes ought to have done.

CHAPTER SEVEN

GLASTONBURY

In July 1890 a branch line from Bridgwater to Edington Burtle (which thereby was elevated to the dignity of Edington Junction) provided a direct rail link between Bridgwater and Glastonbury. For sixty-four years this route across the Sedgemoor country to Bawdrip, over the western tail of the Poldens to Cossington, and then through the peat moors of the Vale of Avalon to Glastonbury, was the most enchanting way of seeing the landscape of central Somerset. In later years the train was a single coach; those who travelled in it will remember the journey as a childlike toyland experience. One almost expected to find Father Christmas driving the engine. And when the inevitable closure of the line came it was genuinely mourned as the loss of one of life's minor pleasures.

Unlike most railway journeys it was far too short. There was so much to see — the wooded slopes of the Poldens, green and gentle, and then the wilder expanse of the moors, dotted with conical stacks of peat, ribboned with quiet waters, picketed with inclining willows that seemed to be absorbed in their own slow, vague, vegetative dreams. At Shapwick the train halted in a little station reminiscent of Edward Thomas's Adlestrop — except that no express ever came to Shapwick. Solitary, except for its attendant pub, the station was lapped round on all sides by the pervasive atmosphere of the turbary. Wild irises grew thickly on the adjoining land, and snipe and wild duck haunted the vicinity.

Beyond Shapwick the railway ran past dense mysterious thickets of the primitive waste, a squamous jungle of scrub alder and what the natives call 'dun-withy'. And as you moved up the Vale of Avalon you became increasingly aware of the compelling presence of Glastonbury Tor. The curiously formal triangular outline of the hill, surmounted by its ruined chapel, has a visual fascination out of all proportion to its size.

In this excessively horizontal landscape it still asserts itself like the one startling exception to an otherwise inflexible rule. Wherever you are on the moors your eye turns to the Tor as if it had some magnetic power. It is even in a way unnatural, a visionary thing, a cryptic symbol of some kind such as an artist might invent. Certainly no rare sensibility is needed to understand how readily the Tor would acquire a supernatural character. It is so aloof from its context, so geometrically self-contained as an uplifted haven riding securely in these marshy wastes. If ever a landscape provided its own altar, this is it. The air of sanctity is unmistakable. The Tor is an island of the uplifted spirit; its symmetry seems to proceed from a purity of conception that is foreign to the natural order of things.

Geologically the Tor is akin to Brent Knoll: each is a harder lias core from which the softer rocks have been scoured away. But Brent Knoll has the character of a fortress, a military stronghold. Seeing it, one has the impulse to climb to the top, to conquer it, to become king of the castle. The Tor is quite different. It is a landmark that the pilgrim heart rejoices to have found, so that still one pauses and says, 'Look, Glastonbury Tor' — for no apparent reason, since it could hardly be more obvious. But mind and memory gather there, to contemplate eternal possibilities. And so it must have been at the beginning of the long spiritual history of the Isle of Avalon.

Incidentally, the Tor — rising to rather more than 500ft — is virtually an island, for its steep slopes rear up from the southern end of the Isle of Avalon. Westward the long narrow spur of Wirrall or 'Wearyall' Hill thrusts out into the moors, and the town clusters about the westerly slopes of the Isle, inclining down to the moor levels at what is called Paradise. That Paradise should be a suburb of Glastonbury will not seem odd to the student of the Avalon myths: it simply confirms one's fondest suspicions.

At Paradise the railway discharged its passengers for Glastonbury. The walk into the town followed the line of Wirrall Hill, which gave an impressive setting to one's approach.

The town itself offers a sharp contrast to Bridgwater in every way. In Bridgwater it is the river which is still the dominant feature although the town's history as a port has virtually ended. The Parret cuts through the town and opens it up. Its banksides are unencumbered. On each side the buildings stand back from the river behind a roadway, giving an air of spaciousness. And the gulls which float on the river or rise above the old bridge are a constant reminder that the open sea is near. In its modest way Bridgwater retains the atmosphere that all ports share of freedom and adventure. History has no climax here. It is not taller than the buildings nor stronger than the inhabitants.

But in Glastonbury that is the case. It is a town overwhelmed by its past. The majestic amplitude of the Abbey, even in its decay, dwarfs and belittles the small market-town that clings to it. 'A ragged poor place' is how Celia Fiennes described Glastonbury in 1698, 'very ragged and decayed'. And so it must have been, for the destruction of the Abbey hit Glastonbury as hard as, say, the demolition of the dockyards would hit Devonport, or as the annihilation of the university would hit Cambridge. What survives in

Glastonbury is the afterglow of a great tradition, a posthumous glory. And the present has no part in it, except in the menial roles of custodian and gatekeeper. The mighty legends are today irrelevant and yet all-consuming — an almost ludicrous paradox.

To the town pilgrims and tourists, visitors of every degree of curiosity from the devout to the inane, flock in their thousands. And the local inhabitants have somehow to come to terms with their heritage and the swarms it attracts. The solution inevitably is to cash in on assets which, visible and invisible, are so productive. The magic name of Avalon spreads like a rash among the tradesmen. Some years ago there was one enterprising cafe proprietor who — for a modest subscription — was prepared to enrol all-comers as Knights of the Holy Grail. As for the local guide-books, their plight is almost pitiable. Faced with so much more history than any town could possibly need, they plunge into a style of breezy jocularity which sounds suspiciously like a small boy whistling in the dark. And dark indeed are the shadows that enshroud Joseph of Arimathea and King Arthur and the Holy Grail and that band of saintly churchmen — headed by St Patrick and St David — who made Glastonbury a kind of primitive Athenaeum club.

To criticise in such circumstances is absurd. In a mature civilisation it is the fate of some places to become parasitic on their own past. Modern Glastonbury has no option but to engage in the tourist trade, and it suffers inevitably from the rule by which visitors, when they become customers, lose some of the gentler manners that visitors show to a host. I sympathise with the people of Glastonbury. They must weary of being told that their modern brick villas look shoddy by medieval standards. So majestic a past can be as much of a burden as it is to have a world-famous grandfather in one's family. Keeping up with a venerable genius is altogether more formidable than merely keeping up with the Jones's.

And just consider what Glastonbury was, in its heyday. Here, by strong and credible tradition, stood the oldest church in Britain, the first Christian altar in these islands. Here Arthur and Guinevere were laid to rest — or so it was asserted, with the support of evidence that is at least worth examining. Here St Dunstan revived the monastic ideal in England, and after him a succession of great builders and administrators created an ecclesiastical dominion of such prestige and influence that Glastonbury outshone all its rivals. The Abbey itself was about 180m in length and must have been one of the wonders of the Middle Ages. Noblemen sent their sons to Glastonbury to be educated and the Abbey could entertain 500 'persons of quality' at a time. The last abbots, in the climax of their prosperity, were accompanied on their journeys by never less than 100 retainers.

Over the centuries Celt and Saxon, Dane and Norman acknowledged the eminence of Glastonbury and fostered the growth of the Abbey's wealth. The original settlement, the famous twelve hides of land, were given to the first missionaries by a local British 'king'. Ine the Saxon, that great warrior and devout man who retired to Rome to end his days in piety, was one of

Glastonbury's chief benefactors. He is reputed to have rebuilt the church in the year 708, 'using 2,640 pounds of silver and 264 pounds of gold', and he confirmed all existing grants and added new territory to the Abbey. King Canute decreed that nobody might enter the district without the Abbot's permission. The Norman Conquest left the Abbey in possession of forty-one manors, and in the four centuries that followed the monks prospered so notably that there was a popular saying to the effect that 'if the Abbot of Glastonbury could marry the Abbess of Shaftesbury their first-born would inherit more land than the King of England'.

Perhaps that was Reformation propaganda, but there is no doubt that Glastonbury was one of the foremost ecclesiastical centres of Europe. As you wander among the ruins today you may grasp something of the size and grandeur of the buildings, but it is more difficult to envisage the Abbey's part in the life of medieval England. For more than 1,000 years the fame and prestige of the Abbey grew. Spiritually it gave precedence only to St Albans. The sacred relics it enshrined brought pilgrims from far and wide. The Abbot was as powerful as any man in the realm. Like the King he even had his own personal champion to fight for him, if the occasion arose. In the reign of Henry III the post was held by Henry of Farmborough, which is a village near Bath and was anciently rendered Ferenberge. "Henry de Fernbureg' is recorded as being engaged to fight as the Abbot's champion against the Bishop of Bath and Wells, the Dean of Wells 'and all other his champions whatsoever', in defence of certain manorial rights in Cranmore and Pucklechurch.

The effective life of the Abbey buildings was surprisingly short. The first great Norman church was destroyed by fire about sixty years after its commencement. The buildings that now stand were begun towards the end of the twelfth century and were not completed and dedicated until 1303. For 200 years after that additions and alterations were in progress, and the Abbey had probably just reached its peak of perfection when one of Glastonbury's greatest builders, Abbot Bere, died in 1524. That his successor could be counted anything but fortunate must have seemed most unlikely in 1524, with the Defender of the Faith on the throne of England. Moreover the monks of Glastonbury could pardonably congratulate themselves on their political sagacity in asking Cardinal Wolsey to nominate Richard Bere's successor. To achieve his high office under the auspices of Wolsey was for Abbot Whiting an extremely propitious start. If any danger threatened Glastonbury in 1524 it was the peril of smugness.

But fourteen years later Wolsey was ruined and dead; and Abbot Whiting, tied to a hurdle, was drawn up the steep slope of the Tor to be hanged there, and then drawn and quartered. To the people of Glastonbury the events of that November day in 1538 must have been beyond belief — their Abbot humiliated like the commonest of felons and butchered without mercy. Did anyone really believe it could happen, until it was no longer possible to doubt?

Nowadays it is a death that we do not much care to remember. One can hardly help thinking that the worst of martyrdoms is to be martyred in a lost cause — or at least an ambiguous one. The pitiful but noble figure of Whiting is obscured by the great issues of the Reformation. Perhaps good came out of it. Perhaps it was on balance well that the Abbey fell. Perhaps later events justified that horrible scene on the Tor. It is a controversy beyond the power of any one of us to judge, except in a sterile sectarian way. But the blood still sticks to the memory of some singularly dirty hands. One does not easily forget Cromwell's cynical memorandum — 'Item. The Abbot of Glaston to be tryed at Glaston and also executed there with his complycys.' Such determination must have made the trial an extremely simple affair. And if public consciousness be reluctant to dwell on the death of Abbot Whiting and the two monks who suffered with him as 'complycys', at least the integrity of that elderly and frail but valiant man is not gainsaid. After his own fashion he followed his Lord to the end, and of such men history is not always the best nor the only judge.

The dissolution of the Abbey cut Glastonbury at the root. Church and monastery were 'quarried' for building stone, and the only intact surviving building, the kitchen, was leased. In 1667 some local Quakers hired it as a meeting house. What remained of the Abbey fell into complete neglect, but its atmosphere was strong enough to impress so sturdy a freethinker as Defoe, who confessed he was struck with 'some unusual Awe' and concluded, 'I cannot so much blame the Catholicks in those early Days for reverencing this Place as they did.'

How deep and enduring may have been the shock of the Abbey's destruction I do not know, but its ruins have still an awe-inspiring power. And it is a curious fact that a local slang name for Glastonbury is 'Killmantown'. Of course, there were American troops there during the last war, there was at least one notable brawl, and they could easily have coined such a name. Alternatively and just possibly the troops might have picked up an expression which had survived in a disreputable way under the surface of polite conversation. Killmantown! One's mind turns unbidden to the Tor four centuries ago, to whatever group of incredulous peasants who may have seen as swift and savage an overthrow of human dignity as can be imagined. Such tales are never lightly forgotten. And memories are not short on the moors.

CHAPTER EIGHT

THE LAKE VILLAGES

Books about Glastonbury are many, and they range from factual studies of the Abbey architecture to speculative flirtations with the possibility that Jesus Christ visited the place and even that it was the original Garden of Eden. There is really no limit to what you may believe, if you are so minded, in this shadowy world of fantasy where truth and superstition play their obstinate game of hide-and-seek and sometimes seem to change places with each other in the most provocative way. There is an extraordinary imaginative power about this place which cannot but fascinate anyone who comes in contact with it. Even Dr Armitage Robinson, who made a thorough and objective study of the two main Glastonbury legends — of King Arthur and of St Joseph of Arimathea — concluded his admirable book, *Two Glastonbury Legends*, with this cautionary summing-up:

> The two Glastonbury Legends are not very ancient, when the long life of the abbey is taken into account. From first to last they occupied only the last three centuries and a half of its history. They were unknown to William of Malmesbury when he wrote his book, On the Antiquity of the Church of Glastonbury, about the year 1125, although he had free access to all the abbey's records before the Great Fire and made, as we now know, excellent use of his opportunities of investigation. Our earliest date for any of them is 1191. Yet they claim respectful treatment on very various grounds. He who rejects them as unworthy trivialities, and will have nothing but the unclothed skeleton of historically attested fact, cuts out the poetry from life, and renders himself incapable of understanding the fulness of his inheritance. Even the severe historian may not neglect the beliefs and fancies which have come to weave themselves about a people's daily life: their very vogue has become a fact of history itself. Still less can the student of medieval literature afford to miss the lesson here presented to us of the progressive modification of great popular themes, long after they have ceased to be subject to the vicissitudes of merely oral transmission and have been enshrined in famous writings — a modification due to the instinct of appropriation and the desire to give them local colour.

It is not therefore a matter merely for facile debunking, nor for the denunciation of what some like to call 'monkish forgeries'. Like our predecessors we look back into the shadows, discern what we can, and interpret by the light of our understanding. And shadows they are indeed, for the history of Glastonbury comes to us in fitful glimpses between patches of dense obscurity. We know a lot about the people who inhabited the district 300 years before the birth of Christ, and very little about the people here 300 years after His birth. We know something of the Romans who conquered and colonised Somerset, but practically nothing of their descendants who tried to resist the Saxon invasion. Most curiously we almost lose sight of Glastonbury in the reign of King Alfred, and that obscurity persists until the time of St Dunstan.

And it is in the darkest corners that we must look for the keys to the major riddles. If St Philip the Apostle sent missionaries from Gaul, it was before Roman order was established in Britain. If St David and St Patrick came to Glastonbury, it was during the confused decay of Roman rule. If Arthur came to the Tor, it was when Saxon fire and slaughter darkened the land. The legends wreathe up mistily from the most vaporous cauldrons of our history. If only Alfred, the champion of Christendom, had loved Glastonbury — how much might he or Asser have chronicled, if indeed there were much to chronicle. But the Danes had overrun the place, and Alfred was not moved by its desolation. His act of thanksgiving after victory was to found a new abbey at Athelney.

Controversy and doubt, then, are inevitable from the very nature of the context. We can expect no sudden clinching proof — or disproof — of much that is in debate. But the very beginning of the story comes in one of those rare glimpses of a lucidity that is almost freakish. Thanks to the preservative powers of peat, and the skill of modern archaeologists, we know more of pre-Roman life about Glastonbury than William of Malmesbury could have found out when he was writing his history eight centuries ago, and probably more than St Patrick could have heard during his supposed visit in AD 439. In the neighbouring parish of Godney, and a little further westwards at Meare, there were settlements of a cultured and resourceful people which passed unrecorded until 1892. These settlements were first discovered in that year by Arthur Bulleid, a doctor with antiquarian interests who had been closely following recent research on lake villages in Switzerland. Dr Bulleid saw that the peat moors round Glastonbury might well have been colonised by the same type of prehistoric settlement, and he went out with the deliberate purpose of seeking what he did in fact eventually find.

The Godney village was the first to be uncovered. Excavations continued from 1892 to 1898, and were renewed again in 1903 when Mr H. St George Gray joined Dr Bulleid in charge of the work. The Meare village was discovered in 1895 but excavations did not begin until 1908, when the work at Godney was completed. It should be said at once that there is nothing of interest to see at the village sites in Meare or Godney, except for a short period in the summer when some fresh excavation may be in progress. The materials

Glastonbury Abbey — 'The buildings that now stand were begun towards the end of the twelfth century'

Above Burrow Mump; *left* the King Alfred Monument on the 'isle' of Athelney

recovered from the lake villages are to be seen at the Lake Museum in Glastonbury or in the County Museum at Taunton. And very remarkably they are, both in bulk and in quality. They speak in vivid detail of a people, skilled in the basic arts and crafts, who lived an organised community life in a village enclosed within a palisade.

The question of how long the villages were occupied and by what sort of people is difficult to answer with close precision. The inhabitants were of the Iron Age, using bronze in the manufacture of ornaments but not of weapons. About 250 BC has been a widely accepted date for the commencement of the villages, though E.K. Tratman suggests that the date for the Godney village might be about 100 years later. There is no certainty as to why they were abandoned. The original theory that the villagers were massacred, propounded by Boyd Dawkins, was not accepted by Bulleid and is wholly rejected by current archaeological opinion. The first century AD, when the occupation of the villages apparently ended, was a period when the pressures of invasions from the continent could have menaced the villagers and might have forced them to abandon their territory and move elsewhere but they certainly were not slain in a battle to defend their homes. The probable explanation is that a worsening of the climate raised the flood level in the vicinity and made the villages untenable.

The importance of Dr Bulleid's discovery and the value of the excavations he made with St George Gray can not be gainsaid. It is in no spirit of denigration that more recent archaeologists have ventured to reinterpret some elements in the broad picture of the villages and their inhabitants. If a layman may attempt to summarise current discussions, there appear to be two major topics of speculation. Taking the Godney village first, Bulleid and Gray considered the 3½ acres site to have been occupied by sixty to seventy dwellings, circular in shape, constructed of wattle and daub and with thatched roofs. The buildings were raised on mounds of clay supported on a base of timber and brushwood and stood in the relatively shallow water of Meare Pool, with a causeway 1½m wide and extending for over 48m from the palisade. This causeway was skilfully made and presumably served as a landing place for boats.

But are the villages truly to be considered as 'lake' villages in the sense that they were raised artificially and surrounded by water? And were the inhabitants from first to last the same kind of people, showing therefore a continuity of method and style in their working lives? Dr Tratman argues for two quite distinct occupations of the Godney site by peoples of notably different cultures. In his view the builders of the round huts were preceded by people who built square or rectangular houses raised on oak piles which, like stilts, lifted the buidings several feet above ground (or water) level. These first settlers were skilled woodworkers and they practised agriculture. Their successors apparently scrapped whatever remained of the houses and built their own kind of circular house; and they had no use for wheeled vehicles or ploughs (unlike their predecessors). Perhaps adjacent land that had hitherto been cultivable was now flooded.

Mention of flooding leads to the other problem — the level of water surrounding the village. Fishing and trapping have been regarded as an important part of the community's life, and bones that survive give us some interesting information on this point. Bones of roach, trout, shad, perch and pike have been identified, and with them many varieties of birds — some that one would expect, like geese and swans and cormorants and several kinds of duck, and a few that would nowadays be very welcome in Somerset. The white-tailed sea-eagle and the goshawk knew the lake villages. So did the crane and the kite. The bittern was there in the marshes, of course, as it might be again if it can be left unmolested. But the most surprising is the pelican, which was not just a rare vagrant, for its seems to have been relatively common and must have bred in the locality. Among the pelican bones are those of young birds.

From these details it is tempting to imagine scenes of hunting and catching wild animals as the main preoccupation, but R. Trow Smith in his *History of British Livestock Husbandry* asserts that the bones of wild animals represent only just over 2 per cent of the total examined and that the overwhelming preponderance comes from sheep — no less than 88 per cent. To have grazed their flocks of sheep and used their ploughs the first villagers must have had an extent of dry land nearby. And some additional evidence for dry land comes from the great work on pollen analysis in this area with which the name of Sir Harry Godwin has been connected for many years. His research shows the presence of a number of trees near or even on the Godney site.

These awkward facts have to be reconciled with what is known of the distribution of surface water. The river Brue at this period may well have flowed northward through the Panborough Gap to join the river Axe. Dr Williams considers this was probably the case until the Glastonbury monks realigned the river system. 'The diversion of the rivers Brue and Hartlake', he writes, 'and perhaps even the Sheppey away from the Axe valley and towards Meare Pool in the thirteenth century must have led to a great increase in the amount of water entering the pool.' We have then to think of a landscape about 1,000 years earlier than that and with the assumption that Meare Pool and the Brue were not at that time connected. Dr Tratman's view is that the square houses of the first settlement were erected 'along the edge of a main water-course, which had side channels'.

Bulleid and Gray continued their excavation of one group of mounds at Meare until 1933. Subsequently they worked on a second group to the east until 1956. They published detailed reports on the first group but both died without publishing their later work. It is on the second (eastern) group that Michael Avery began working in 1966. Perhaps the most important difference between Meare and Godney is that the Meare villagers, though near the edge of Meare Pool, were building on a dry site, a raised peat bog which had dried out and did not require stilt-like piles or raised 'islands' of timber, brushwood and clay. The Meare people built the round houses of their lakeside village on a wooden frame that had no more foundation than the driving of posts into the dry peat. In Mr Avery's view the raised hearths and clay floors described by Bulleid and Gray as domestic features are more likely to be rubbish tips and he suggests that the villagers used their abandoned houses as middens when they moved away, perhaps to the slightly higher ground nearby. This in turn creates a fresh problem, in determining the motive for depositing such large quantities of clay. If it had no part in the construction of any sort of building why was so much clay manhandled in this area?

It is in the nature of archaeology that each new discovery leads to a reinterpretation of existing knowledge, from which fresh problems emerge. No one would claim that we yet know enough to speak with precision of the way man lived in the neighbourhood of Meare Pool and the Isle of Avalon during the two or three centuries before the Roman occupation. But the great discovery that Dr Bulleid made, and the patient work of Bulleid himself, St George Gray and their successors, give us a lively picture in which some fascinating details stand out clearly. Whether the people were of two, three or more different tribes or races they bequeathed to us a collective legacy of tools and ornaments that can tell us much about their daily lives.

The craftsmen in the villages made brooches and bracelets, pins and studs, harness trappings, finger rings and yet more ambitious things like a bronze mirror and the wonderful bowl of hammered bronze which is the *chef d'oeuvre* of the lake village finds. From bone they made handles and buttons and beads, and domestic implements like needles and weaving combs. Some of these, from the bone of a horse or a deer's antler, are delicately shaped and patterned with obvious delight in the way good craftsmanship can subtly transform the crude original. They still used flint, principally for arrowheads, and they had a flint saw. They also worked tin and lead, and one object of tin appears to have been some sort of mace or sceptre and was probably gilded.

The occupation of the villages persisted for a few decades into the Christian era. About 50 AD extensive flooding seems to have ended their story though there is some reason to think that the site at Meare was reoccupied briefly in the third or fourth century AD. The flooding that covered the villages with silt to a depth of 6–18in was the climax of what must have been a growing threat to their existence. The warm dry weather of the Bronze Age began to worsen about 500 BC and gave way to the cooler and wetter climate of modern times. The old Bronze Age trackways over the moors were gradually flooded and abandoned. The Vale of Avalon must have become a vast morass with lakes and pools covering much of the landscape, particularly in winter time when the floods were high. Such land could only continue to be inhabited by people who were at home in boats and, like the 'web-footed' men of the fens, had adapted themselves to these conditions.

In some ways, though, the scenery surrounding the villages would have been very similar to the Avalon of today. Plant remains show that climatic conditions and the level of the sea were much as we now know them. There were buttercups in spring time, and yellow flags later, and blackberries ripening in the autumn. And no doubt the children of the lakeside villages picked them as eagerly as children do now. It is not difficult, indeed, to picture for a moment a little party of those children of the Iron Age, coming across the mere in a dug-out canoe — perhaps the one now in the museum at Glastonbury — carrying in their hands some small treasured collection of flowers or fruits as the boat drifts alongside the landing-stage and they run along the causeway to the village, the last generation of inarticulate prehistory, the nameless ones who lacked the ability to commemorate themselves. By the works of their hands, and not by any written record, they tell us as much of their story as we can decipher.

CHAPTER NINE

THE FIRST ALTAR

One interesting consequence of the discovery of the lake villages is that we now know a good deal about Glastonbury at the time of the birth of Christianity. Godney is only a couple of kilometres from the Isle of Avalon and Meare no more than five. The villagers came to the Glastonbury hills for some of the materials they needed, so the present site of Glastonbury was either a part of their territory or it was in friendly hands. If Joseph of Arimathea or any missionary sent by St Philip the Apostle crossed from Gaul and came to Avalon he must presumably have made contact with those who were still living in the round wattle-and-daub huts on the edge of Meare Pool. And if 'King Arviragus' did indeed give the missionaries twelve hides of land in the locality, it would seem to be an odds-on chance that he was an Iron Age gentleman whose habits and customs can be described with some accuracy. For example, he ate bread made of crushed wheat and honey, and he sometimes whiled away a dull hour by playing dice. If he was a wise king he picked his company rather carefully, because someone in the village had a dice with two sixes on it.

Those twelve hides of land were to be the cradle of British Christianity, for it was here that the legendary first altar was raised. How swiftly the fame and the sanctity of the little church spread is impossible to determine but when the West Saxons crossed the Mendip Hills and swept forward to the river Parret they treated Glastonbury with considerable respect. Clearly they regarded it as a holy place of the religion which they themselves had adopted only a generation earlier. Fifty years after their victorious invasion of Somerset they rebuilt the original church.

The two questions which have exercised the mind of every student of the subject are these — when was that earlier church built and by whom was it founded? The standard Glastonbury legend, in its full flowering, asserts that the *vetusta ecclesia* — the 'old church' — was founded in AD 31 by a party of missionaries sent from Gaul by St Philip the Apostle and led by Joseph of Arimathea, who brought with him the Holy Grail. St Joseph, according to legend, landed on Wearyall Hill — the steep spur that juts from the Isle of Avalon into the westward moors — and then proceeded to perform two minor miracles. He buried the Grail at a point from which ever afterwards a blood-red spring has flowed, and he planted his staff, which thereupon put forth leaves at Christmastide and became the celebrated Holy Thorn of Glastonbury. And so, to the accompaniment of these miracles, the first Christian altar in England was raised. And today no tourist likes to leave Glastonbury without seeing St Joseph's Chapel and Chalice Well and the Holy Thorn.

That, then, is the legend in its final detailed form. There is no need to dwell on the latest fancy, which hints that Jesus Himself may have been brought here on a visit with His 'father'; presumably that arises from a fairly simple-minded confusion of Josephs. But the main legend has flourished for some hundreds of years, and it is certainly plausible. Rome had her contacts with Britain before she invaded; the more intrepid travellers and traders must have had some acquaintance with the western peninsula and the Severn Sea, and there is no inherent impossibility in the idea of a party of missionaries following the Roman trade routes and adventuring across the sea to a little known but not wholly unfamiliar land which might seem to promise them the conditions they were seeking. To the hermit the little islands of the Somerset marshes offered a peaceful retreat, while among the neighbouring tribes there was a challenging field of endeavour for the evangelist.

But did Joseph in fact come, with his miracles, in the year 31? The evidence, such as it is, is not very satisfying. The first reference to hawthorns 'that bear green leaves at Christmas' comes in a poem of about 1500, which ascribes no holy qualities to them and makes no mention of Joseph's staff. The Grail legend, according to the same authority, Dr Armitage Robinson, 'never at any time received ecclesiastical sanction'. One must add, though, that there was certainly some ecclesiastical flirtation with the idea, for the so-called 'arms of St Joseph' clearly commemorate the Grail legend and they were a popular symbol with the later Glastonbury abbots. Two examples that come to mind are a stone carving in Meare church and an exquisite panel of stained glass in the east window at Langport.

But setting aside the Grail and the Thorn, what of the central question of the church's foundation? An authoritative answer should come from the Abbey's first historian, William of Malmesbury, who stayed at Glastonbury in 1125 and seems to have been an honest and scholarly man with little inclination to encourage old wives' tales. Of any earlier written records than his concerning the Abbey there is now no trace, but he would certainly be acquainted with such documents as the Abbey preserved and with a considerable oral tradition. He was aware of claims that the old church was built during the lifetime of St Philip, but he inclined to the view that it was founded in 166 by missionaries sent from Rome. In any case he did not mention Joseph of Arimathea. It was later editors of William's writings who argued in favour of the earlier mission from Gaul. According to them the missionaries from Rome — whose names were Phagan and Deruvian — restored the wattle church but could not be credited with having founded it. And later still a thirteenth-century editor concluded positively that Joseph led the mission from Gaul and received from a pagan king twelve hides of land and the island of Yniswitrin — Yniswitrin being the Celtic name for what the Saxons later called Glestingaburg. John of Glastonbury, writing in the fourteenth century, translates the Celtic word as meaning the Glassy Isle or the island of glass — in which some commentators have seen a reference to the sheets of water that surrounded the isle.

To Yniswitrin, then, came missionaries at about the dawn of our Christian era. Call them Phagan, Joseph, Deruvian, what you please — but still the central fact appears to be unshaken, that in that isolated place among the swamps and lakes between Mendip and Polden a little company of pious men gathered their bundles of rods and twisted them about stouter stakes — as the men of Sedgemoor still do today — and set up their hurdles under a roof of thatch, in honour of the new God. A tenuous and insecure foundation it must have seemed, but that first light was never afterwards to be completely extinguished though twice a pagan invader swept victoriously westwards.

The affection and reverence that Glastonbury has inspired down the ages are easy to understand. Hers was the mother church of England, and perhaps we need look no further for a reason to account for the awe and wonder which our forefathers felt in this place. Yet it is tempting to speculate about that first choice of a site for the wattle church. What influenced the founders — was it mere chance? Was it the geographical advantage of an inaccessible hill site, promising security and privacy? Or were there already some strong religious traditions centred on that spot? It may not be altogether fanciful to suppose that the Tor, that indelible landmark, may already have held some sacred power for the lake dwellers or the Bronze Age herdsmen of the moors. Support for this possibility comes from an eminent archaeologist, Dr Ralegh Radford, who has devoted so much of his life to the study of Glastonbury's early history. He points to the existence of a massive earthwork at Ponter's Ball on the tongue of land which connects the Isle of Avalon to Pennard Hill and the general range of uplands extending southwards from Mendip; and he argues that this bank and ditch at Ponter's Ball, which is of pre-Roman construction, could not have been a military defence work. He therefore concludes that:

> It is most easily explicable as the Temenos or enclosure of a great pagan Celtic sanctuary. Analogy suggests that the focus of this sanctuary, the sacred grove or high place, must be sought near a hill beside a spring. Chalice Well, the principal spring on the island, lies immediately below the highest summit, Glastonbury Tor.

If the Isle of Avalon were indeed already a sacred place, an honoured burial ground where the kings and nobles of the Celtic tribes were interred, it might on that account be specially attractive to Christian missionaries. Establishing their individual cells and hermitages, they would have taken over the 'goodwill' that their Celtic predecessors had already invested in the place. Such a hypothesis helps to explain the apparent speed with which the fame of

Glastonbury spread. By the fifth century there was quite a colony of holy anchorites. St Indract was on a pilgrimage to Glastonbury when he was murdered at Shapwick; and St Patrick, who is said to have been born at or near Glastonbury, returned after his labours in Ireland to gather the individualist hermits and holy men into an organised monastic life. William of Malmesbury considered St Patrick to be the first abbot, with St Benignus as his successor.

The century that followed the death of St Patrick was a time of obscurity and confusion and growing peril, and it was the West Country — with Glastonbury as its shrine — that nursed the flickering light which was never quite extinguished. At Canterbury and St Albans the cross was thrown down and replaced by the worship of pagan gods. Naked without the shield of Roman power, Britain was ravaged to a degree that we in our generation can perhaps understand better than many of our predecessors. Consider for a moment this remarkably graphic account by an eyewitness of the Saxon invasion:

> Terrible it was to see, in the midst of the streets, tops of towers torn from their lofty fittings, the stones of high walls, holy altars, fragments of bodies, covered with clotted blood, so that they seemed as if squeezed together in some ghastly wine press. There was no burial of the dead, save in the ruins of their homes, or in the bellies of beasts and birds . . . Some of the wretched remnant were caught in the mountains and all murdered there; others, forced by famine, surrendered; others with great wailing sought the regions beyond the sea.

In this nightmare conflict the valiant and magical name of King Arthur like a comet streaks momentarily across the darkling sky and then is lost. The rumoured fame of his victories still lingers, and for some years the Saxons were halted. But in 539, if one can put a date to the event, Arthur died. In 552 the West Saxons won a great victory at Old Sarum and spread across Wiltshire. By 577 they were in Cirencester and Gloucester and Bath, with three British kings lying dead on the battlefield at Deorham. Little more than a day's march separated them from Glastonbury, but in between lay the barriers of the Avon, the Mendip ridge and the old forest of Selwood which then stretched from Chippenham to the Dorset Downs at Cerne Abbas. At this point the Saxons halted and — apart from an unidentified battle at Beandun in 614 — they made no major move westward for eighty years. And during that momentous lull Cynegils, the victor of Beandun, was converted to Christianity. Even if one calls it no more than a coincidence it is at least remarkable that both Saxon and Dane were halted and converted within sight of the Tor.

To the Saxons Glastonbury owes a great deal. In the long line of illustrious men whose names are linked with the Abbey there is none to surpass Ine, the royal patron, or Dunstan, the saintly abbot. Guided by such men, the Glastonbury story begins to take on a firm outline as it develops from a quasi-mythical colony of hermits and becomes one of the vital centres of European churchmanship.

Cynegils was converted in 635, but he may never have entered Glastonbury. The victory of Penselwood, which carried the Saxons to the Parret in 658, was won by his son, Cenwealh, and the Isle of Avalon may well have remained in British hands until then. From the outset the Saxons treated the shrine with reverence and generosity. The whole area of Sedgemoor and Avalon seems to have had a special attraction for the conquerors and was to become the 'home-estate' and favoured hunting-ground of the royal house. The new kings made grants of land and revenue to the church, and we do no more than add sagicity to their piety if we follow the suggestion, made by Albany Major, that their benevolence may have had a political value. Speaking of Centwine, who completed the conquest of Somerset, Major observes:

> The lavish generosity of the early Saxon conquerors to Glastonbury suggests that they had set their hearts on winning a shrine which both Briton and Saxon held sacred . . . It is possible, too, that motives of policy led Centwine to value the possession of the Isle of Avalon, for we find evidence that he endeavoured to make the Abbey a mediator between the two races who were drawn to worship at their holy spot . . . On the other hand, it is hardly conceivable that the hope of regaining Glastonbury did not animate the West Welsh at least in the early days of the long warfare, while from their frontier posts on the Blackdown hills they could still look undisturbed across the fenlands and the Polden hills to where the Tor marked the lost shrines. Year after year, moreover, the dispute between the two Churches was brought home to the pilgrims from the west and from across the Severn, as they found their Easter disregarded, and reached the shrines either too late for the Saxon festival, or too early.

This confusion between Roman and Celtic practices was brought to a head in Britain by the arrival of Augustine in Kent in 596. The religious unification of England was achieved by Archbishop Theodore in 672, but the Celtic West retained its own practices after that. When King Ine founded the bishopric of Sherborne — 'the west of Selwood' — in 705, one of the first tasks of its bishop, Aldhelm, was to write to Geraint, king of Dyvnaint (or Devonshire), in an attempt to persuade the British Christians to conform with Saxon ecclesiastical rules.

Aldhelm's death in 709 cut short his attempt at reconciliation, and it was left to Ine to settle the issue. This great ruler, who seems to have been warrior, statesman and saint in one, occupied Taunton in 710 and by 722 his people were fighting on the river Hayle in Cornwall. He thus consolidated the kingdom of the West Saxons, and on that basis pursued his ideal of organising the many separate monasteries and missions of the older tradition into a corporate church. And in that single unified body he envisaged Glastonbury as a chief member. In 704 he built the first Saxon church at Glastonbury, dedicated to Dominus Salvator and SS Peter and Paul. After his victory over Geraint in 710 he gave to Glastonbury ten hides of land at Brent, one at Bleadon and ten at Sowy. He also confirmed all previous grants and exempted Glastonbury and her subordinate churches from episcopal authority.

And then, towards the end of his reign, he took a further step which was designed to secure his patronage from the hazards of changing circumstance: he asked the Pope to take Glastonbury under his protection, and he went in person to Rome and secured the Papal assent. After his return to England he seemed to feel that his work was completed. He laid aside the kingship and returned to Rome, with his queen, to end his days in a private life of great simplicity and humility. And one wonders indeed if any man deserves to be remembered more kindly in the West Country which he did so much to form.

The invasion of the Danes followed a very different course from that of their Saxon predecessors, so far as the western counties are concerned. In the vital civilising faculties they were the inferior race, and their many successes in battle at no time gave them the essential mastery. Their first real disturbance of the tranquillity of Glastonbury came in 845, when the monks were doubtless stirred by reports of a victory by combined levies from Somerset and Dorset at the mouth of the Parret against a Danish force which was trying to thrust its way up the river. Twenty years later a great Danish army overran East Anglia, and refugee monks would have reached Glastonbury with appalling tales of the savage destruction suffered by every monastery that fell into Danish hands. In 870 the danger came ominously close when the Danes invaded Wessex. For eight years they were checked by a skilful mixture of counter-attack and negotiation, but in 878 they completely outmanoeuvred the Saxons with a surprise march from Gloucester to Chippenham, and organised resistance to them virtually collapsed.

What happened in the following months is far from clear, but it is all but certain that Glastonbury must have fallen into Danish hands for a short time, between January and early summer. Alfred at Athelney was in no position to defend the Isle of Avalon, so the Danes could move at will in the district and so rich a prize must have been an inevitable attraction. On the other hand, the Danes never succeeded in crossing the Parret. Their most advanced positions were perhaps along the line of the Polden Hills, and they could not have been long established there before they suffered the shattering defeat which led to the conversion of their leader to the Christian faith and their permanent withdrawal from Somerset. Once again, then, Glastonbury witnessed the turning of the heathen tide, though on this occasion she herself suffered momentarily the agony of desecration as the tide of war ebbed and flowed about her.

What treasures were lost then, what jewels and furnishings and still more — what ancient documents, we do not know. Nor do we know if the Danes destroyed the place in the fury of a single raid or for a time occupied it. Perhaps some of the brethren escaped and hid in the vicinity, perhaps some of the treasures were hidden in the marshlands as they were at Ramsey. One might expect a few survivors to return and restore the old life in some measure, but the sorry truth is that all monastic life throughout the country had collapsed under the long and severe strain of the Danish war. When King Alfred tried to revive churchmanship and learning, his first act was to found a new monastery at Athelney rather than attempt to restore Glastonbury. Those occasional pilgrims who came to visit the first church of Britain, the old 'Mother of Saints', found there only a little community of clerks who used the place as a schoolhouse and laboured to teach the local children something of their native tongue, of their history and of their duty to God. It was a poor state of affairs, but up and down the land every other monastery was in the same case. So the clerks laboured to kindle in the children what they were themselves unable to restore. And at Glastonbury that tenuous thread of continuity, never quite broken, led to a recovery so remarkable that it swiftly eclipsed even the great days of Ine. Among the children of the district who visited the desolate abbey and heard their elders describe the departed glories of the olden days was the son of a neighbouring thegn, born probably at nearby Baltonsborough. Today the church of that parish is dedicated to him. His name was Dunstan.

CHAPTER TEN

ST DUNSTAN AND THE NORMANS

In his survey of the history of Glastonbury William of Malmesbury pokes fun at the belief that Dunstan was the first abbot. Of course he was not. Chronologically he stands at about the middle of the span of centuries during which some kind of monastic life flourished here. He could perhaps be described as the first paragraph of the last great chapter, as the founder and architect of that monastic system in Britain which — both spiritually and politically — was to play so dominant a part in our medieval history. From the initial visionary dreams of Dunstan to the last days of Tudor destruction there is a clear unity of purpose and style.

In particular Dunstan stands as the British prototype of the statesman-priest, as the forerunner of Becket, of Wolsey, of Richelieu, of a whole line of ecclesiastics whose political influence has been a distinctive element in European history. For most of his life Dunstan was a public figure of great consequence at court. He publicly rebuked one king, imposed a severe penance on a second, and crowned two others. He was for many years a trusted counsellor in matters of state, and it was by the support of the Saxon royal house that he achieved so much.

In early youth Dunstan won favour with King Athelstan by his ability to play soothing music when the King was fatigued and wanted entertainment. As a result of some hostile intrigue the young man decided to leave in some haste and fled to Winchester, where the bishop was a relative of his. The bishop — Elphege the Bald, as he is usually called — nursed Dunstan through a fever and then persuaded him to go abroad to a Benedictine monastery. It was this period of exile which settled the course of Dunstan's future career, for he returned to England with a passionate devotion to the Benedictine ideal. It is said that he immediately went to Glastonbury and there built a cell, only 5ft long and 2½ft wide, in which he designed to live the traditional life of a hermit. And here, according to legend, Dunstan on a famous occasion seized the Devil by the nose when he ill-advisedly visited the young saint's cell for his customary purpose of temptation.

Was it perhaps another and subtler temptation that came in the form of an invitation from the new King, Edmund, who had succeeded his brother Athelstan? After consideration Dunstan decided that he might do more good at Court than in his narrow hermitage, but he was once again involved in a web of intrigues and accusations and Edmund was persuaded to send him away. This time, however. the triumph of Dunstan's enemies was extremely short-lived. King Edmund went hunting on Mendip, and his horse bolted towards the edge of Cheddar Gorge. Nobody who has looked down into that impressive chasm will underrate the terror that the King must have felt as he struggle to rein his horse, and it is natural enough that he should have been in a chastened and contrite mood when he did eventually succeed in halting on the very brink. As many another man has done in similar circumstances, he made a rapid survey of the life he had nearly lost and decided penitently to make one or two desirable alterations. The unjust dismissal of Dunstan was evidently on his conscience, for he recalled the young monk, made him Abbot of Glastonbury and offered to sponsor the necessary work of rebuilding.

It was the opportunity for which Dunstan had been waiting. Years before he had had a dream in which an elderly man in white robes escorted him to Glastonbury and showed him, not the ruins with which he had all his life been familiar, but a magnificent new church. And now he was Abbot, with the King's treasury at his command for the great task of reviving the 'old church' and breathing into it the new spirit of the Benedictine resurgence. The accession of Eadred, who succeeded Edmund in 946, brought even more enthusiastic support. A pupil of Dunstan's became the first abbot of a new monastery, at Abingdon, founded by the King; and by degrees a movement spread throughout the country to restore old buildings and erect new ones. While Eadred lived, Dunstan's influence grew steadily, but the death of the King in 955 led to a crisis which broke Dunstan's long and fruitful association with Glastonbury.

The new king, Edwy, was a young man with an independent outlook. At his Coronation banquet he upset the company by walking out early, and scorned the advice of Dunstan who entered the King's private apartments with the intention of persuading him to return to the banquet. The fact that the crown was thrown carelessly on the floor scarcely helped to endear the new monarch to Dunstan, who without more ado proceeded to grasp the young man by the shoulders, clap the crown on his head, and push him back to his royal seat in the banqueting hall.

The banishment of Dunstan follows this lively incident with an air of inevitability. One kingdom could scarcely contain such a king and such an abbot. Dunstan first returned to Glastonbury to break the news to the brethren there, and for a time he seems to have been shielded by the privileged nature of the Abbey, as an inviolable sanctuary. But Edwy's soldiers were bound to seize him if he remained, so he escaped overseas and settled at Ghent.

It was hardly to be expected that Edwy should not also have his troubles. He had to submit to a partition of England with his younger brother, Edgar, who promptly recalled Dunstan and made him Bishop of Worcester. Mercifully this division of the kingdom, with its growing animosities, was summarily terminated by the obscure and convenient death of Edwy. Edgar was now King of a reunited England, and Dunstan stood on the threshold of almost unlimited power. In 960 he became Archbishop of Canterbury and Legate of the Holy See.

For the remainder of his life Dunstan of Glastonbury was the vitalising force of the nation. We can see in him the consummation of that lively faith which sustained King Alfred — the faith that, in the darkest hour of the Danish ravages when scarcely a church or a book survived, there would nevertheless be a future time when learning would flourish again and men would once more devote their lives peacefully to Christian worship. On the brink of disaster Alfred clung grimly to that belief, though his country was exhausted with fighting and he had to send outside his kingdom for a handful of scholars to make a fresh start with the task of teaching his people. Yet a generation later Dunstan was born, to give a copious and splendid reality to Alfred's fondest hopes. New churches replaced the ruins of the old, libraries were built up again by the patient labours of the monastic scribes, and England had a king who loyally supported Dunstan in his work.

The way was not always smooth, but Dunstan was inflexible. When he met opposition he defied it, just as on occasion he resisted the Pope and censured the King. There is indeed something touching about the way in which Edgar accepted the justice of a long and severe penance, which among other penalties forbade him to wear his crown for seven years. At the end of the period a jubilee was held at Bath, and Dunstan placed the crown again on the head of the King, without the pride of the one or the vanity of the other being any the worse for what must have been a severe strain on their personal relations.

Before he died Dunstan was to crown two more kings — Edward the Martyr, who was assassinated at Corfe Castle, and the ill-starred Ethelred. On Ascension Day in the year 988 Dunstan preached his last sermon, in the knowledge that his life was ending. Like John Donne in a later age, he told those who heard him that he would not have the opportunity to speak to them again. And when he had finished his address he indicated the spot where he wished to be buried.

So great a man steps inevitably from the local to the national scene, but Glastonbury does not relinquish its special claim to commemorate him. He was a child of the neighbourhood, and for much of his life he was its Abbot. He made the Abbey the central seminary from which the monastic revival flowered, and his work was a source of inspiration to the later abbots of Norman times who strove to emulate their famous Saxon predecessor. His ascetic, spiritual nature had also its practical side, embodying the Benedictine rule that religious devotion should be combined with some form of labour. It may well have been he who set to work to restore his own countryside after the neglect of war-torn years, for we read that Ulgar of the Beard built the bridge at

Baltonsborough in Dunstan's time, and it is thought that some of the earliest embanking of the river near Glastonbury was carried out by the monks during St Dunstan's years of office.

Two of the kings most closely associated with Dunstan were buried at Glastonbury — Edmund, who made him Abbot of Glastonbury and helped to rebuild the Abbey, and Edgar, who made him Archbishop of Canterbury. A third Saxon king was later brought to lie beside them — Edmund Ironside, the last of England's heroic defenders against the Danes. And when Dane and Saxon were finally united in one nation, Canute the Dane came to Glastonbury to lay a cloak of peacock's feathers on the tomb of his old adversary. It was just a century and a half since the first Danish invaders under Guthrum reached Glastonbury and were there halted and flung back by Alfred. But now, where Guthrum had come with fire and sword, Canute came to kneel and to declare formally his respect for the established privileges and rights of the Abbey. In that contrast there is a moving tribute to the courage of those — priest and soldier, king and peasant — who in the concert of their various ways wrought a transformation as dramatic as anything in our history. It is an old, far-off story, admittedly, of which many details are lost, and Alfred and Dunstan seem remote indeed from the present day. But such men are rare, and we do well to cherish their memory.

The date of Canute's visit to Glastonbury was 1030. The next and final invasion of England, by the Normans, offered no great threat to the Abbey, though it gave rise to some unhappy moments. William the Conqueror took away some of the Abbey lands, but he was pledged to uphold the Church in general, and the Domesday survey shows Glastonbury as holding 442 hides of land, with a tenth of the population of Somerset living on Abbey properties.

What was perhaps more serious was the high-handed way in which William appointed a Norman as Abbot, for his appointment of Turstin of Caen began a series of scandals which in the following centuries sprang from the desire of powerful personalities to gain control of the wealthy Abbey and its enviable revenues. Turstin himself was far from being a bad choice, for he defended the rights of the Abbey at a difficult time and he was zealous in his duties. But he had the disadvantage of being a foreigner imposed by conquest on his own community, and he showed little tact in his dealing with the English monks. They disliked his Norman innovations, and after a dispute in the chapter house Turstin made the fatal mistake of calling in Norman soldiers to subdue his monks. The monks promptly barricaded themselves in the church, and a disgraceful scene followed when the soldiers broke in and opened fire on the defenceless rebels. A salvo of arrows killed one monk and wounded fourteen others; and another monk was slain with a spear as he clung to the altar. The height of the uproar was reached when one of the brethren held a wooden cross in front of himself in self-defence, and a soldier shot an arrow into the cross. This act of sacrilege apparently spread a panic among the troops, for they lost their nerve and were driven out by the surviving monks.

After such behaviour, Turstin had to go. A complaint was made to the King, and the Abbot returned to Normandy in disgrace. Towards the end of his life he was restored to office by William II, but he had little further influence on the Abbey.

Little more than a century later Glastonbury became the plaything of a quite fantastic intrigue, which continued for many years in a cloak-and-dagger atmosphere of backroom plotting, ambushes by night, savage imprisonments and general skulduggery. Most jealously guarded of Glastonbury's privileges was its independence from the bishop of the diocese, and it was this privilege which began to be undermined on the day when an extremely smooth gentleman, by name Savaric, took it into his head to visit Richard Coeur de Lion. King Richard, on his way home from the Crusades, had fallen into the hands of the Emperor of Germany, and was in fact a prisoner. Savaric being a cousin of the Emperor, was in a position to be of service to Richard, and he had not omitted to calculate the price of his services. Put bluntly, he wanted the bishopric of Bath. And to sweeten the bargain he was inclined to insist that the Abbey of Glastonbury should be included in the diocese.

Now the ecclesiastical quarrels between Bath, Wells and Glastonbury, between bishop and abbot, are a recurrent theme down the centuries. One was always trying to win supremacy over the other, and some commentators have pointed out that the ruin which ultimately overtook Glastonbury might have been avoided if Henry VIII had had to deal with a bishop and not an abbot. And so, even in Savaric's day, there were sincere churchmen who saw dangers in the lordly independence of Glastonbury and were prepared to support the plan for its incorporation in the diocese. But there is no reason to suppose that Savaric's motives were so subtle or so selfless as that, nor to question the honest indignation of the monks when they discovered that the reason why their Abbot had been summoned to the King in his imprisonment was to learn that his personal compliance was to be bought with the bishopric of Worcester. True it might be that Dunstan also, after being Abbot of Glastonbury, became Bishop of Worcester — but this was an ironical way of following in the saint's footsteps!

Having gained his bargain, Savaric may well have felt that he had nothing more to do but enjoy it. However, the stubbornness of the monks had still to be reckoned with. They petitioned King Richard as soon as he returned to England. They petitioned the Pope. They walked out of the chapter house when Savaric's agents read out what was claimed to be a mandate from the Pope, and year after year they kept up a running fire of appeals and counter-appeals to anyone who could help them. Sometimes Savaric gained the upper hand, forced his way into the monastery and punished his opponents: at other times the monks won the support of Pope or King or Archbishop, and proceeded to elect their own officers and throw out Savaric's men. Before the great dispute ended, almost every dignitary in Europe must have burned his fingers in an attempt to end the conflict. In 1199, for example, the Archbishop of Rouen was surprisingly involved, when Savaric seized Eustace, the Glastonbury chamberlain, in Rouen and contrived to have him shut up in the city gaol. The Archbishop promptly released Eustace and sent him back to Glastonbury.

In the following year Savaric made his most savage bid to crush resistance, and once again there was fighting at the altar. Some of the monks were carted off to Wells and imprisoned, and two attempts to get messengers out of the country to appeal to Rome were foiled in dramatic hold-ups on the road. The unyielding determination of both parties in the long struggle is something to marvel at, and it eventually became evident that the only workable solution was some form of compromise prepared by a high-powered committee of arbitration. Savaric died before the affair was concluded, and may well have wished that he had never set eyes on Glastonbury. As for the monks, they may well have sung a particularly vigorous Te Deum when in 1219 they read the last words on the subject from Pope Honorius III — 'The union of Bath and Glastonbury is dissolved. The Abbey is to be under its own Abbot, freely elected in the usual way.'

CHAPTER ELEVEN

THE MEDIEVAL ABBEY AND
THE HOLY THORN

The more peaceful history of Glastonbury during the Middle Ages is a story of steady achievement under the wise guidance of a number of distinguished abbots. The arrival of the Normans had brought a new impetus to building, and both Turstin and his successor, Herlewin, undertook additions or fresh constructions in the new Norman style. But the great innovator was Henry de Blois, nephew of King Henry I and brother of King Stephen, who became Abbot in 1126 and held that post by special dispensation until his death in 1171, although he also became Bishop of Winchester and Papal Legate. According to Adam of Domerham, Abbot Henry built 'from the foundations' a belltower, chapter house, cloister, lavatory, refectory, dormitory, infirmary (with its own chapel), a brewhouse, a palace and many other works. He was also a keen administrator and tightened up some of the laxities of his predecessors.

In this connection an amusing story has come down to us, about a piece of land in Brent Marsh which bore extremely good crops. Abbot Henry, making a visit of inspection to the Abbey estates at Brent, noticed a wonderful piece of wheat neatly fenced off by a raised bank of earth and asked what the field was called and who was its owner. He was told that it was called 'No Value' and had been ceded to a local knight by Abbot Herlewin. This evidently roused the suspicions of Abbot Henry, for he made inquiries and discovered that the land had been given away on the knight's assurance that it had always been of no value, was of no value, and would ever remain no value. Perhaps the Lord Abbot was good-humoured enough to smile at this explanation, but of course land was land and that wonderful golden wheat was the last crop the knight was allowed to take from 'No Value'. Thereafter the field made its contribution to the census of Abbey production, which in 1252 showed that the monks had 892 oxen, 60 bullocks, 23 colts, 223 cows, 19 bulls, 153 heifers and young oxen, 26 steers, 126 yearlings, 6,717 sheep, 327 pigs and enough wheat to last the year until next harvest.

The new monastery buildings erected by Henry de Blois probably completed the Abbey's major architectural plans for the time being. Much of the previous 200 years had been spent in expansion and new building, and there should now have been only minor additions and normal repairs to undertake. But in 1184, thirteen years after Abbot Henry's death, fire broke out at the Abbey and completely gutted the whole place. The precious relics and emblems of antiquity, for which Glastonbury was so famous, all perished in the disaster. It was a national tragedy, and fortunately it was treated as such by King Henry II. He appointed Ralph FitzStephen to rebuild the Abbey, and in noble and dignified terms the King gave a pledge that:

> Because whatsoever a man soweth, that shall he also reap, I, in the act of laying the foundation of the church of Glastonbury (which, being in my hands, has been reduced to ashes by fire), do decree, by the persuasion of Heraclius, the patriarch of Jerusalem, Baldwin, archbishop of Canterbury, and many others, that, God willing, it shall be magnificently completed by myself or by my heirs.

With this royal backing FitzStephen repaired the burnt-out shells of the monastic buildings and laid the foundations of the great church which in part still stands at Glastonbury. In particular he created the exquisite Lady Chapel, the most sacred of Glastonbury's buildings since it is reputed to stand on the original site of the primitive wattle church. And not time or the folly of men has yet wholly suppressed the loveliness of what is still the choicest treasure Glastonbury has to offer to its visitors. The graceful, effortless interlacings of curving stone seem to echo and crystallise the entwined wattling of the 'ealde chirche'.

The task of rebuilding, so briskly and propitiously begun, was sadly slowed down when Henry II died. The dispute with Savaric still further weakened and impoverished the community, and the new church was not advanced far enough to be dedicated until 1303. It must by then have been roofed in, but additions and embellishments continued for long afterwards, and indeed the work of enriching and perfecting the vast building was never finished. Two of the great builders of Glastonbury came very late in the succession of abbots — John Selwood, who built the superb church of St John's in the latter half of the fifteenth century, and his successor, Richard Bere, whose handiwork — with sometimes his monogram — is to be seen in several buildings in the district. Abbot Bere, who also rebuilt St Benedict's church and added a chapel to the great Abbey church, was one among that group of urbane and cultured churchmen who shared the friendship of Erasmus. Bere travelled to Italy as Henry VII's ambassador, and no doubt he shared Erasmus's high hopes of the young Henry VIII. Death spared him from the disillusionment that was to come so swiftly and brutally.

After the Dissolution of the Monasteries and the judicial murder of Abbot Whiting, the Abbey passed to the Duke of Somerset. It had, of course, been pillaged by the King's commissioners, and no doubt there were other robberies and transferences of ownership on a lesser scale. The clock which is now one of the show-pieces of Wells Cathedral is said to have been removed thence from Glastonbury at this time, although there is a slight mystery about it. Maxwell Fraser dismisses the story as a fable, on the ground that there is a reference to the clock in a Wells account roll of 1392–3. On the other hand, there is strong evidence that the clock was at one time at Glastonbury. John of Glastonbury, who was the Abbey's official historian, asserted that Adam of Sodbury gave 'the great clock, which was remarkable for its processions and spectacles'. And Leland, reported that he saw the clock — inscribed 'Petrus Lightfote, monachus, fecit hoc opus' — in the southern part of the transept of the Abbey church. Adam of Sodbury was Abbot from 1322 to 1335, so there are various ways in which the conflicting evidence could be reconciled. Peter Lightfoot might have been engaged to make for Wells a second clock of a similar design to his one at Glastonbury. Alternatively, the Glastonbury clock might have been taken to Wells at the time of the Dissolution and, as it were, 'grafted' on to the cathedral's existing clock. After all, such 'marriages' are not unknown to clockmakers.

In general, though, it is surprising how swift and complete was the plundering of the Abbey, and how little — apart from the buildings — remains identifiable. A young soldier who visited Glastonbury in 1635 wrote: 'Heere had I soone a sight at full of the stately ruines, and demolish'd downfalls of that ancient, rare, and unparallel'd Abbey, stuffe enough left to reare up a new History.' But, alas, the 'demolish'd downfalls' of Glastonbury were too engulfing for those who at various times have tried to rear up a reasonably comprehensive history of the Abbey. Commenting on the paucity of our knowledge of the later abbots, one historian complains justifiably that the Abbey's own manuscript history had had all the latter pages torn out 'for common purposes' before it was rescued.

Occasionally some item of Abbey property has come to light in later years, and on one occasion this happened in a most diverting way. In the seventeenth century an old mantelpiece from the Porter's Lodge was thrown into the street and left there for several years. Its current owner seemed unable to find a use for it, so a fellow townsman made him a bid of 3s for it. I am unable to say whether that was a fair price for a mantelpiece in those days; but probably it was, because the owner said he was prepared to let it go for 3s 4d. By normal standards of rural haggling the two were so close together in their valuations at the very outset that one would have expected them to come to an accord in the neighbourhood of 3s 2d with no more than an hour's light teasing over a mug of cider. However, these were obdurate men, of inflexible will. The would-be buyer refused to advance beyond his opening bid of 3s. And the owner as steadfastly refused to bate a penny of his declared price of 3s 4d. Argue as they might, they made no progress in their mutual attrition and the affair terminated without result. The mantelpiece remained where it was, in the street.

At this point the owner's daughter intervened in the story. She evidently despaired now of ever getting rid of this confounded thing, which was making the front of the house look so untidy. And since her father would neither use it nor sell it, she decided to solve the problem in her own way. Without more ado, she gave orders for it to be cut up. Some handy fellow with a saw accordingly set about it, and in so doing he opened up a secret hole inside the mantelpiece which contained 100 gold coins minted in the reigns of Richard II and Edward III.

The ruined buildings have passed uneasily through many hands. Their first secular owner was attainted for treason, and only the Devonshire family — who held the property through the seventeenth century — have been in possession for any length of time. The last sale was in 1907, when various proposals were put forward, including a scheme to convert the remains of the Abbey into a neo-Arthurian 'school of chivalry'. As in the case of Stonehenge, there was also the terrible rumour of an American plan to ship the entire place across the Atlantic. However, the purchaser was a nominee of the Church of England, and in 1909 — as part of the celebrations of the millenary of the diocese of Bath and Wells — the deeds were handed to the Archbishop of Canterbury. Among other things, time and misfortune had healed the long acrimony between Glastonbury and its episcopal rival.

The place has been dead for four centuries; but the supernatural atmosphere which enshrouds it has remained curiously potent. At a comparatively minor level there was, for example, the strange case of Matthew Chancellor's dream in 1751. Chancellor, a lifelong sufferer from asthma, dreamt that he could be cured by drinking water from the Chalice spring. He obeyed his dream, which required him to drink, fasting, on three consecutive Sundays, and he subsequently reported himself to be cured. The effect of this on a public which already had a positive mania for drinking curative waters was electric. By the following May, according to Collinson, there were 10,000 visitors in Glastonbury and the surrounding district. A Pump Room was built, and for a while the little town was stirred from its lethargy by such a host of pilgrims as it had not seen for 200 years and more. Some hard-hearted doctors analysed the water and declared that it contained nothing more than the bare essentials of which water is composed — putting it crudely, two of hydrogen to one of oxygen — but nevertheless it was necessary for someone to drink too much and expire before the boomlet collapsed.

And then, on a far bigger scale, there is the fascinating case of the Holy Thorn, with all its ramifications. To distinguish it from the common hawthorn, which it so closely resembles, it is now dignified by the name *Crataegus oxyacantha praecox*, and its reputation for bursting into blossom at Christmas has been widely known and reported for some centuries. William Turner's Herbal of 1562 refers to a hawthorn 'in ye park of Glassenbury' which is green all the winter; and Gerard, in 1597, claims more specifically that the tree 'bringeth foorth his flowers about Christmas'. But earlier than the herbalists a poet wrote the following lines in a poem entitled 'The Lyfe of Joseph of Arimathia', published in 1520:

> Three hawthorns also, that
> groweth in Werall
> Do burge and bear green
> leaves at Christmas
> As fresh as other in May.

Two interesting features of the poem are its omission of any suggested link between the Thorn and Joseph's staff (which comes in later versions of the legend) and its reference to not one hawthorn but three. Later writers make rather a cult of the 'original' hawthorn. It was said to have two trunks, one of which was cut down by an Elizabethan Puritan, the other by a Roundhead during the Civil War. And the wicked Roundhead is alleged to have been killed by a splinter from the Thorn.

For a time the Glastonbury Thorn had to compete with an oak tree in Hampshire which, in the words of Thomas Fuller, 'is generally reported to put forth green leaves yearly on or about Christmas Day. It groweth nigh Lyndhurst in the New Forest; and perchance I could point more exactly at the position thereof, but am loath to direct some ignorant zealot, lest he cut it down under the notion of superstition, and make timber of this oak, as some lately have made fuel of the hawthorn at Glastonbury.' John Aubrey also knew about the New Forest oak. He recalls several years when his father received some of the leaves at Christmas and he adds that 'old Mr Hastings, of Woodlands, was wont to send a basket full of them every year to King Charles the First'.

The Lyndhurst oak, lacking association with a 'holy place', does not seem to have aroused any notion of superstition (in Fuller's phrase). By contrast the Glastonbury Thorn rapidly acquired supernatural attributes. Its 'miraculous' aspect seems to have come into vogue around 1600. James I and members of his Court paid large sums for cuttings, and in 1645 a clergyman, John Eachard, cited the Thorn as evidence in favour of 25 December as the positive date on which Our Lord was born. In *Good News for all Christian Souldiers* Eachard wrote:

> I knowe that England doe keep the right day that Christ was borne on, above all the Nations of Christendome, because we have a miracle hath often been seene in England upon that day, for we have a tree in England, called the Holy Thorne, by Glassenbury Abbey, nigh the Bathe, which on the 25 day of December, which is our Christmasse day, hath constantly blossomed; which the people of that place have received from antiquitie, that it was that kind of thorne, wherewith Christ was crowned.

In 1698 Celia Fiennes visited Glastonbury and jotted down a brief note on the Thorn — 'There is the Holy Thorn growing on a chimney; this the superstitious covet much and have gott some of it for their gardens and soe have almost quite spoiled it, which did grow quite round a chimney tunnell in the stone.' Again there is no reference to any connection with St Joseph. It seems that the Thorn originally gained its reputation for 'holiness' by its habit of flowering at Christmas: the idea that the first true and authentic Holy Thorn sprang from the staff that St Joseph thrust into the ground when he arrived is evidently a later refinement. According to Vaughan Cornish, the first specific reference to St Joseph in this connection is as late as 1714.

Here, then, is a quite remarkable case of a legend growing up in comparatively modern times and over quite a short period. The sixteenth-century references to the Thorn which I have quoted show no inclination to treat it as holy. As late, even, as 1635 there is an almost flippant attitude about Lieutenant Hammond's description of 'the Christmas-day-blossoming Hawthorne, looking as if it would not flourish in Summer, much lesse sprout forth on that nipping day in Winter'. And incidentally he mentions that he saw another and younger hawthorn in a tavern garden. However, from then onwards the tree seems to have acquired a settled title to the designation of 'Holy Thorn'.

By the beginning of the eighteenth century the association with Joseph's staff had come into the picture and by the end of the century the touring clergy who wrote so many of the travel books of the period recognised the Glastonbury Thorn as one of the obligatory subjects to be mentioned. Perhaps it is no exaggeration to say that it had become one of the official wonders of the West Country. It could not be ignored, even when it was dismissed as a vulgar superstition by a writer like Richard Warner, who decided not to ascend '*Weary-all*' Hill, the former scene of this wonder' after he had been told by 'a sagacious cobbler' that the original plant had been destroyed. Nevertheless Warner was not deterred from giving a fully detailed account of the legend (with the interesting variation that it was St Peter who dispatched Joseph of Arimathea to England) before dismissing it with the assertion that

> though the vulgar still regard its descendants in the neighbourhood with veneration . . . yet the progress of botanical knowledge has, with the more enlightened, dissolved the wonder by discovering that the individuals of one whole species of the thorn possess the same peculiarity.

Between the vulgar and the enlightened the division of opinion was extreme. Warner passed through Glastonbury in 1799. At about the same time John Clark erected a memorial stone with the simple inscription 'J.A.Anno D. XXXI' (Joseph of Arimathea, in the year of Our Lord 31).

At this point one must pause to ask if there is anything at all in the Thorn legend which can survive the debunking that it seems to invite. Perhaps there may be, because so often the wilder extravagances of this type of legend are the result — oddly enough — of late attempts to rationalise them. The idea that the whole thing sprang out of the staff of the first missionary is, in its way, a tidy explanation. It gives shape and logical pattern of a kind to what otherwise is just a vaguely superstitious veneration of the unaccountable. But if we scrape off this superimposed rationalisation we may find that the underlying superstition had some quite realistic motive which later became confused and distorted.

The key to this motive may be found, not very surprisingly, in the nature of the tree itself. If we doubt that one and the same thorn tree flourished for 1,700 years we must ask how it propagated itself. The answer looks easy enough, since the way trees do these things is familiar to most of us. But Dom Ethelbert Horne pointed out some years ago that seeds of the Holy Thorn yield only common hawthorn. This means, of course, that the winter-blossoming habit could have been propagated only by grafting. Is it too fanciful to suggest that at one time this knowledge may have been confined to the monks of Glastonbury?

In earlier times it was among the monks that the arts of husbandry were most assiduously developed. Having acquired one example of the stock, either from a local sport or from an imported specimen, they may understandably have conserved among themselves the knowledge of how to propagate it. Equally, they would scarcely be averse to the fostering of popular admiration for this unusual plant which greeted so pleasantly the festival of Our Lord's birth. The sheer force of association with Christmas would be enough to exalt the Thorn above its conventional fellows. It was in fact an endearing example of the pathetic fallacy, of the eternal human desire to read sentiment into natural phenomena. And there is no reason to think that the monks would want to discourage such a wholesome turning of men's thoughts to the Christmas theme. The engrafted thorn was one more symbol, with a direct and simple message that anybody could understand. And to that extent it was holy, as ikon or vestment or abbot's ring was holy; because, of its nature, it called men to remember their Heavenly Lord.

But there may be more to it than that. Vaughan Cornish suggests that the Glastonbury tree may have had a much more positive value for the monks at a time when they had to combat the pagan worship of the thorn, which was particularly a cult of the Belgic tribes. Heathen ideas and customs survived in a sort of spiritual underworld for a long time after their official conquest by Christianity, and it is well known that the Church was often content to transform what it found difficult to eradicate. The solitary thorn, as landmark, as boundary post, as meeting place, might easily retain an unspecified magic long after its conscious worship had died out. Superstitions and half-forgotten beliefs would cling to it, and its adaptation to the Christian calendar as the herald of Christmas would sweeten the tree's reputation and exorcise its ancient evil.

Of this theory it must be said that it at least does no violence to our powers of credence. The tenacious hold that the Glastonbury Thorn still has on popular imagination suggests the probability that it may stem from some remote and powerful source, of which the symbolic propriety remains though the explanation be lost. It could be that the Thorn of Avalon was once the focus for some pagan act of worship; that the monks later diverted its veneration into the forms of Christian practice; and that by the thirteenth century or thereabouts the tree had settled down to a holy reputation because of its quasi-miraculous blossoming at Christmas time. From then until the Dissolution the monks followed an increasing tendency to rationalise their own legends, and in particular the Joseph myth began to take hold but never apparently became

A completed 'tree' or 'gallus' of teazles

The teazle harvest at Fivehead, near Langport; handfuls of teazles, tied with another, are slipped on a pole to dry

Cattle grazing near Westonzoyland

Peat extraction on Shapwick Heath

associated in any precise way with the Thorn during the life of the monastery.

Some very striking evidence at this point comes from a letter written in 1535 by Dr Layton to Thomas Cromwell, who had sent him to inspect the Somerset monasteries. Layton enclosed what he described as 'two flowers wraped in black sarsnet, that in Christmas Mass even, at the very hour when Christ was born, will spring and burgen and bare blossoms'. Identification with the Nativity could hardly be more complete, and we may take it that this was the extreme claim for the Thorn during the existence of the Abbey: that it had, by the operation of the pathetic fallacy, a synchronism with Christmas and was to that extent holy.

The Elizabethans were very chary about the pathetic fallacy — except when they went to the theatre. Poor Camden bends over backwards to save himself from seeming the teeniest bit superstitious. 'I should be esteemed credulous in our age', he writes, 'were I to mention the cornel or hawthorne at Glastonbury which buds at Christmas Day, as if it was May. Yet many credible persons, if we may believe their testimony, vouch these things for truth.' To be esteemed credulous was worse than death to an Elizabethan, for superstition had so recently been rooted out of the land. A hundred years had to pass before educated persons could start to toy with the Thorn legend. But holy or not, the fame of the Thorn held its place as one of the minor wonders of England. It even became acclimatised to the needs of Restoration verse, for Charles Sedley turned it into a neatly gallant metaphor in his praise of Cornelia who

> Blooms in the winter of her days,
> Like Glastonbury Thorn.

In the eighteenth century, Bristol merchants did quite a flourishing trade in sprays of the Holy Thorn, including some export business. I like to think that no common hawthorn found its way into the warehouses, particularly as many a good honest seaman would buy a piece and carry it as a charm against peril on the ocean.

And now the lingering superstition gathered force again, with the Gothic Revival and the Victorian taste for medieval romance. Joseph and Arthur emerged as the two heroes of Avalon, and the old half-forgotten stories were finally tidied up and given a sort of heraldic formalism. The romantic antiquarianism, which flowered in the poetry of Tennyson particularly, posed the legendary figures against a tasteful backcloth and placed the Thorn artistically in the hand of Joseph — where it showed to the best advantage. And every subsequent guidebook strengthens the grasp.

In 1929 George V revived the old custom of accepting a gift of Holy Thorn from Glastonbury at Christmas, and this gift is now sent to the ruling sovereign each year. The custom probably began when the Bishop of Bath and Wells gave a spray to the consort of James I. It is a pleasant custom, and long may it continue.

CHAPTER TWELVE

ARTHUR AND AVALON

For the modern visitor enough remains to recapture an impression — perhaps quite a strong impression — of the ancient glory of Glastonbury. The massive broken columns of the great tower, groping upwards to the sky, have the moving dignity of blinded giants. The Lady Chapel, though damaged and incomplete, has an impassive eloquence for which it has been justly described as 'the swansong of Romanesque art'. The vast choir and the whole immense ground plan make still a silent but undeniable challenge. Here was a superb vision, realised in stone, to which men, generation after generation and century after century, dedicated themselves. Here is still one of the great monuments of human purpose and devotion. To walk among these ruins is both a humbling and an inspiring experience.

And not all the work of the Abbey's masons is ruined. The jewel of their craft is shattered, but their lesser works survive in some abundance. The little town still points with justifiable pride to its fifteenth-century inn, to the Tudor court house or tribunal, to the Abbey barn and to its parish churches. Passing through the vicinity of Avalon the most casual eye will hardly fail to notice some building which commemorates the name of Abbot Bere or Abbot Selwood or one of their predecessors. And within the Abbey grounds indeed one fabric remains intact — the abbot's kitchen. It was probably built at the beginning of the fourteenth century, when Abbot Fromond was adding various new buildings, and no timber was used in its construction. This was doubtless a lesson learnt from the great fire of 1184. The kitchen has four large fireplaces and an ingenious louvre-system for regulating chimney draught. The double lantern which surmounts the kitchen and regulates the airflow can now be seen in a reflecting mirror which was provided by the squire of Butleigh, Neville Grenville. The squire, a man of character, was one of the earliest motorists, and fragments of a solid tyre from his first mechanical monster now serve as rubber stops for the mirror in the abbot's kitchen.

There is one aspect of the Glastonbury story, however, which still remains to be mentioned. It is the most elusive and tantalising of all the legends — the legend of King Arthur, which gives the Isle of Avalon its name. I have kept it separate from the main story because it is an auxiliary myth, drawn here perhaps by the magnetic power of the Abbey's medieval prestige, but not necessarily an integral part of the history that develops from the 'ealde chirche'. I feel also that the best way to put Arthur in some sort of perspective is to consider him side by side with King Alfred, for there is to my mind a strong affinity between the two men. Both were defenders of the Faith against a pagan invader, and Alfred's unofficial title of 'England's Darling' fits Arthur even more aptly. The primary difference between the two men is that Alfred has a firmly documented historical existence, whereas Arthur has not; and perhaps because of that, Arthur retains a kind of mystical glamour which Alfred lacks.

The immediately striking thing about Arthur is that he is so much of a household word. He is commemorated in song and story, and on the map of these islands only one name occurs more frequently than his — and it is hardly fair competition, even so, because that one name is the Devil's. Yet the foundation on which this almost boundless fame reposes is, to put it mildly, exiguous. One eminent authority, E. K. Chambers, observes in a rather tart and cautionary way that most of the Arthurian legend 'can be no more than the play of imagination about the meagre details furnished by Harleian MS 3859'.

And meagre indeed are the established facts to which we can refer with any confidence. There is no firm evidence that he was a 'king'. Nennius, writing in the early part of the ninth century, says that Arthur was the leader of the Britons in war, which may mean that he was a military overlord commanding the forces of an alliance of petty kingdoms. He fought against the Saxons, won the battle of Badon and eleven other battles, and fell at Camlan in the year 539. Argument continues as to where the battle of Badon was fought, but there is no doubt that it was a major and decisive victory for the Britons. A period of peace followed, lasting for at least twenty and perhaps forty years. Gildas describes the battle as 'almost the last slaughter of these gallows-birds, but by no means the least'. Nennius says definitely that Arthur was in command at Badon, and he certainly made his presence felt if we are to believe that 960 of the enemy fell 'from the onslaught of Arthur only, and no one laid them low, save he alone'. But what is very curious is that Gildas, who was born in the year that the battle of Badon was fought, seems never to have heard of Arthur. At any rate he makes no mention of him. And it is just that kind of tantalising mystery which surrounds Arthur at every turn.

Piecing together the fragmentary story as best one can, it does seem that Arthur succeeded for a time in giving a coherent leadership to the crumbling resistance of Romano-British civilisation to the invading Saxons. Like Alfred, he stood as the champion of Christendom against the heathen. In the eighth of his twelve great battles, at Castle Guinnion, Arthur carried a representation of the Blessed Virgin Mary, and by the sight of it the enemy were turned to flight.

However, advantages won in the field were largely dissipated by internal jealousies and treacheries, and it is suggested that Arthur's death was occasioned by a brawl during a private quarrel; possibly after a previous quarrel, in which his wife's reputation was involved, had been healed by the intervention of the monks at Glastonbury. That at any rate is a rough pattern of events which can be inferred from the scanty evidence.

The connection with Glastonbury is so far very slight. For the suggestion that the wounded Arthur was brought from Camlan or Camelot to die at Glastonbury, 'anciently called insula Avallonia', there is no earlier authority than Giraldus Cambrensis. And he made this claim at some time in or near the year 1194 — at any rate between 1193 and 1199. And that date is of special significance because of what happened at Glastonbury in the ten years following the disastrous fire of 1184.

At about the time of the fire — presumably shortly afterwards — Henry II suggested to the monks that they should try to find the remains of King Arthur, and he gave them a remarkable reason for his suggestion. He told them that he had heard an old British singer prophesy that the body would be found at Glastonbury in a hollowed oak 16ft below the ground.

This old British singer belonged to what we now call the Celtic peoples, among whom Arthur had become a legend of great potency. Giraldus, for example, records that they still await his coming, 'even as the Jews their Messiah'. And Alain de Lille, writing in the latter half of the twelfth century, says:

> Go to the realm of Armorica, which is lesser Britain, and preach about the market-places and villages that Arthur the Briton is dead as other men are dead, and facts themselves will show you how true is Merlin's prophecy, which says that the ending of Arthur shall be doubtful. Hardly will you escape unscathed, without being whelmed by the curses or crushed by the stones of your hearers.

To the defeated Celts, driven into the hilly corners of Cornwall and Wales and Brittany by successive invasions from northern and central Europe, Arthur was the heroic saviour of their nation who would one day come again in triumph. And Welsh and Cornish and Breton bards kept his memory green with song and prophecy.

But why was Henry II so interested in what an old singer told him? There are two explanations, and regrettably they are both nefarious. One, put forward by E. K. Chambers, bids us to consider Henry's policy in Brittany. There the King had secured the dukedom for his son by a politically convenient marriage, but unfortunately the young duke ruined the whole stratagem by changing sides and supporting Breton resistance. What was worse, when his wife bore him a son he named him Arthur. As the significance of this could hardly be lost on the Arthur-worshipping Bretons, it may be that Henry II felt the time had come to prove that Arthur the King was as plainly dead as anybody else who last breathed six centuries ago. And as he was now proposing to rebuild the Abbey at considerable personal expense, Henry could perhaps be forgiven for assuming that the monks would find Arthur — or somebody else of the same name — if it was humanly possible to do so.

An alternative explanation is that it was clearly necessary for the monks to face the fact that many of the things which had always brought pilgrims and donations to Glastonbury were lost in the flames. A new Abbey, be it never so fine, would not have the compelling attraction of the old one unless new relics and curios of great rarity and sacredness could be found. There was thus every incentive to search in remote corners and under the ground for fresh treasures, and it is noticeable that some quite remarkable discoveries — including the bones of St Dunstan and a manuscript of St Patrick — were made in a surprisingly short time after the fire.

So we have a real cloak-and-dagger plot by a crafty king and unscrupulous monks to rig a phoney exhumation. It is always easy to believe that other people, particularly those who have been dead for some time, are more wicked than one is oneself, and perhaps more ingenious too; but we may be as credulous in our own way as those we so confidently slander. It is almost a modern superstition to believe in the most uncritical way in what is after all the fairly astonishing thesis that the lord abbot would one day rise up in the chapter house and announce that he was proposing to discover a completely non-existent grave, from which he would palm off two fictitious corpses as Arthur and Guinevere. One cannot say positively that it did not happen, but such a proceeding would not be quite the commonplace everyday piece of monkish perfidy that we are sometimes asked to assume. Moreover it is fair to allow that the very ruin caused by the fire would provide special opportunities and incentives for excavation. We have seen in our own day that the bombing of cities and the destruction of buildings can lead to archaeological discoveries that would otherwise have been impossible. Let us hope no one will later say of us that, as a consolation for the blitz of the 1940s, we hurriedly trumped up a lot of bogus finds.

With that lingering degree of openness of mind, we may return to the little party of monks digging beside the charred walls of their abbey. At a depth of 16ft, between two stone pyramids, they found, or said they found, a hollowed oak — just as the bard had foretold. Inside the oak were two skeletons. One was a woman's and a lock of golden hair crumbled to dust as a monk grasped it. The other was of a man of immense stature, with ten wounds in his skull.

If suspicion is to fall on this, it must surely be confined to the identification with Arthur. There is no reason to doubt that the monks, in their digging after the fire, might well have unearthed an ancient burial of this kind. And they may have had their reasons for considering the male corpse to be Arthur's. Remote and almost mythical though he be to us now, the finding of Arthur would seem no more improbable in 1190 than the finding of Edward I would be at the present day. And it does no outrage to truth to remark that the man had to be buried somewhere.

On what grounds did the Glastonbury monks claim that it was indeed Arthur they had exhumed? Giraldus Cambrensis says unequivocally that he saw a leaden cross, which was alleged to have been found with the bones, and which bore the inscription:

HIC JACET SEPULTUS INCLITUS REX ARTHURUS CUM WENNEVERIA UXORE
SUA SECUNDA IN INSULA AVALLONIA

Giraldus may have been fooled or he may have been lying, but he wrote shortly
after the discovery and presumably reported the official account. That the
leaden cross was a forgery, or that at least it was made after the exhumation as a
sort of museum label, is an obvious and legitimate suspicion. And like so much
in the Arthurian legend this cross disappears in the most maddening way, after
being copied and measured by Leland in about 1540, and after remaining in
the possession of a Wells family named Hughes until the eighteenth century.

Even though we discount the authenticity of the leaden cross, however,
there remains the possibility that Arthur's last resting place would be
remembered with reverence among his own people and not revealed to Saxon
or Norman. And where more likely than in the hallowed ground beside the old
church in the Isle of Avalon, under the protection of that most holy shrine
which Arthur's courage had helped to save from the fate which befell
Canterbury and St Albans? The monks of 1190 may not have had all the
positive evidence that was later claimed. But they may not have been so far
wrong, for all that.

What is perhaps surprising is the speed with which the non-Celts adopted
Arthur. Shortly after the discovery Richard I presented Tancred of Sicily with
Arthur's sword 'Caliburnus'. In 1278 Edward I, who was spending Easter at
Glastonbury, ordered the reopening of Arthur's tomb and inspected the relics.
The tomb was subsequently removed to a position in front of the high altar. In
1344 Edward III vowed to re-establish the company of the Round Table, to
the number of 300 knights, and Philip of Valois replied with a rival Round
Table. By 1348 English knighthood was established as the Order of the Garter,
and from then onwards the Arthurian boom was well under way. In the
fifteenth century the University of Cambridge claimed Arthur as its founder,
and by the time of Caxton it was possible to see Gawain's skull, Cradok's
mantle and Launcelot's sword in various parts of England. That old spell-
binder, Geoffrey of Monmouth, who either preserved or fathered the early
Celtic legends of Arthur and his company, has much to answer for — and some
reason for pride in the power of his pen.

Close identification of the Arthur story with the neighbourhood of
Glastonbury had become an antiquarian hobby by Tudor times. Leland refers
to 'a Bridge of Stone of four Arches communely caullid Pontperlus, wher men
fable that Arture cast in his Swerd'. In 1415 the bridge was called 'Pons
periculosus', and in John Overton's Map of Somerset, of 1668, it is
'Pomperles'. Rebuilt in 1912 and spanning the muddy and unimpressive
waters of the Brue, a less romantic bridge than Pomparles would be difficult to
find. However, Sir John Harington quoted in 1591 a 'fabulous' report that
Arthur was carried away in a barge 'from a bridge called Pomperles, near the
said Glassenbury, and so conveyed by unknown persons [or by the Lady of the
Lake] with promise to bring him back again one day'.

Camelot, like everything in the Arthur legend, is the subject of much dispute. It could be in the Camel country of Cornwall. Tintagel is a well-known claimant. Malory considered it to be Winchester; Caxton thought it was in Wales. Another possibility frequently canvassed is Cadbury Camp which is about a dozen miles from Glastonbury and looks out over the upper course of the river Cam and the villages of West Camel and Queen Camel. Cadbury has a long history of human settlement, dating back to the Early Neolithic people before 3000 BC. When the Romans invaded Britain Cadbury was a fortified township or large village and it must have been an important centre of resistance. Vespasian stormed the place and slaughtered the inhabitants.

Leland noted that many Roman coins had been ploughed up at Cadbury and it was he who first identified the Camp as 'Camallate, sumtyme a famose toun or castelle'. He questioned the local inhabitants in the hope of picking up some sort of confirmation, but they could tell him nothing more than that they had heard that 'Arture much resorted to Camallate'. The site has been examined on several occasions by archaeologists. The most recent and very thorough work of Leslie Alcock has thrown a fascinating light on the Arthurian period as he has been able to show that the Camp was reoccupied in the late fifth and sixth centuries, when the whole 18 acre site was equipped with new fortifications — perhaps designed to oppose the westward drive of the Saxons. Within the fortress the remains of a large hall have been uncovered. It is reasonable to assume that the place must have been a major military headquarters during the period when Arthur was the British Commander-in-Chief and it is hardly reckless to suggest that Arthur may at some time have entered the great hall, but when one looks for some final clinching proof it is as well to heed Mr Alcock's cautionary words:

> It is altogether unlikely, on the nature of the evidence, that we will ever be able to identify a fortress, or other site, with Arthur in a personal sense.

With so little fact to build on, the story of Arthur takes its wayward and fanciful shape as chance suggests. Leland's attempt to identify Camelot in the vicinity of Avalon may lack justification, but he picked up a piece of gossip that helps to enrich the Arthurian legend. Someone told him about a silver horse-shoe that had been found at Cadbury-Camelot within living memory — that is to say, probably not later than 1500. This horsehoe has its place in a popular belief that on Christmas Eve Arthur still rides with his knights to Glastonbury on horses shod with silver shoes. The path they follow is known as 'King Arthur's hunting track'. An interesting modern record of this legend was noted as recently as 1890 by the rector of South Cadbury, who preserved this account from one of his parishioners:

> Folks do say that on the night of the full moon King Arthur and his men ride round the hill, and their horses are shod with silver, and a silver shoe has been found in the track where they do ride; and when they have ridden round the hill, they stop to water their horses at the Wishing Well.

And so the legend persists. In the early years of this century an archaeologist, excavating at Cadbury Camp, was asked, 'Have you come to take the king out?' The king — king that was, king that shall be. With those words one's mind turns back to the verses written early in the fifteenth century:

> But for he skaped that batell, y-wys,
> Bretons and Cornysch seyeth thus,
> That he levyth yet, parde,
> And schall come and be a kyng aye.
>
> At Glastonbury on the queer
> They made Artourez toumbe there,
> And wrote with latyn vers thus,
> Hic jacet Arthurus, rex quondam, rexque futurus.

CHAPTER THIRTEEN

ALFRED AND ATHELNEY

As you pass through the village of East Lyng your eye may be caught by a stumpy little obelisk on a whaleback of land that elevates itself above the surroundings flats. It is there to commemorate King Alfred. The gently contoured ridge is the Isle of Athelney, and its memorial was erected as a local tribute to 'England's Darling'. A closer inspection is not particularly rewarding. The Alfred monument, put up in 1801 by Colonel John Slade who then owned the estate, is a rather meagre and unlovely object. And its inscription is not even accurate: Alfred's stay in Athelney was not of a whole year's duration, but of a few months only, and it was in the year 878 not 879. However, the piety of Colonel Slade's intentions deserves our respect for he did at least recognise that something was due to the memory of one of England's greatest kings. And it was here, at Athelney, that one of the most momentous periods of our history originated. When the Danish barbarians were burning and destroying the centres of a Christian civilisation in England, the defeated Alfred hid at Athelney, secure among the surrounding marshes, until he was ready to launch his victorious counter-attack.

Athelney is no longer an island at any time of the year and it retains little of its earlier character. Today it is a countryside of small orchards, withy-beds, paddocks and pastures, carefully tended and cultivated — quite unlike the natural fastness to which Alfred retired in his hour of greatest peril. Asser, who was Alfred's friend, adviser and biographer, described Athelney as 'surrounded on all sides by vast impassable marshes and pools, so that it was totally inaccessible except by boat or by a single causeway'. And this causeway was defended by a fortification at each end. The island itself was densely wooded with alder thickets which sheltered an abundance of game. The cleared dry land scarcely amounted to a couple of acres.

To this marshy waste Alfred came as the beaten leader of a crumbling kingdom. His soldiers were dispersed, many of his people had already fled overseas, and the Danes plundered where they pleased. Yet within a few months he had rallied his people and achieved the most resounding and decisive victory. It is almost a fairytale of heroism: no wonder legends and fables gather about it, and no wonder one's curiosity plays about the character of the man himself. As a king, Alfred had advantages of ancestry. He was of the illustrious line of Ceawlin. His grandfather was Egbert, who learned the arts of war as an exile at the court of Charlemagne, and came home to make himself master of all England. Before he was seven Alfred had made two journeys to Rome — one with his father — and perhaps may thereby have acquired a rather wider horizon than was usual in a young Saxon noble. But he could not read English until he was twelve, and Latin he mastered painfully in middle age. From his mother he learnt to love the old songs of his people, and here he may have found the imaginative wealth that inspired him. As the fifth son he was unlikely to come to the throne, and his first battles against the Danes were fought under the command of one of his elder brothers.

For thirty years Danes had been raiding England sporadically, but in 865 they intensified their campaign and radically altered their tactics. Hitherto they had relied on their ships to give them mobility and striking-power in raids up the river valleys, but now they landed a large army in East Anglia and launched fast-moving cavalry attacks. With this new method they conquered Northumbria, slew St Edmund of East Anglia and — in 870 — turned to attack Wessex. Once again the West Country faced the peril of full-scale invasion by a European people intent on conquest.

It was in these circumstances that Alfred came to manhood. He met life sword in hand. Against the later picture of the cultured and pious ruler, we must set the younger glimpse of the impatient captain leaving his elder brother at Mass and hurrying to give battle orders because the moment was ripe for an attack to be launched. Impious must Alfred's action have seemed; but is there not a striking foretaste of Cromwell in that hard-headed sense of what 'the Lord's work' required? And it is not irrelevant to recall that, in the outcome, the Lord blessed the deed with victory.

The first campaign ended indecisively, and may therefore perhaps be counted as a negative success for Wessex. The Danes were not conquered but they were halted; and at the battle of Ashdown they quite certainly had the worst of it. Wessex was the most effective military power of the Saxon kingdoms, and the Danes — disappointed of yet another easy triumph — had to concede that they had met their equals in the field. The reputation of Danish invincibility took a heavy knock, and Saxon morale must have risen correspondingly.

In April 871 Alfred became King, following the death of his brother, Ethelred. The continuing struggle was profiting neither side, and Alfred was content to buy peace and gain time. Wessex remained unmolested until 875, when the Danes made an astonishingly swift sortie from Cambridge to Wareham. They had perhaps intended to establish contact with a Danish fleet in the Channel, but a storm wrecked the ships off Swanage, and the land force was quickly surrounded. Another peace treaty was made — but this time in more humble form than the Danes were accustomed to — and they withdrew. They seem to have decided that Wessex was still too hard a nut to crack, for they turned away into Mercia and left Alfred to enjoy three untroubled years.

It was in 878 that the blow fell, in a sensational and catastrophic way. In the depth of winter, in January, when armies were normally disbanded and warfare was considered to be impracticable, the Danes moved out of Gloucester, struck at Chippenham and captured the town. A large part of Wessex submitted, and the national spirit of resistance seems to have collapsed. Prominent men fled abroad, and it was as something of a fugitive that Alfred came to Athelney, to the two acres of inaccessible dry land in the flooded waste of marshland and bog.

The completeness of the defeat is bewildering. One might have expected the Saxon leadership to fall back southwards and start rallying support in Winchester perhaps or Sherborne. It was the men of Hampshire and Dorset who eventually joined the surviving Wiltshire men in the counter-attack, and Alfred clearly had difficulty in making liaison with them from his headquarters in Athelney. It looks as if the surprise attack on Chippenham in some way separated Alfred from the main reserves of Saxon resistance. Possibly he was wintering in the royal 'palace' or villa at Wedmore and his routes into Wiltshire or Dorset were thought to be already cut or too dangerous to risk. Yet only three years earlier the Danes had moved from Cambridge to the Dorset coast without apparently disorganising the Wessex defences. One wonders why the loss of Chippenham was now so paralysing.

In the temporary security of Athelney, with the winter floods at their height, Alfred built a fortification of some kind and constantly sallied out after Easter to attack and harry the enemy. And in the seventh week after Easter he was able to link up with the southern forces and to bring the Danes to battle at Ethandun. Victorious in the field Alfred pursued the enemy into a fortress where he besieged them for fourteen days and compelled them to surrender. The capitulation of the Danes was complete. The conditions imposed on them included the adoption of the Christian faith by their leaders. Beyond any doubt the Battle of Ethandun must be reckoned one of the great turning-points in our national history.

Outlined in this simple fashion the facts of Alfred's achievement are incontrovertible enough. But when one tries to go into any detail the doubts and confusions and controversies swiftly multiply. There is uncertainty about the location of 'Ethandun' and also of the place on the Somerset or North Devon coast called 'Cynuit' (where a Danish force landed with the presumed intention of outflanking Alfred). There are difficulties in any attempt to interpret the military strategy of the two adversaries. And there are problems inherent in the timescale. More than enough acrimony has already been generated by the disputes between the so-called 'Somerset historians' and the place-name experts; their conflicting viewpoints are by now so familiar that any fresh partisanship would be quite out of place. What is needed is a reconciliation of what is demonstrable and what is plausible.

The 'place-name' argument can be stated very simply. The study of the evolution of place names from the dawn of literacy to the present day is a science in its own right. Because the historical documentation on which it relies is neither complete nor free from error it is an imperfect science — like any other — and may sometimes come up with a wrong answer. But it is the best tool we have for this particular job. To reject it categorically is the act of a bigot.

The argument of the Somerset historians is that the identification of 'Ethandun' and 'Cynuit' must be consonant with a plausible reconstruction of military strategy within the framework of the Saxon narratives. To put it crudely, if one accepts the account of those months after the defeat of Chippenham, as reported by Asser and the Chronicles, it must be wholly implausible to locate 'Ethandun' on the banks of the Clyde and 'Cynuit' in the Lizard peninsula.

Each approach therefore imposes a limit beyond which the possible becomes impossible. With that in mind, let us trace the course of events from Chippenham onwards. On that January day when the victorious Danish leader, Guthrum, took stock of his success and decided his next move, did he plan to destroy Alfred personally, to capture or kill him? Did he seek to envelop Athelney (assuming that he knew Alfred was hiding there)? And was Guthrum in command of the Danish fleet that crossed the Bristol Channel from Wales and made an abortive landing on the Wessex coast? Were the movements of the Danes co-ordinated by land and sea in an overall strategy aimed at Alfred?

What may be called the 'official' view of modern historians is that Guthrum's main army stayed in or near Chippenham, that the sea-borne landing was at Countisbury, and that 'Ethandun' was fought at what is now Edington in Wiltshire, whence the defeated Danes fled either to nearby Bratton Castle or back to Chippenham. The more heretical view of the 'Somerset' school is that the Danes would have met no opposition to prevent them from advancing to Mendip. Glastonbury seems to have met the familiar fate of monasteries and churches in Danish hands, since nothing survived there to aid Alfred's rebuilding of religious and cultural life after the Danes were expelled. And there is a probability that the Danes occupied the Polden ridge, if we are to believe Asser's statement that after Easter Alfred constantly harried the enemy in sorties from Athelney. 'De ipsa arce semper . . . contra paganos infatigabiliter rebellavit' is how Asser describes Alfred's efforts, suggesting frequent forays against forces that were therefore reasonably near. It is not easy to interpret this as requiring a round trip of a hundred miles into Wiltshire each time.

The landing of the cross-channel force commanded by Hubba could conceivably have been a quite unrelated attack, in the sense that Hubba and Guthrum may not have been in touch with each other, and Hubba may not have known that Alfred was at Athelney. So much depends on whether the Danes were a single disciplined army, with a higher command pursuing a strategy, or were unco-ordinated bands of marauders chancing their luck in an

Withy fields near Oath

Withies drying beside the River Tone in flood

The lonely foreshore of Bridgwater Bay

opportunist way. But if one seeks to find a meaning in Hubba's expedition it is worth looking more closely at what Alfred had managed to achieve since the loss of Chippenham.

The defensive works described by Asser are generally held to be a degree of fortification on the hill known as Burrow Mump, from which a causeway or bridge passed to the 'island' of Athelney. The old English name for Burrow Mump, incidentally, was Tutteyate or Tote Yate, which suggests a combination of 'look out' and 'gateway'; in more modern times it has been known as 'King Alfred's Fort'. From a military point of view what Alfred had gained by his Athelney-Burrow Mump fortifications was a firm grip on the junction of the Tone and the Parret. North of the Parret and its winter floodwaters lay Sedgemoor and the morass of the river Cary before the first usable dry land to which the Danes could advance — the Poldens. All in all Alfred had secured an excellent defensive position from which a growing force could make damaging sorties by way of the obscure, hidden, waterlogged routes that so greatly favoured the Saxons with their local knowledge.

In these circumstances a move to force the Parret with a naval attack, or to outflank it, would make good sense. It is at any rate plausible to suppose that this was Hubba's intention. The fact that his warriors were engaged and defeated promptly would seem to suggest a degree of preparedness by the Saxons. If indeed they had taken some counter-measures to protect their coastal flank one would expect them to do so along the Parret estuary and immediately to the west of it. There are inducements therefore to look for 'Cynuit' (where Hubba was defeated) in the country adjacent to the left bank of the Parret. The 'Somerset' historians have seized on a local legend which places a victory over the Danes at Cannington, and this has become their 'Cynuit'. Unfortunately the etymological analysis of 'Cannington' does not support the identification with Cynuit.

Where then was Cynuit? Increasingly, though with some hesitations, the place-name experts incline to what we today know as Countisbury. Sir Frank Stenton takes this view. So too does Dr Ekwall in the *Oxford Dictionary of Place Names*. On the other hand Asser's editor, W. H. Stevenson, who poured scorn on the place-name identifications of the Somerset historians, considered that Countisbury was 'impossible phonetically and formally' — a judgement not supported by Professor Dorothy Whitelock, though, in her revaluation of Stevenson. Here then is one of the obstacles to our comprehension of these events. One does not lightheartedly question such a weight of authority but it is surely difficult to believe that Hubba's fleet landed for the purpose of besieging a company of Saxon thegns on Countisbury Hill. Setting aside the difficulty of getting troops ashore there, in the face of even light opposition, one must wonder what their destination could be. If they had succeeded in fighting their way to the top of the hill, what would they have gained — except a view of Exmoor?

Wherever Hubba landed he failed to check Alfred's counter-attack. Seven weeks after Easter Athelney saw the departure of the King as he journeyed to his rendezvous with the men of Hampshire, Dorset and Wiltshire in Selwood Forest. From Selwood they moved to a night halt at Aecglea and the following morning they went into battle at Ethandun. And again, as with Cynuit, one has to ask where the two armies met. Were the Danes defeated at Edington in Wiltshire, or Edington Polden, or somewhere else? The place-name argument favours Edington, Wilts. According to Stevenson Edington Polden would have been known in the ninth century as Eadwinstun. Edington, Wilts, would have been called — or could have been called — Ethandun. This in itself is not conclusive: just as there are many Suttons and Charltons, so there could be more than one Ethandun. But it is obviously no good to consider as a possible site a place which could not have been named Ethandun.

Any consideration of Edington, Wilts, ought to take into account the decisions that Guthrum and the Danes would have taken if they chose to make this the battlefield on which to meet the Saxon counter-offensive. At least until Easter the initiative was clearly with the Danes, after their crushing victory at Chippenham. The coming of spring could be expected to bring the first signs of any Saxon resurgence, and we know from Asser's account that Alfred now started his sorties from Athelney. Any Danish consolidation of the Chippenham victory would therefore have to take account of this renewed activity from the Somerset marshes, and one might expect a movement in the general direction of the Fosse Way if not on to the Polden ridge itself. And again the presumed fate of Glastonbury emphasises the likelihood that the Danes had in fact passed through Bath in some strength.

Edington, however, lies to the south of Chippenham and is perched on the northern scarp of Salisbury Plain. Nearby Bratton Castle similarly looks northward across the lower land, and one would expect any commander who positioned his forces here to be expecting an attack to be launched against the chalk uplands from the north. But of course the Saxon advance was virtually certain to come from the south or the south-west. Even if the Danes had judged that Alfred's frequent thrusts from Athelney were a diversion and had therefore decided to drive southward deeper into Wiltshire in order to confront the main Saxon force they would surely not have seen any value in pausing to refortify the old Iron Age positions at Bratton Castle, nor would they have elected to meet an enemy advancing across the plateau of Salisbury Plain when they themselves had no more than a toe-hold with the steep scarp at their backs. In such a position they were facing the wrong way.

After the battle the Danes fled, according to Asser, 'ad arcem'; and Alfred thereupon deployed his entire force 'before the gates of the heathen fortress' ('ante portas paganicae arcis'). If the Danes fled the fourteen miles or so back to Chippenham one would expect the town to be named instead of the reference to an anonymous 'arcem' (a fortified place). This has perhaps encouraged the theory that Bratton Castle was the fortress that Alfred besieged for fourteen days, but a consideration of the local geography does not offer much encouragement. The Saxons advancing to Edington from the direction of Warminster would have passed Bratton Castle, unless they made a wide detour

— which there is no reason to suppose. It is therefore difficult to see how any significant number of men, defeated in close combat at Edington, could have retreated to a visibly prepared position to the westward: the Saxons would surely have forestalled them. And if such a move seems implausible in theory it becomes even less likely when one walks over the ground. The awkward contours of the land between Edington and Bratton Castle would compel the vanquished survivors to scramble downhill before making the stiff climb up to the old fortifications at Bratton — an uncomfortable and dangerous action to take with a victorious enemy in command of the higher ground nearby.

One final difficulty remains in our attempt to understand the implications of Asser's text. Some historians have suggested that the Danes surrendered because, after fourteen days, they had no water. Asser gives us specific reasons for the demoralisation of the defenders and names them as 'fame, frigore, timore': hunger, cold and fear. The word for 'hunger' might perhaps be taken to include 'thirst', but 'cold' is a rather surprising factor seven weeks after Easter. Night frosts in late May are not unknown in Wiltshire, but Guthrum's men can scarcely have suffered more than discomfort from exposure to the springtime temperatures of southern England.

All in all it is a tantalising story — in some ways so circumstantial, in others so baffling. The more one looks at the available evidence, the more necessary it seems to keep an open mind. The etymology of place names can tell us much but it is worth recalling that Professor Finberg, a contemporary historian of undoubted authority, wrote as recently as 1964 — 'The study of place names is comparatively new, and the principles of its historical application have not yet been fully worked out. Until this is done, it will remain exposed to faulty reasoning and erroneous conclusions.' To that one might add that our knowledge of ninth-century warfare is no less embryonic: the professional strategist and the military historian have much still to do before we can piece together with confidence the few facts that have come down to us.

After Ethandun the scene changes indisputably to central Somerset, to Aller and Wedmore. One of the conditions imposed by Alfred on the defeated Danes required Guthrum and some of his henchmen to accept the Christian faith; and it was at Aller church that the Danish leaders were baptised. The choice of Aller is interesting. Nothing in its history before or since can suggest that it was other than an obscure and insignificant place which happened to suit Alfred's purpose for a reason that we can only guess at. Perhaps it was near to where he was or where he intended to be. Perhaps it was a hasty substitute for a recently destroyed Glastonbury. Possibly he wished to associate nearby Athelney with the moment of triumph. Conceivably its setting may have recommended it to Alfred. Aller stands on the lower slope of the hill north of Langport, with a commanding view across Aller Moor and North Moor to the Sowy villages and Burrow Mump. A ceremony outside the church could be conveniently attended and witnessed by large numbers, and that perhaps was an important factor.

The ceremony of Chrism-loosing — the putting off of the white baptismal robe — took place at the royal villa at Wedmore, to the accompaniment of the giving of presents and appropriate celebrations. The fact that the villa was presumably undamaged offers no comfort to the Somerset historians, though it could be argued that a Danish advance to the Poldens might have 'bypassed' the Isle of Wedmore, which would have been secured by the Panborough Gap and the winter flooding of Brent Marsh. It is an odd fact, incidentally, that Wedmore's southern slope inclines down to a second 'Aller Moor'. The coincidence of two Allers so near Wedmore is an amusing postscript to the place-name controversy. It is a not uncommon Saxon name deriving from the tree, alder. Locally it is still pronounced 'awler' or 'oller'. Alder thickets grew freely on the moors and in Henry VIII's reign Aller Moor was described as a place where 'no chase could formerly be made by reason of the thickness of the alders and the depth of the morasses'.

With the conclusion of a peace treaty Guthrum retired to East Anglia and honoured his pledge by never again taking up arms against the Kingdom of Wessex. But the Peace of Wedmore did not mark the end of the Danish wars. Fresh immigrations led to renewed fighting, and in 886 Alfred occupied London to protect it from the Danes. However, there was never again any real danger of an English collapse. Wessex had survived, as the one intact Saxon kingdom, and Alfred came to be recognised as the king of all free Englishmen throughout the land.

For this decisive victory Alfred declared his thankfulness by founding a church and an abbey at Athelney. Again the neglect of Glastonbury is striking — but Athelney Abbey was not destined to supplant its illustrious neighbour, and no trace of it now remains. William of Malmesbury visited the church and described it as having four piers sunk in the ground. Each side of the building formed an apse, and it stood in its original form until 1320, when it was restored. At the Dissolution the Abbey revenue was given as £209. The buildings disappeared quickly; the latest reference to its existence that I can find is in 1674, when workmen uncovered some of the foundations.

The first Abbot of Athelney was John the Old Saxon, and his appointment indicates Alfred's policy. Abbot John was a famous scholar — one of the few remaining after the violent years of fighting and pillage. The whole fabric of Saxon culture and learning had been torn to pieces by the Danish destruction of the monasteries, and Alfred set himself the task of salvaging and restoring the precious heritage. Asser records that Alfred gathered monks of different races, and brought priests and deacons from the Continent to Athelney. Asser himself came from St David's to live at Alfred's court and read to the King 'whatsoever books he would, such as we had at hand. For this is his own most special wont, despite of every hindrance, mental or bodily, either to read books to himself or to listen to others reading, day and night.' In the dark night that had descended on war-torn Wessex, men like Abbot John were virtually an extinct race, and Alfred was glad to recruit four learned Mercians and three foreigners to help him in his great task of translating into English those books 'most necessary for all men to know'. The few remaining scholars were to translate, and all free-born children were to be taught in schools to read — that was the great conception which inspired Alfred after his victory. And at Athelney, in his new abbey, he lit the first flame to illuminate the prevailing darkness.

Meanwhile what had been secured needed to be protected. To ward off further raids Alfred built a navy to guard his coastline, and covered the country with an organised system of fortresses. This vast undertaking, completed by Alfred's son and summarised by him in the Burghal Hidage, called for one man from each hide of land to serve in his local fort or burh — so that there were four men to each perch of wall or earthwork. When the scheme was completed, no village in Wessex was more than twenty miles away from a fort. To support these efforts with good government, Alfred prepared a new code of laws based on the earlier codes of Ine of Wessex, Offa of Mercia and Ethelbert of Kent — a significant amalgam which welded the best of the past into a national code which was to be respected in all England outside the Danish territories. The old legal distinction between the Saxons and the conquered British peoples disappeared: they had fought together against the Danes, and they were now united as a nation.

In spite of the calls of leadership Alfred still pursued his own scholarly vocation, translating, making notes and adding to his knowledge by conversations with the travellers who came to his court. His survey of central and northern Europe has been praised by Sir Frank Stenton as an achievement which 'stands alone in the Dark Ages as a piece of systematic geography'; and he adds that Alfred was 'on any estimate, the most effective ruler who had appeared in Western Europe since the death of Charlemagne'.

For those who venerate the memory of this great man — as every Englishman should do — the Athelney countryside has a special fascination. The legendary fame of Arthur is scattered up and down the land with no certain location, and it is to Athelney that we look for a clear and undisputed association with one of the heroes of our remote antiquity. Whatever the transformation made by drainage and cultivation, this is still one of the secret places of the West — with its dense withy-beds and narrow roads and glistening rhines, with overhanging orchards and bushy willows shading into the wider green of the moors and softening enigmatically in the mists of evening.

One feature stands out, a natural monument to the Wessex king — the Mump at Burrow Bridge which guarded the bridge over the Parret and the approach to Alfred's headquarters. Although it rises only 75ft above its surroundings, the Mump is strongly reminiscent of the Tor at Glastonbury. Like the Tor it too is crowned with a ruined chapel dedicated to St Michael. Limited excavations in 1939 by Harold St George Gray revealed the skeleton of a young man shot with a bullet, a quantity of medieval ridge tiles and pottery fragments, and the foundations of an earlier chapel and of a Norman building which may have been a castle. The original chapel was a cruciform building belonging to Athelney Abbey. William of Worcester in the fifteenth century, and Leland in the sixteenth, refer to the place as Michaelborough, and during the spoliation of chantries and free chapels in Edward VI's reign the chapel on the Mump was listed as 'the Free Chapel of St Michael at Burrowe'. A free chapel was one built on royal land and not subject to a bishop.

The present building is sometimes said to be an eighteenth-century folly, though I doubt if this could mean more than a whimsical restoration in the fashionably 'ruinated' style. A chapel of some sort was certainly standing on the Mump at the time of the Civil War. Thomas Gerard in 1633 noted that 'on the topp of it [the Mump] now stands a chapell dedicated to St Michaell, which gave it the forename', and two years later Lieutenant Hammond passed by and observed Burgh church 'mounted on a round hill like a castle'. It may have been damaged in the fighting for Langport in 1645, as Goring tried to cover his retreat by garrisoning the Mump with 120 men who held out against Fairfax for three days. An uncompleted restoration is said to have begun in 1724 or 1730, but in 1762 the chapel — then belonging to the rectory of Aller — was portrayed as being in ruins. However, its obscure and rather mysterious history has a fine ending, for it was given as a memorial to the men of Somerset who died in the last war.

There remains to be mentioned one other local object associated with Alfred. In 1693 a 'jewel' was found in North Newton Park, four miles from Athelney. Presented to the Bodleian Museum in 1718, the object was of gold and enamel and bore a representation which is said to portray St Cuthbert. It had perhaps been designed as the top of a staff and it bore a Saxon inscription — 'Alfred had me made'. Those simple words are the King's most fitting epitaph, remembering the practical energy with which Alfred addressed his valour and his wisdom to the building of the English nation. A thousand years and more have passed since his death, but there is still much that is lively in our national heritage which could truthfully echo those words: *Aelfred mec heht gewyrcan* — Alfred had me made.

CHAPTER FOURTEEN

CHEDDAR CHEESE AND TEAZLES

A Wedmore farmer of the old school, describing his childhood, said, 'At eight years old we all had a little pail bought for us, and we had to learn to milk. That's what we were taught — fill the milkpail, nothing else matters.' For him, and for generations of Somerset farmers like him, it is the milkpail and not the plough that has ruled their lives. The philosophy of such men could not be expressed with a finer simplicity than the words he used to sum up his thoughts – 'We just like the cows.'

In recent years there has been a tendency to break some of the peaty land which has been improved by new drainage works and to take a chance on successful cropping. Changes in the level of the water-table are crucial in such circumstances. Conversely there is a danger of the light topsoil's drying out and starting to blow. The more traditional arable areas are on the safely raised land of the 'islands' and in the good ploughland of the alluvial clays along the coastal belt. Some of this land is extremely fertile. For example in 1829 John Rutter noted that some fields in Burnham, Huntspill and Mark had borne crops of wheat continuously for twenty years without any manure, and were still yielding remarkably heavy crops.

But whatever changes may result from the steady improvement of drainage and the introduction of modern machinery it is difficult to believe that central Somerset will easily or rapidly change its traditional character as one of England's premier dairying regions. The area of Pawlett Hams has been described as the richest grazing in the country and some of the moorland pastures fetch high prices. The waterlogging of land from late autumn to early spring and difficulties of access must always have deterred the would-be cultivator, but to the eye of the dairyman the wide moors promised lush grazing when the winter floods withdrew and the deposited silt nourished the new year's herbage. Today the flooding is controlled as never before and the modern dairy farmer rejoices in his ability to turn his beasts on to the levels three weeks earlier in the spring, and to leave them for three weeks longer in the autumn, than was possible thirty years ago.

There are no farm buildings, no milking-parlours, on the moors where the cows graze: the milking bail is the modern method but you may still see men and women, with no more equipment than a stool and a pail, settling to milk their beasts in the open. The one universal innovation is to have some form of transport for bringing the milk back from the moors. The horse-drawn milk float, once a familiar sight, is now a thing of the past and the usual way is by a light van or perhaps a couple of churns in the boot of the farmer's car. But not so long ago the milk was carried home by the milker. Victorian men, and women too, were accustomed to walk as much as three or four miles with their milkpails balanced on their heads. And they were seven-gallon pails — 'none of your four-gallon buckets'. There were recognised places for stopping and resting on the way, and the feat of balancing the weight on one's head was as much second nature here as in the London markets. One Wedmore man took a pride in his ability to shoot a snipe as he walked, without spilling a drop of milk.

The traditional use of the milk was for cheese-making. As early as 1625 the quality of cheeses from the Cheddar district was recognised and they were 'in such esteem at Court that they are bespoken before they are made'. In 1662 Thomas Fuller made a similar complaint about the scarcity of Cheddar cheese: 'they are so few and dear', he wrote, 'hardly to be met with save at some great man's table'. Half a century later Defoe declared Somerset cheese to be the best in England and noted that it sold for 6d to 8d a pound, as against Cheshire cheese at 2d to 2½d. In 1797 John Billingsley, surveying the general agricultural scene, wrote:

> The cows of this district are intended chiefly for the purposes of cheese-making. The cheese is much admired, particularly that made in the parishes of Meare and Cheddar. It is for the most part purchased by jobbers, and sent through the medium of Weyhill, Giles's Hill, Reading and other fairs to the London markets, where it is sold under the name of double Gloucester.

At Weyhill Fair — immortalised by Thomas Hardy as 'Weydon Priors', where the Mayor of Casterbridge sold his wife — the Somerset cheeses were much sought after, and in the great exchange of commodities that took place at the Fair in its heyday the West Country merchants sometimes traded their cheese for the hops of Kent and Hampshire. What seems strange to modern eyes is Billingsley's assertion that the Somerset cheeses were sold 'under the name of double Gloucester'. The true double Gloucester, from the Vale of Berkeley particularly, is a moister and faster-ripening cheese, although it has close affinities with Cheddar; both are hard pressed cheeses made from full-cream milk (unlike the single Gloucester which may include skimmed milk). But before the nineteenth century the naming of cheeses gave little guide to the nature of the cheese and was usually no more than an index of the district where it was made. The hard pressed cheeses of Somerset, Gloucester and north Wiltshire showed plenty of individual variation in their quality but were generically the same kind of cheese. Somerset cheeses bought by the big wholesale buyers at Reading or Weyhill could quite reasonably go on to the London market as 'double Gloucester'.

For an idea of what the big cheese fairs were like in the 1830s we have Mary Russell Mitford's account of Reading in *Belford Regis*, which was

> one of the principal marts for the celebrated cheese of the great dairy counties. Factors from the West and dealers from London arrived days before the actual fair-day; and wagon after wagon, laden with the round, hard, heavy merchandise, rumbled slowly into the Forbury where the great space before the schoolhouse, the whole of the boys' playground, was fairly covered with stacks of Cheddar and North Wilts. Fancy the singular effect of piles of cheeses several feet high, extending over a whole large cricket ground, and divided only by narrow paths littered with straw, amongst which wandered the busy chapmen, offering a taste of their wares to their cautious customers the country shopkeepers (who poured in from every village within twenty miles), and the thrifty housewives of the town.

The stabilisation of a recognisable standard for Cheddar cheese was the achievement of a Somerset man, Joseph Harding, who was born in 1805. In a period when new scientific and technological thinking was being applied to agriculture and food production Harding emerged as a great teacher of improved methods of cheese-making. Until his death in 1876 he travelled extensively in Britain, lecturing to dairy farmers and expounding his ideas. One of his sons, Henry Harding, introduced the art of Cheddar cheese-making to Australia and thus began the international acceptance of this product of the Somerset dairies.

In its earliest form Cheddar cheese would have come from the milk of ewes or goats. These were the milking animals of Saxon and Norman England, when cows were kept primarily to supply the oxen that pulled plough and wagon. Before the enclosures and reclamations of the thirteenth century the levels would have been great open expanses of common land where animals roamed at will as they grazed. Once a year a 'drift' would have been organised to round them up and penalise the owners of any beasts found grazing illegally. In addition to the four legged herds and flocks there was another abundant grazer — geese. These were kept primarily for their down and feathers, for bedding, and they were an important element in the primitive economy, particularly for the poorer commoners. Moreover they were well adapted to pick a living on the poor and overgrazed pastures. As the poet John Philips notes, even the worst land can be put to good use:

> Thus naught is useless made; nor is there land,
> But what, or of it self, or else compell'd,
> Affords Advantage. On the barren Heath
> The Shepherd tends his Flock, that daily crop
> Their verdant Dinner from the mossie Turf,
> Sufficient; after them the Cackling Goose,
> Close-grazer, finds wherewith to ease her Want.

As the grasslands were improved the cows came into their own as the more profitable beasts, and the growth of urban communities meant an expanding market for milk and cheese. To his praise of Cheddar cheese Defoe added an interesting account of the system used by the cheese-makers of his day. On Cheddar Moor — which lies between Wedmore and Mendip — the day's milk was pooled and cheese was made communally from it: each contributor was entitled to the price received for the cheese when his individual quota of milk amounted to the quantity needed to make one.

The most famous of all collectively-made cheeses was the one produced in 1839, when the farmers of the district combined to make a quite stupendous cheese as a wedding present for Queen Victoria. Into it went a day's milking from 737 cows. The result was a cheese measuring 9ft in circumference and weighing half a ton. Made at West Pennard — a couple of miles east of Glastonbury, in a good cheese-making country — the mammoth cheese was exhibited in London at the Egyptian Hall while it was maturing. It must have excited a great deal of admiration, and doubtless it would have gone down in history as the Cheese of all cheeses, but for one fatal defect: when the moment at last came for it to be tasted, it proved to be so frightful, so execrable a cheese that it had to be disposed of in a most ungracious manner. What had begun as food for a queen ended as food for pigs.

The traditional Cheddar cheese was coloured on the outside with reddle, or redding as it is sometimes called. The travelling reddle-man used to be a familiar figure in the countryside, for his red powder was also used for marking sheep; there is a celebrated description of one of his kind in Thomas Hardy's *The Return of the Native*. The reddle for the Somerset cheeses came from the Mendip Hills, and it is still quarried near Winford. Nowadays its main use is in the manufacture of paint.

Wells was the chief market for Cheddar cheese. The other kind of cheese made by the moorland farmers, Caerphilly cheese, went to Highbridge, and before the 1939 war a great deal of it was sent across the Bristol Channel to the colliery districts of South Wales, where it was much in demand among the Welsh miners. Wartime rationing put an end to the Caerphilly cheese, and the cheese-makers of Somerset were obliged to concentrate on Cheddar. Cheddar is, of course, a keeping cheese, whereas the Caerphilly is perishable.

The decline of cheese-making as a farmhouse industry is easily understood. It was good policy where there was difficulty in getting liquid milk away to a satisfactory market, and where there was available labour for the work of the cheese house. Improved transport has eliminated the risk of milk souring while it waits for collection; and labour is, of course, more costly and more reluctant to come to grips with a seven day week task like cheese-making. Even more decisive perhaps is the changing status of the farmer's wife. Those epic matrons of the past whose entire conscious life was apparently devoted to the arts and crafts of the farmhouse took cheese-making in their stride, along with the little matters of curing hams, drying herbs, rearing poultry and children, brewing, preserving and generally coping with all household affairs. You may regard them as senseless drudges or as superwomen, but in any case they are extinct as a race — even though there be a survivor here and there.

And with their passing the farmhouse cheese nearly went too. Nearly, but not quite. Today there are about three dozen farms in central Somerset where the tradition of cheese-making persists in a modern form. In volume it may be insignificant in comparison with the mass-production of a world-wide Cheddar that comes indifferently from the factories of Canada, New Zealand or Europe, but it is made to exacting standards of quality and it can fairly claim to be 'the real thing' in an age of imitations. The modern Cheddar is smaller than the great cheeses of the past, which were 3ft high, weighed up to 2cwt and took four or five years to mature. The last of these giants was made at Castle Cary in 1914.

The contemporary cheese house is like a miniature laboratory, with its scientific layout, its stainless steel vat, its white-coated young lady perhaps with her pipette and her farm institute diploma. And the prize cards proudly displayed on the wall are sufficient testimony that the traditional skill and care of the cheese-maker have been unharmed by this transformation. Is it still worth while? One farmer answered in this way — 'Cheese-making is like a lot of other things: it doesn't pay unless you're good at it.' The test comes with the verdict of the grader. It is his examination of the cheeses that settles their worth.

The tendency today is to stay small, without hired labour, or to develop a larger unit than in the past so that labour costs and capital investment are spread over a bigger output. Another development in recent years is the revival of Caerphilly cheese as a less demanding product in terms of labour — 'a four hour cheese', to quote one cheese-maker, 'where Cheddar is an eight hour cheese. And', he added, 'I like to finish in the cheese house by midday.' There is the further attraction of a quicker turnover. A Cheddar cheese takes four to six months from making to paying, a Caerphilly only one month. And nowadays there is small chance of the price of Caerphilly falling to its ruinous pre-1940 price of 3d a pound.

The cheese houses have a distinctive atmosphere that is pleasing in its sweetness and serenity — an atmosphere compounded of the great vat of warming milk, the white rubbery curd, and the drum-like cheeses sleeping and ripening on their shelves. The cheese-maker will tell you that no day's make is ever quite like the next. If the cows have moved to another pasture, the difference in the milk will be recognised as soon as it comes into the cheese house. For a show-cheese the cows will be put on to the choicest grazing, specially reserved for important occasions. I recall one farmer who retired from cheese-making after a wartime order to plough up his most cherished grassland. He had won championships with his cheese off that grass, and he believed that without it he could never again produce anything worthy of his reputation; so he gave up. Right or wrong, that is the mood of the artist.

Equally famous in days gone by were the fat oxen of the moors. Defoe described them as being as large and good as any in England, and Billingsley asserted that 'in the London market, to which fat oxen are brought from all parts of the kingdom, the Somersetshire [next to the Galloway Scot fatted in Norfolk and Suffolk] appear to bear the bell, both in respect to fineness of grain and internal fatness'. The oxen were red, of the Devon strain. Used in teams of six for ploughing, they were reputed to be the best labouring animals in the kingdom. For the production of veal, the custom was to keep calves in a dark place and feed them on milk laced with small doses of metheglin, which is a sort of mead.

Stock-breeding was, in fact, a large part of moorland farming. In the eighteenth century colts were bred in large numbers and sold to the Midlands and the North. Defoe mentions that the horse-copers of Staffordshire and Leicestershire were accustomed to buy the Somerset colts and sell them to London for coach-horses and cart-horses. He adds that the breed was very large — unlike the primitive pony of the moors, which was not unlike the modern Exmoor type of pony.

A remarkable byproduct of this widespread grazing of the moors by cattle and horses was the cucumber industry of Somerton. The children of Somerton were sent with donkeys to King's Sedgemoor to collect dung — particularly horsedung. This they loaded into donkey carts or on to the backs of their donkeys and took it back to the market gardens of Somerton; and in due course cartloads of cucumbers, grown on hillocks of dung, were sent away from the district. The practice must to some extent have impoverished the grazing of Sedgemoor: I wonder if it could be construed as poaching. Or was it perhaps stealing by finding?

The various Enclosure Acts towards the end of the eighteenth century and into the early years of the nineteenth gradually extinguished the commoner's right to let his animals range freely under the general supervision of a steward or overseer called a 'reeve'. Collinson, in his *History of Somerset*, refers to a reeve in 1792 who was appointed to 'drive the moors' of West Sedgemoor, Stanmoor, Curry Moor and Hay Moor. He must have been one of the last of his kind. The enclosure of Hay Moor and Curry Moor began in 1797; West Sedgemoor followed in 1816. Altogether about 20,000 acres between Mendip and the Quantocks were enclosed in the last quarter of the eighteenth century and the value of the land was reputed to have trebled as a result.

Collinson, writing his county history at the time of the enclosures, mentioned hemp, flax, teazles and woad as being cultivated in substantial quantities. Jeboult, writing about eighty years later, mentioned the first three but omitted woad; presumably its cultivation died out in the earlier half of the nineteenth century. As a crop it had its drawbacks if Fuller is to be believed, for he stated that woad 'doth greatly impair the ground it groweth on . . . it being long before it will recover good grass therein'. As a dye its fortunes were probably bound up with the Cotswold cloth industry — which was certainly the case with teazles. Woad, which contains the glucoside Indican, from which indigo is made, is usually understood to colour blue; but it can also dye green or black. Pliny the Elder refers to a plant 'like plantain, called Glastum in Gaul, with which the wives and daughters of the Britons paint their bodies in certain ceremonies, which they attend coloured like Ethiopians'. It has been held — though not very convincingly — that this word 'glastum' may have given its name to Glastonbury; however that may be, Glastonbury was a centre of the woad trade.

The disappearance of woad is complete but hemp and flax survived until comparatively recent times as crops in the Fosse Way country south of Langport. This hillier area between Ilchester and Ilminster provided flax for the famous sailcloth that was made in the Coker villages. Before the days of steam Coker sailcloth was an important item for the Royal Navy and farmers hereabouts had their own flax-working shops. The rise of pleasure sailing provided a new market but in the 1920s flax was replaced by Egyptian cotton, which in turn has given way to man-made fibres. Similarly the cottage industry of the eighteenth century became a factory industry in Crewkerne in the nineteenth century: in 1828 there were twenty-seven firms manufacturing sailcloth. Today flax is no longer a local crop. The last flax-mill, a wartime revival at Lopen, closed down in 1947–8 and polyester fibres are certainly not a Somerset speciality, but Crewkerne retains its importance in the new market of synthetic sails for yachtsmen. And it still weaves flax for the webbings required for such things as parachute harness.

Teazles are a curious exception to the usual story of the long persistence in a locality of some traditional crop or craft. It is in the valley of the Isle, and mainly in the village of Fivehead, that you will see the mauve or purple flowering heads of this unusual crop; and although you are likely to be told that they have been grown there from time immemorial or at least since the Romans, this is not so. The teazle is a comparative newcomer in that part of the county. Roughly a century and a half ago two surveys of Somerset were made by men who must be regarded as on the whole authoritative. One was John Collinson, whose interests were mainly antiquarian but did nevertheless embrace a great deal of miscellaneous information. The other was John Billingsley, whose interests were strictly agricultural. Collinson's reputation is perhaps higher than it deserves to be, for he is a fairly uncritical retailer of historical fables, but there is no reason to doubt his reporting of what lay before his eyes. And he endears himself by at least one classic example of what might be called clergyman's mock-Augustan — when he writes that Long Ashton is 'so denominated from its prolixity'. Billingsley, by contrast, sounds like a county secretary of the NFU. He marshals facts and quotes prices in good sound utility English.

On this question of teazles, Collinson says that they were grown in his day on the northern slope of Mendip, from Wrington to Harptree — that is to say, in the valley of the Congresbury Yeo. If there were any teazles in the valley of the Isle, Collinson failed to notice them. Perhaps it might be an omission, if his were the only testimony; but Billingsley's account is precisely the same. In even more specific terms Billingsley locates the teazle industry in the parishes of Wrington, Blagdon, Ubley, Compton Martin and Harptree. Here, he says, they are much cultivated, for sale to manufacturers in Somerset and Wiltshire and also — 'by water conveyance from Bristol' — to Yorkshire.

There seems, then, to be no doubt that teazle-growing flourished in the valley of the Congresbury Yeo until at any rate about 1800, and was not developed in the Isle valley until after that date. It is a curious story, this wholesale transfer of a specialised crop from one district to another: perhaps one or two of the leading growers were obliged to move and took their knowledge with them, to be emulated by the new neighbours and forgotten by the old ones. In general, the method of cultivation as Billingsley describes it is very similar to what is practised today. The teazles were sown in April — preferably on a strong rich clay — and were subsequently weeded three or four times with long narrow spades. Hoeing was tried, without success, but men accustomed to the spade were 'so dexterous they will even thin carrots with it'. Today a rotavator is used. In the 1930s and '40s a horse-hoe was the usual method but the older practice was remembered, and a cultivator in the early fifties still owned and used one of the narrow spades described by Billingsley.

November was the month for thinning. The following summer the teazle plants were again weeded and 'speddled' — that is to say, earthed up. When the heads were cut and dried they were divided into three grades by size, known as kings, middlings and scrubs. The three grades were cut at fortnightly intervals. Nowadays there are only two cuttings — first the kings, and then the middlings or 'twerts'.

The teazle is valued for the natural brushing power of its bristles. In its wild state it is common and familiar enough, but for those who do not know what it looks like it may perhaps be described as a tall and extremely plump sort of thistle. Botanically it is not anything to do with the thistles, of course, but as a rough and ready comparison there is something of a thistly nature in the teazle's prickly purple head. An old name for the plant was Fuller's Thistle. In the days when men looked for suitable tools in the natural objects that surrounded them, the teazle was selected for scouring newly-woven cloth; and as the West Country cloth industry grew, so the teazle became an object of deliberate cultivation.

The growing plants are interesting to see — ingenious plants, I would call them, for they have an engaging method of storing water and at the same time of catching insects on which they feed. Look at a teazle and you will see how its pairs of stalkless leaves form a cup embracing the plant's stem. Each cup holds rainwater, which is a most useful parlour trick for any plant to be able to perform, and by a notable economy of invention these tiny reservoirs act as traps for the insects that try to creep up the stem. One false step, and into the water they go to drown. And having drowned they obligingly dissolve into a digestible sort of food that the teazle's stem can absorb. Incidentally the water stored in the leaf-cups was recommended by Culpeper as a collyrium to cool inflammation of the eyes and as a cosmetic to render the face fair.

The harvest of teazle heads is cut with a quite extraordinarily small knife, so small that the gloved hand of the harvester completely hides it and he appears to be picking the teazles. The knife is curved and will lie in the crook of a man's first finger. The gloves, incidentally, will be black, and look as if they have been coated with tar for some reason. It is not tar, however, but a black sticky sap that exudes from the plants when they are cut. The cutting is done by an upward slice, so as not to 'bow' the stem, and the teazles are transferred to the harvester's free hand until they accumulate to a 'handful'. Each handful is tied with another teazle, which is not counted in the total — 'we give 'em that one' — and the handfuls are slipped on a pole to dry. And when they have been 'lugged' in that way on the poles, the poles are leant on a 'gallus' until the teazles are ready to go away. The teazles dry naturally in the sun; their enemy is too much wet at the wrong time. As one grower put it, 'A wet July, and, oh dear, you'll have some soldiers.'

In olden days the teazles were packed in a very attractive way before they were sent from the farm. Staffing the teazles, as it was called, was a wintertime job and it was done in this way: a hazel stick of about a yard's length was split, like a clothespeg, and teazles in fans of about twenty-five were slid on to it and then fastened with a withy, so that none of the stems showed. The finished staff appeared to be simply a tight fan of teazle heads. I have seen them mounted in this way, and very neat they looked; but the practice of 'staffing' them has quite gone out of use. Nowadays they are tumbled loose into a large cloth in lots of 20,000, known as a pack. Billingsley gives the price of teazles in 1797 as 40s for a pack of either 20,000 middlings or 9,000 kings, and he estimates the average yield as 7 to 10 packs an acre, with an occasional bumper harvest of 15 or 16 packs. On the face of it, it looks a profitable crop; but it takes two years to yield, it needs a lot of labour and there can be heavy losses from dampness or plant disease. 'A very temperamental crop,' was the verdict of one grower, speaking from long experience, 'it can easily lose money for you.'

For a variety of reasons the acreage devoted to teazles is declining. In the first half of the present century the highest grades of English cloth — the hunting pinks and naval blues and green billiard cloths — were scoured with teazle heads clamped in rows in a metal frame which gripped the cloth as it passed under the teazle spines. Fitted into one of these Yorkshire-type teazle raising gigs the naturally grown spines had a blending of 'firmness' and 'give' that was very difficult to match artificially. The Italians developed a plastic teazle, but it failed to reproduce the essential qualities of the natural head. Brass wire has been a more successful substitute, but it is factors of other kinds that have really damaged the teazle trade. New man-made fabrics compete with wool and high standards of finish tend to be the casualties of mass-marketing.

The more recent call for teazles is in a type of machine which gives a different finish from that of the Yorkshire gig. This uses only the largest teazles, which are drilled through the centre and fitted to a rod which is inserted through them — usually in groups of three teazles. The rods are then fitted to a revolving drum which brushes up blankets, knitted fabrics and mohair. From the grower's point of view a demand for king-size teazles only is tantamount to a rejection of much of his crop; and, as the prices of grain and livestock farming have improved, the teazle crop has become correspondingly less attractive. In concentrating on the production of 'kings' exclusively, the Somerset grower meets severe competition from growers in the south of France who have the natural advantage of ample sunshine and sometimes the artificial one of irrigation. One must perhaps concede that Avignon is more favoured than Fivehead for this particular crop but it will be a sad day if the teazle disappears entirely from the Isle valley.

CHAPTER FIFTEEN

WILLOW AND PEAT

On Sedgemoor I collected a poem which never appears in any normal anthology, so I offer it herewith to any enterprising editor who likes to make use of it:

> I can rand
> At your command,
> Put on a decent border,
> Upset tight,
> Wale alright,
> And keep my stakes in order.

If you find it a little slow to give up its meaning — and it has a meaning — I should explain that it is a poem of basket-making or withy-working. To 'rand' is to interlace the single withy; to 'wale' is to make the stronger border of each section, which is called a wheel and usually consists of several withies twined together and closely interwoven. 'Upsetting' means turning the bottom of a basket — the 'upset' is the bottom wale.

The withy country of Sedgemoor lies mainly to the west of the Parret below Langport — in the neighbourhood of Athelney and Lyng and Stoke St Gregory. Occupying about 500 acres, these withy-beds of Sedgemoor provide about 80 per cent of the entire English crop. The tall beds of growing withies and the cut bundles drying and weathering by the roadside give to this area a unique character.

The modern industry is a product of the Enclosure Acts, for the laying down of cultivated withy-beds dates from the early years of the nineteenth century. Billingsley's survey says that:

> The low lands are badly wooded, and planting in general shamefully neglected, particularly a very profitable part of it, viz the elm and the willow, both of which thrive in this soil, and the latter is much wanted for the purposes both of the thatcher and the fisherman.

Collinson's description of the Athelney district reinforces this impression.

> The situation is low, damp and unhealthy. These moors contain neither peat, heath
> nor sedge, like those on the north side of Poldon-hill; nor are they divided by ditches,
> planted on each side with willows, like those about Glastonbury; but are rich, flat,
> open commons, skirted with high lands, and producing most excellent pasture. The
> muddy slime of the Parret affords fine manure.

It is significant that Billingsley says that willows were wanted by the thatcher
and the fisherman, but does not mention the basket-maker. The boom in
basket-making came later, with the Victorian taste for wicker furniture, wicker
bird cages, wicker this and wicker that; but the craft of basket-making is an
old-established one in the Sedgemoor country. So early as 1225 there was a
basket-maker in Langport: his identity happens to have been recorded because
he had the misfortune to be murdered. What is now interesting about him is
that basket-making was his trade, his fulltime employment: a simple skill in
twining willows for some single object, for containers or fishing-pots, has been
diffused among farming and fishing communities since time immemorial.

Until the seventeenth century individual craftsmen in Europe relied mainly
on 'uncultivated' willows, growing in the wild, natural state. The production
of withies as a crop to be sold is a relatively modern idea, though some osier
beds have a longer history than might be expected. In the mid-seventeenth
century John Aubrey noted 'great plenty of osiers about Bemarton near
Salisbury, where the osier beds do yield four pounds per acre'. But it was in
Germany, France and the Low Countries that systematic commercial growing
and cropping really developed first. Britain imported from Holland until the
Napoleonic blockade gave a stimulus to home production. The Royal Society
of Arts offered a prize to encourage British growers, and the enclosure of
suitable land in Curry Moor and West Sedgemoor came at a timely moment.

What was probably the pioneer large-scale planting in Britain was located in
about 1825 in West Sedgemoor, where the ability of the withy to survive winter
flooding after being planted in the autumn made it a particularly attractive
proposition. Production reached its peak in 1900, since when a steady decline
has been checked only when wartime conditions have put a premium on home
production to offset the lack of imported withies. The boom associated with
World War II was prolonged into the mid-fifties by a continuing shortage of
European crops; but after 1957 the total acreage, which for a generation had
been reasonably steady at about 1,500 acres, declined sharply to 500 acres in
1970.

Some withy-beds have remained undisturbed for forty years but the usual
life is about twenty years, by which time the land would be foul with weeds.
The bed would be at its most productive from its seventh year to its fifteenth.
Grubbing out an old withy-bed with a mattock was a laborious task. Rotavators
now do the job so easily that in some cases withies are being cropped once only
and then grubbed out as part of an arable rotation in which they are treated as a
short-term planting. There could be no greater contrast with one of the old

practices, which was to plant apple trees among the withies, so that — when the time came to grub out the withy stools — the land was occupied with a well-established cider orchard. And a very handsome sight it was to see the dense green jungle of willow wands tapering up to a height of 6 or 8ft, with the foamy white apple blossom stirring above.

The coming of autumn used to signal the withy auctions, which were important events in the Sedgemoor calendar. They began to decline in the 1960s and they are now a thing of the past. Their disappearance is bound up with the disappearance of an unusual class of man — the 'landless master', who could acquire crops without owning or renting land. With withies, as with teazles and peat, the landowner could make a kind of partnership with a craftsman who, as the saying went, 'bought for work'. In the case of teazles a farmer might agree to provide the land and do the ploughing, in partnership with a grower who provided the seed and the labour. A peat-cutter would rent the right to extract peat for a term of years from a landowner. And in the case of withies a farmer might plant a withy-bed and auction the crop each year to anyone wishing to cut the withies, boil them and strip them, and in turn sell them to a merchant or a basket-maker. These landless masters — like the bodgers in the Chilterns and the hurdle-makers in Cranborne Chase — must have added a distinctive element of social and economic independence to their communities. Today that kind of independence is obsolescent, like seasonal work and casual labour generally. Coinciding with a declining demand for withies it has tended to concentrate the growing and processing work as a unified operation. The grower nowadays has planned the cutting and disposal of his crop before he raises it.

Anyone who remembers the withy auctions must regret the loss of them as a social occasion. The traditional custom was for everyone to be given a free pint of cider or beer on entering the saleroom, which was probably in a village inn. This jovial benevolence extended yet further to individual buyers, who received a token entitling them to another drink after each successful bid. Such a custom was defended tenaciously by the participants but it was declining in the 1950s and increasingly customers were expected to buy their own refreshment. Even so the convivial atmosphere was very much a feature of a withy-sale.

What was auctioned was the right to go to the appropriate withy-bed and cut withies 'after the fall of the leaf'. That pleasant phrase was part of the conditions of sale. The right was held for one winter only. The following year the buyer would have to bid for the same plot again — if he wanted it a second time. A part only of the price was paid at the time of the auction — anything from a tenth to a quarter. The balance was not due until the end of the season, so there was an opportunity for the man with limited capital to cash his crop before he had to pay for it.

The style of bidding showed that variety of technique in which countrymen excel. It ranged from the silent wink and the tap of a foot on the floor to a stentorian 'Goo on then' from somewhere at the back. As the price rose the auctioneer, becoming increasingly morose, reminded the company that their bids fell far short of what they offered for the same lots last year. And the company, with a touching delicacy of feeling, refrained from contradicting him.

After they are cut, the withies have to be boiled and stripped. Stripping peels off the outer skin and is done with a pair of prongs, known as 'breaks'. The humbler method is to pull the withy through a pair of fixed prongs, and you may still see this type of stripping being performed in cottage gardens — often by women and children, who attend to this while father gets on with the heavier tasks of cutting and boiling. A more efficient type of stripper is a pair of mechanically driven rollers — like a mangle — with rows of prongs. With a machine of this kind a number of withies can be fed through the rollers and stripped at the same time.

The two processes of boiling and stripping give the withy its variations of colour. The typical buff withy is subjected to both processes; the white is stripped but not boiled; and the chocolate-coloured withy is not stripped, but is boiled in water used for previous boilings. By these simple alternatives the withy is given that variety of colour which makes it so much more attractive.

Like many other things, withy had its unexpected hour of wartime glory. In the 1940s it proved to be the answer to the problem of finding a material sufficiently rigid and yet resilient enough to provide containers to be dropped by parachute. Where wooden cases were apt to break up, panniers of withy could take the stress of impact. This was a more belligerently military contribution than withy had made in its more traditional form — as frames for bearskins. The productiveness of Sedgemoor's withy-beds accordingly became a matter of some national concern — the more so as cheap imported withies from the Argentine were not so easy to come by as in peacetime.

After World War II the withy industry retained its buoyancy, partly because of the slowness of the reappearance of competitive imports and partly because of the organising energy of the then MP for Taunton, Victor Collins (later Lord Stonham). Its subsequent decline may be traced to a variety of factors. A wider choice of more sophisticated and remunerative crafts has become available to blind workers, who were traditionarlly large users of withies: in 1960 blind and disabled workers used 35 per cent of the British willow crop. Cheap imports of withies and the use of synthetic materials in basket-making have replaced a proportion of home-grown withies. Modern marketing techniques call for large quantities of a few standardised types, whereas British basket-makers tend to work as small, individualised producers.

All in all, the lost acreage is unlikely to be replanted but the present scale of growing seems to have settled to a new stability where it again meets a firm demand. Mechanical cutting is far from perfect yet but it takes some of the cheerless, hard labour out of the winter's work. And in an increasingly 'plasticated' world the withy's appeal is strengthened by the feel of life in it and the homeliness of its country style — qualities which appeal to the visiting tourist, for whom the crop itself also happily enriches the scene. The deep and secret withy-beds, favoured as a hiding-place by snipe, add a distinctive bass note of green to the lighter greens of the open moor. Encircled by rhines, dense and shadowy, they are natural sanctuaries. And the buff wands, drying after being boiled, and turning from honey colour to a warm golden brown in the changing light as they loll against a hedge, add a gay and almost frivolous vivacity to the countryside of Sedgemoor.

The frontier-like character of the Polden Hills is most marked in this matter of special crops. Just as withies are a distinctive feature of Sedgemoor, so does the country on the other side of the Poldens — the Vale of Avalon — have its own special but quite different crop; that is, if peat can be called a crop. William Stradling, the somewhat eccentric antiquary who built Chilton Priory on the Poldens in the early nineteenth century, looked across to the Isle of Wedmore over what he described as 'the immense turbary'. Billingsley, referring to the peat moors, wrote:

> This country has been heretofore much neglected, being destitute of gentlemen's houses, probably on account of the stagnant waters and unwholesome air. On these bogs scarcely any pasturage at present grows. They are a composition of porous substances, floating on water and imbibing it like a sponge. They are observed to rise with much wet, and sink in dry weather.

Still earlier, Camden summed the matter up tersely in good Elizabethan phrases. 'So wet and weely,' he wrote, 'so miry and moorish it is.'

In spite of the changes that time brings, those descriptions are still pretty accurate. The turbary is still fairly immense. The landscape lacks all trace of those gentlemen's houses which elsewhere are numerous in the county. And if you care to walk across any of the heaths that separate the Polden villages from Meare and Westhay, you will agree with Camden that the way is distinctly miry and could be fittingly described as moorish. But do not for that reason postpone your walk, for this wild country has a fascinating and quite magical spell of its own. It is a very primitive landscape with few inhabitants. You may find a cottage, perhaps a small farmstead, where the ground swells up slightly; and on the rising ground there will be a few acres of good grass. And then as you skirt down to the low levels you cross one of the margins of civilisation and pass over to the waste land, to the bog which 'floats on water and imbibes it like a sponge'. Here there is only one crop and one industry. The stacks of black peat assert themselves whichever way you turn, like a repeated monosyllable; black, clumsy-looking heaps, glistening with a subdued rough vitality.

Peat is something of a paradox, for it is termed a mineral and a permit is therefore needed to cut it; but its vegetable nature is immediately obvious. Crumble a piece in your hand and you will see the mummified pieces of stem and leaf. The Oxford Dictionary defines peat as 'vegetable matter decomposed by water and partly carbonised by chemical change'. What happens in the formation of peat is that normal decomposition into humus and mineral salts is arrested by the excessively wet and acid conditions, which are harmful to bacteriological action. Different types of peat reveal changes in climatic conditions when the peat was being formed. For example, peat containing heather and cotton-grass indicates an earlier dry condition which later deteriorated. Sphagnum peat would be formed in really wet periods, when the moss grew so fast that it is still sometimes found to be undecayed. Sedge peat comes from land that was flooded intermittently, from lagoons and shallow lakes that dried out and filled again. In the hands of a skilled investigator like Harry Godwin, the peat can disclose a great deal of information about prehistoric changes in climate and vegetation.

The oldest peat comes from reeds and sedges, growing five or six thousand years ago in the swamps which formed when the sea finally withdrew after filling the valleys with clay. On top of this lowest layer of peat there is a woody peat, which shows that birch, alder and willow were able to establish themselves in the bogs, perhaps as the result of a period of lower rainfall and higher temperatures. This was followed in the Neolithic period by sphagnum moss, cotton-grass, ling and deer-grass in swamp conditions that suggest increased flooding and must have made necessary the first wooden trackways. The upper layers of the peat show alternating periods of moister and drier conditions, with sphagnum predominating in the wetter climate, whereas drier conditions favoured ling, cotton-grass and tree-scrub, and produced the best burning peat.

In dry periods the surface of the heaths would have been firm enough for men and animals to walk on. The people of the Bronze Age would have had a warmer and drier period until the last millennium BC, when the climate again deteriorated and fresh-water flooding submerged the heather-covered raised bogs and turned them into wet sedge fens. It was in these circumstances that the Bronze Age men, like their Neolithic predecessors, laid down trackways to maintain what they must have regarded as important routes across the heathland where hitherto they had walked without difficulty. Some of their trackways appear to be designed for wheeled vehicles. During the cool, wet years of the Iron Age the sphagnum continued to grow, until renewed flooding around AD 50 brought back areas of sedge-fen — and incidentally saw the abandonment of the lake villages. The formation of peat continued until late Roman times.

The finding of archaeological objects in the peat throws an important light on the sequence of peat-levels and the dating of the climatic changes associated with them. As layer after layer of peat was formed, the 'turf' enclosed here and there some article that had been dropped or discarded. In addition to the sections of trackway there were weapons, pottery and coins — some now in museums, others treasured privately by their finders. In one cottage where I was visiting years ago, my host — a peat cutter — went into his toolshed and brought out for my inspection a Bronze Age whetstone which he had uncovered in a peat-working. The deepest recovery is a Neolithic pot of about 2000 BC excavated in Meare Heath. It was lying in a type of peat which showed that the climate was then passing to wetter but still warm conditions, with heather flourishing in the vicinity. The Bronze Age is represented by

Huish Episcopi Church

The Hood monument at Butleigh.

The Fish House at Meare, built to supply Glastonbury Abbey with fish from Meare Pool

Muchelney Abbey

implements and weapons, particularly spear-heads. At a still higher level Meare Heath disgorged a La Tene scabbard of the Iron Age; and near the surface of Shapwick Heath were coins and other objects deposited before the end of the Roman occupation.

Considered in its traditional character, as a fuel for burning in the domestic hearth, the Somerset peat is of two main kinds. The two top levels, which are brown, are good for kindling but 'bury themselves in ash'. The best fuel comes from the upper of the three layers of black peat which separate the brown peat from the two lowest levels, the wood peat and the original sedge peat. Disregarding the last two, which lie too low to be excavated without pumping away floodwater, the peat was therefore divided for practical purposes into brown peat and black; and the black peat was considered to burn as well as the coal from the Somerset coalfields at Radstock and Midsomer Norton.

But who now burns peat? In this age of swift and radical change no industry has changed more swiftly and radically than the peat industry. From being obsolescent in its traditional usage peat has moved into a boom as a horticultural requirement. Its 1954 output of 16,000 tons was up to 63,000 in 1966 and could reach 100,000 tons a year in the 'eighties. If demand continues to develop at the present rate the whole of the immense turbary could be extracted and worked out in the next fifty years, giving the industry a history from first to last of only a century and a half.

The commercial working of peat began about 1870 when it was sold for fuel or as a litter for livestock. The idea of using granulated peat in horticulture as a compost-ingredient or mulch was introduced in a small way about 1900. It was one of several innovations for which credit is due to the Alexander family, who came to the moor in 1869 and subsequently applied scientific research and modern machinery to a craft that had persisted without change from time immemorial. The original founder of the Alexander fortunes was long remembered with awe for his habit of firing a shotgun over the heads of his workmen if he judged them to be slacking — a patriarchal custom not carried on by his descendants.

The importance of peat historically as a solid fuel has tended to be overshadowed by coal, so it is worth recalling that in his portrait of a shepherd in Victorian Wiltshire W. H. Hudson noted that the only user of coal in the village was the blacksmith, to whom it was transported by a team of donkeys. The shepherd was permitted to use his master's wagon and horses to go from Cranborne Chase to the New Forest to fetch a year's supply of peat. In the rural economy of south-west England before industrial development — and particularly before the railways — the peat of the New Forest, the Somerset Levels and Dartmoor must have been a considerable asset. Its importance can easily be imagined by anyone who recalls coal-rationing and the general fuel shortage in the 1940s and who remembers how readily peat from Somerset could then be sold in the big urban areas of Bristol and Bath. The gipsies and others who hawked their cartloads through the city streets could be sure of selling every turf they could get.

As it burns peat gives off a pleasant odour. Its traditional uses included the smoking of hams and the burning out of spirit barrels. Those accustomed to it praised it for its healthy smoke, claiming that its freedom from sulphur made it kind to asthmatics. Its great disadvantage is the dustiness of its powdery ash, which seems to penetrate everywhere if there is the slightest movement of air to carry it. However the very fineness of peat when it is pulverised was to be a virtue in its new role. As wartime conditions receded the demand for fuel died away and the needs of horticulture climbed rapidly until they required 90 per cent of the whole output. Granulated, screened and blended in various grades, the peat went increasingly into composts and fertilising compounds. Some, of the finest grade, was used as a grass-dressing on race courses and training-gallops and on golf courses up and down the country. Other modern uses for peat have given it a role in the manufacture of blotting-paper, the malting of whisky, the growing of mushrooms, the purification of gas and the spraying of grass-seed on motorway embankments.

Accompanying these changes there has been a transformation of the outdoor working scene. The heavy hand-labour of many smallholders has been largely replaced by the mechanised cutting and carting of large-scale operators. About three-quarters of the gross output belongs to one company, Fisons, in which the pioneer Alexander interests are embodied. About an eighth of the whole total is accounted for by the second largest operator. The cutting-machines, of German manufacture, do the work of fifteen men. They cut a trench 3ft deep and over 2ft wide; and they slice the peat into manageable pieces which they stack beside the trench to dry. Handwork is still needed to build up the peat into the drying positions which have always been a familiar sight in this landscape — the smaller 'stooks' or 'hiles' which allow for the shrinkage of the blocks as they dry, and the larger 'ruckles' in which they complete their drying. To remove them to the processing-sheds Fisons use thirteen diesel locomotives on fifteen miles of 2ft gauge rail-track.

All this amounts to such a transformation of the peat-moors as I first got to know them forty years ago that it is worth recording some of the contrasting features of the older more haphazard ways before they pass out of living memory. The customary basis for cutting peat was to rent a section of the moor for a 'term'. This was usually a period of twenty years, and rent was paid for the first fifteen years; the last five were given free. Sometimes a piece of turbary was rented when a baby was born, with the idea that the peat would pay for the child's upbringing.

The season of cutting was from March until August — after the winter floods had abated and before autumn conditions put an end to the prospect of hauling peat to the roads. Where peat is still cut by hand the method is unchanged. The peat is cut in cubes with a hay-knife or a kind of spade called a scyve, and it is heavy work. The cubes, known as 'Mumps', will measure about 10in long, 12in thick and 8in deep. In their freshly-cut-waterlogged state they may each weigh as much as a ¼cwt. One cutter claimed that, in his prime, he had cut from 5,000 to 6,000 mumps in a day; but he added 'you want your jacket and waistcoat off for that'.

The peat-cutter marks out a six-mump head before he starts cutting, and he will go down to a depth of three mumps. Each mump is cut into three with a chopper and placed on end for two or three days. It is then ready for 'hiling' which is a sort of preliminary drying.

Hiling used to be regarded as women's work, when husbands and wives worked together and divided the tasks, and it followed a traditional pattern. Fourteen turfs were stood upon the ground in the form of a cross, with each arm of the cross then being made likewise in the form of a cross. It is perhaps inevitable that the influence of Glastonbury should be suspected as the origin of the cruciform hile. Local memory and folk-legend might throw some light on its origin but it was certainly cherished and displayed with pride by the older generation of peat-cutters, if only as a sort of conjuring trick. I recall being given a single quick demonstration of the method and then challenged to take some turfs and hile them correctly — in rather the mood of performing some sleight of hand with a pack of cards.

The hiles stand for about six weeks. The peat has then shrunk by drying sufficiently to be ready for 'ruckling'. The turfs are built up in a series of diminishing rings, one on top of the other, to form a sort of conical 'beehive' 8ft high. Spaces are left between the turfs, so that air can circulate freely and complete the drying of the peat. These 'ruckles', standing in groups, are the familiar signs of the peat-cutter's work. North of the Poldens they are the one man-made symbol that stands out and catches your attention.

An old alternative word for 'ruckle' was 'tunniger'. By now it is probably obsolete but until fairly recently you might hear somebody speak of 'putting up the peat in tunnigers'. It is a verstile word, for in Dorset it used to mean a colander. In Tiverton the large wooden funnel used for filling cider barrels was called a 'tunniger'; and in Bridgwater, where it was pronounced 'tinniger', it meant similarly a small wooden funnel used for filling bottles. Colander, funnel and peat-ruckle — what they have in common perhaps is the idea of a shape formed to allow the passage of air or liquid. Whatever the explanation, each was a 'tunniger' to some folk in the West Country.

In the exploration of possible uses for peat nobody in Somerset seems to have experimented with the distillation of naphtha and petrol from peat as was done on Dartmoor. In the mid-nineteenth century, when Princetown Gaol was unused, the building was equipped to distil naphtha from which candles and mothballs were manufactured. The naphtha was also to provide lighting. More recently, in 1937, there was an abortive plan to extract petrol from Dartmoor peat and sell it in roadside pumps. Peat-petrol would certainly be an interesting local novelty on the M5; but it is not one the tourist is likely to find.

CHAPTER SIXTEEN

CIDER, SHEEP AND SHOES

The traditional 'wine of the country' in Somerset is cider. The cider orchards are a pleasing feature of the landscape, and many a conversation is enlivened with fabulous tales of the noble thirsts of ancient worthies. Men cutting corn with the scythe, which is admittedly a thirst-provoking implement, could be relied on to drink as much as forty pints during a day's harvesting and 'sweat it all out'; or so it has been claimed. The normal day ration for a labourer was five pints; but the 'mowing-bottle' was ten pints, in acknowledgement of the harder and thirstier work. The little wooden casks that were carried in the fields may still be seen occasionally in a farmhouse or a cottage, but they have mostly found their way by now into the antique shops. The custom was to leave them empty at the farmhouse door in the evening and collect them filled at the commencement of the day's work.

Just how potent was the labourer's cider is a matter for conjecture. In his advice to farmers on cider-making John Philips wrote:

> Some, when the Press, by utmost vigour screw'd,
> Has drain'd the pulpous Mass, regale their Swine
> With the dry Refuse; thou, more wise, shalt steep
> Thy Husks in Water, and again employ
> The pondrous Engine.

This second pressing was intended for the farmworkers — 'the Peasants blithe'. When one reflects on what the 'pondrous Engine' would squeeze out of the watered husks it becomes easier to credit some of the more phenomenal feats of consumption.

Cider is certainly one of Somerset's most ancient products. A treatise on it was published in the seventeenth century, its history goes back to the thirteenth century, and there is some reason to think that it was introduced by the Normans. It has outlived two of its local competitors — wine and mead. Wine seems to have been made extensively at one time in the Glastonbury area, and the first vineyards may perhaps have been planted by the Romans. The Saxons certainly had vineyards in Somerset, for they are referred to in the Domesday Book. There were seven acres at North Curry and extensive areas in Glastonbury, Meare and Panborough; indeed, a field at Meare is still called the Vineyard. As late as the reign of Edward III — in the fourteenth century — there were at least eight acres in the Glastonbury area (including Meare and Panborough).

This was doubtless a monastic industry, as was the making of mead. A charter of the Archbishop of Canterbury in 1281 refers to the mead-maker as one of the officers of Glastonbury Abbey: he was to receive an annual pension from various churches belonging to the Abbey — half a mark from St Peter's, Ilchester, 5s from Lympsham, 43s 4d from Shapwick, and so on. Mead survived as a local drink into the present century, but the high cost of a spirit licence — which was required where mead was sold — drove it out of the smaller inns and cider houses; and the competition of cheap imported port supplanted it in the modest rural festivities that it had customarily enlivened. It is a pity because good mead is a benign and decently vivacious drink, made from the simplest ingredients and belonging essentially to that tradition of cottage economy which Cobbett so stoutly defended. To have drunk mead at Athelney is an experience for any Anglo-Saxon to treasure.

Like all home-made products mead can vary enormously. Some can be almost as clear and fine as a whisky, and not excessively sweet in spite of the honey content. Others can be so syrupy and foggy that they grip one's back teeth and refuse to let go. And the same extreme variations can be found in the local farmhouse ciders. Nor were the famous tipplings of bygone years always so enviable as memory likes to suggest. The good old days never look better than when they are seen through a bottle, but the hard truth seems to be that the old men drank some pretty poor stuff while all around them their orchards declined and decayed. One writer of authority estimated in 1896 that between a half and three-quarters of the cider orchards were worn out. He may have been exacting in his standards, but in the same year the Gold Medal award for cider-making at the Bath and West Show was withheld on the grounds that none of the cider submitted was good enough, and a few years later the Long Ashton Research Station was called into being, as the National Fruit and Cider Institute, to tackle the general decline in cider-making. Throughout the present century the scientists of Long Ashton have lead the way — by study, experiment, example, instruction and, not least, by their annual cider-tasting ceremony — in reviving a pride in good cider and a recognition of what it demands.

The modern tendency is inevitably for more and more cider to come from fewer and larger factories, and to safeguard their supplies of apples some of the big commercial cider-makers are developing a contract system which enables them to sponsor new plantings in a way that could revolutionise the Somerset orchards. In the first half of this century the total acreage dropped by at least half, largely because, after the 1930s, there was no incentive to plant new trees when apples were in surplus. The ageing orchards therefore degenerated and few of those that remain are worth salvaging. They are in any case unsuited to modern methods of cropping, which are designed to rely as little as possible on seasonal or casual labour. These modern methods include mechanical tree-shakers and various types of machines to pick up the apples by means of spikes or rotating rubber paddles or vacuum suction, with the use of sprays to make the apples hang on the tree a little longer or fall sooner, as the timetable requires. The number of standard trees per acre has been increased from fifty to eighty, and it is reckoned that fertilisers and sprays can double the crop. A more intensive method is to use bush trees on dwarf stocks, planting as many as 240 per acre, leaving just enough room between the rows for the machinery to go through. Acceptance of these progressive methods is not easy for the traditional Somerset grower who values his grazing between the trees and is not operating on a big enough scale to justify an extensive outlay of capital. Here, as with other crops, some of the smaller men will drop out while others create larger and more specialised units. For commercial cider in bulk the poorer grades of the dessert and culinary orchards are satisfactory. The improved cider orchards are needed for the vintage ciders.

The grower who chooses a planting scheme offered by one of the cider manufacturers, would expect his new orchard to have thirty years of effective life. For the first twenty years he would have a guaranteed minimum price. At the same time his contract might include various fringe benefits in connection with the initial planting, fencing and — during the earliest years — spraying and pruning. And if he has anxieties about such a long-term commitment he can take comfort from the probability that demand will run ahead of supply. Selling well below the price of beer, cider is still a popular drink in its traditional strongholds and it has penetrated the beer-drinking areas in its modern factory-made style. Similarly perry, which is made from pears, has an equally buoyant look as an orchard crop.

While it is true that a small number of large-scale manufacturers of cider will increasingly dominate the whole process from orchard to bottle it is also the case that cider is the one drink still made in substantial quantities by traditional home-made methods. The breed of farmers and rural publicans who like to make their own, in the way their fathers did, is not yet extinct. In the old orchards varieties like Kingston Black and Foxwhelp were prized because they yielded a well-balanced cider without the need for blending with other varieties. The alternative was to put two parts of sharp apples with one of sweet and one of bittersweet. This was the rough and ready formula for getting somewhere near the Long Ashton recommendation of 0.5 per cent acid to 0.2 per cent tannin, which yielded a medium sweet cider.

To assist at a farmhouse cider-making is one of the pleasantest occupations Somerset can offer. The apples are shaken from the trees, and in autumn the stillness is punctuated at intervals with this sudden thunder as the apples come tumbling down. They are then heaped on straw to finish ripening. Cider-making begins with the grinding of the apples in a mill. The ground apple or 'pomace' is wrapped in cloths in the form of 'cheeses', which are placed layer on layer in the cider-press. And then the press closes down and squeezes out the juice.

As the work proceeds the natural bounty of the earth comes home to you in the instinctive joy of harvest, the delight that one's senses find in ripeness and crispness and softness and strong sweet scents. At such a time the smallest things become memorable, like the moonbeam green of pulped Morgans coming down from the mill, the bulging opulence of the clothed 'cheeses', the pungent running juice, the drowsy bees walking away across the floor with the sedateness of drunken aldermen, the humour of someone who has put a stick across a runnel in the floor — like a tiny bridge — to help the bees on their way. And then the shadowed coolness of the huge expectant casks, which in a few days will begin to rumble and gasp and snort as the cider starts fermenting and mounts up to a brown frothy head. The control of fermentation is a tricky business, and to this end the maker chooses his moment to 'rack' the cider by drawing off the bulk of it into another cask and thereby separating it from the sediment or lees at the bottom. It was an old Somerset custom to distil the lees and produce what was called 'still-liquors'. It must have been a pretty raucous concoction, but it used to be valued as a cure-all for stomach troubles and colds.

Another and better-known cider custom was the wassailing of the trees, in which the traditional formulas of ancient magic were addressed to the task of stimulating the apple crop — as a sort of primitive Long Ashton research. The custom survived into the present century, though perhaps more for its convivial than its practical value. At Athelney, which was one of the last strongholds of wassailing, a man would climb the tree, put a piece of toast dipped in cider among the branches and lead the singing of the wassail-song. The owner of the orchard had the simple duty of providing cider for the wassailing experts — 'and 'twas cider in buckets in they days'.

The conviviality that is inseparable from farmhouse cider is perhaps its most endearing quality. 'Tanglefoot' and 'Slack Thy Girdle' were some of the less disreputable names for what was the essence of rural hospitality that the cider-maker provided.

> His honest Friends, at thirsty hour of Dusk,
> Come uninvited; he with bounteous Hand
> Imparts his smoking Vintage, sweet Reward
> Of his own Industry; the well fraught Bowl
> Circles incessant, whilst the humble Cell
> With quavering laugh and rural Jests resounds.

Cider has long since ceased to be a part of the rural worker's wage; and we shall never again see the like of the Mendip Feasts, when that high-minded and godly woman Hannah More thought it proper to provide cider for 600 children to drink with their beef and plum pudding. The selling of an occasional drop of cider to the passer-by and the bargee on the canal is no longer a sideline for the cottage housewife; and what Stradling called 'the pestiferous cider house' has given way to the more conventional pub with its vested brewer's interest in beer. Even so cider has found a place for itself in the modern world, neatly bottled and nationally branded. It has moved with the times and changed with the times.

In one of the last of the old-fashioned cider houses — a justly renowned and respected one at Athelney — the cider drinkers used to play a game that I have not come across elsewhere. On the ceiling of the front parlour there is still a black wooden disc, in appearance rather like a gramophone record; this disc was used in a game known as 'Tossing for Quarts'. The procedure was this: two players take it in turns to toss a coin up to the ceiling so that it strikes the wooden disc, and count ten points if it comes down heads and one point if it comes down tails. The game, on the lines of pontoon, is to score as near to thirty-one as possible, and the loser of a rubber of three games buys a quart of cider for the winner, who is then challenged by the man next to him — and so on round the room. Some houses could serve a quart cup, and the signal for its use was for someone to propose, 'Let's drink tonight like the old men used to.' Tossing for quarts became the evening's entertainment, and up went the first coin to the board on the ceiling.

Another and more agile sport, which has quite died out, was running for lambs. This was for the athletic young who competed against each other in pursuit of a lamb which was released on the open moor. The one who caught the lamb kept it. An account written by Adrian Schael, who was rector of High Ham in Elizabethan times, describes the revels of Midsummer Day, when there were wrestling matches in Sedgemoor, and goes on to refer to the lamb-running competition which was held after dinner 'on the Holy Day following'. Schael remarks that the parson of Pitney celebrated Mass on that day before a large congregation of youths who assembled 'in great multitudes' for the games.

Perhaps some of the young men built up a flock of their own from the lambs they captured at the Midsummer revels. Much of Somerset's earlier prosperity was linked with its sheep flocks, and the towns on the edge of the moors were engaged in the 'best and most profitable part' of the wool trade when Defoe visited them. Taunton made serges and druggets, Glastonbury made knitted stockings; and the fine Spanish medley cloths that people of fashion liked were made at Bruton and Castle Cary and other centres along the Wiltshire border. Mantles of serge or linsey-woolsey — known as West Country rockets (or rochets) — were the universal fashion for countrywomen in Somerset when Celia Fiennes passed through the county in 1698.

In the following century the woollen trade was largely lost to the industrialists of the North and the lace and silk trades took its place, but the sheep flocks persisted; within living memory 1,000 ewes grazed Ham Hill, and older men today recall how as lads they each called out their own flock and led them down the hill at night. And Glastonbury retained an industrial interest in sheep after the woollen trade had been lost; in fact, the major industry of the

Avalon area today — the manufacture of footwear — stems directly from the older activities of a sheep-raising district.

Skins from the flocks on the surrounding hills came in quantities to the tanners and fellmongers of Glastonbury and its neighbouring village of Street, and from them there grew up a local manufacture of sheepskin products, of gloves and rugs and the like. The initiative in this new development came from a remarkable family of Quaker farmers — the Clarks — who entered the tanning industry in Street in the first quarter of the last century. The first of what was to become a great industrial dynasty was Cyrus Clark, and when his younger brother, James, joined him as an apprentice Cyrus allowed the lad to deal with the short-wooled skins that were unsuitable for rug-making. With the ingenuity that characterises his family, the younger Clark had the skins made into lined slippers, which quickly became popular with the Victorians. Known as Brown Petersburgs or 'Brown Peters' (as they are still called today), the slippers brought the Clarks into business contact with local shoemakers.

Having employed the village craftsmen successfully for one purpose, the Clarks went a step further and ventured into the making of boots and shoes. The new trade exceeded but did not replace the old. Sheepskin rugs and Brown Peters are still made in Avalon, but it is the footwear industry that now dominates the area. With a global output of well over 20 million pairs a year from its factories in the West Country and overseas Clarks of Street is Britain's biggest manufacturer of footwear.

In its earlier stages the manufacture of boots and shoes was, to a substantial extent, a cottage industry. Until 1858 no machinery was used; the work was contracted out to individual craftsmen for execution in their own homes. In some of the older houses in Street you can still see the typical backroom workshop, built over the kitchen; and a reconstruction in detail of one of these workshops is maintained at Clark's main factory, where the history of their industry is studied and preserved with exemplary diligence. Nowadays the work is done on modern factory lines, though the craft of making hand-sewn boots and shoes is kept alive.

The village of Street, linking Glastonbury with the Poldens, is an exceptional place. A flourishing little township which somehow contrives to retain something of its old village character, it is a centre of up to date industry and fashion in an intensely rural setting. Its products enjoy a worldwide reputation, and a century of success leavened with Quaker paternalism and pioneer welfare work have transformed what might otherwise have been just another village clinging to the skirts of Glastonbury. It was perhaps the first child of the modern age in central Somerset and it is conscious of its modernity, filled with aspirations to clothe the momentary nakedness of sudden growth. The cynic will distinguish it from other Somerset villages by the facts that it has a swimming pool and a zest for organised culture, but I think it is saved from the sterility of the standard industrial garden suburb by its individual blend of homeliness and dynastic genius. All that it is today grew directly from the roots of its past. Its success is an organic success. The enterprise of its own little

Quaker community and the craftmanship of its cottagers have fashioned the Street of today from the opportunities that came to their hands. Their tradition is a real one.

It is a remarkable chance, but surely not an unhappy one, that one family could sustain its resourcefulness and initiative over a century without flagging. The Clarks are an uncommon race of men, for they seem able to throw up in each generation at least one exceptional captain to guide their industrial fortunes. Even their failures are interesting, like that fascinating character John Clark — a cousin of the shoe-making pioneers — who was born in 1785 and died in 1852 after producing what might well be described as the invention to end all inventions: a machine for the making of Latin hexameters. When I first came across a reference to this machine I frankly disbelieved that such a thing could be possible, this side of Wonderland; but I made some inquiries, and to my astonishment I found the machine, intact, in a corner of the factory at Street. For many years previously it had been housed in the now defunct village museum, its purpose almost forgotten and its internal workings falling into disrepair. However, since I first saw it, it has been carefully overhauled and its uncanny faculties completely restored. It does in fact perform exactly what John Clark claimed for it: it composes Latin hexameters, metrically correct (with minor qualifications) and capable of intelligible translation.

The Eureka, to give the machine the name bestowed upon it by its inventor, was originally exhibited in London in 1845 at the Egyptian Hall. It was on show daily from noon to 5 pm and from 7 pm to 9 pm, and the price of admission was 1s — which was a lot of money, when you consider the value of money in 1845. But the exhibition was a success, and John Clark is reputed to have bought himself a house in Bridgwater with the proceeds.

What did our forefathers see for their shillings? They saw a rather ornate gilded wooden case on legs, standing about 7ft high, with six narrow apertures like tiny oblong windows in which, letter by letter, six Latin words would appear when the machine was operating. In more irreverent terms *The Eureka* could be described as a sort of literary juke-box in the Victorian style. Above the little windows where the hexameter would appear were some lines of English verse, calculated to put the beholder in the right frame of mind:

> Eternal Truths of Character Sublime
> Conceived in darkness here shall be unroll'd.
> The mystery of Number and of Time
> Is here display'd in Characters of Gold.
> Transcribe each line composed by this machine,
> Record the fleeting thoughts as they arise:
> A Line, once lost, will ne'er again be seen,
> A thought, once flown, perhaps forever flies.

Having digested that, and having perhaps got his paper and pencil ready, the Victorian spectator might then watch the machine in the act of composition, a process which was said to take about a minute to complete and which culmin-

The Hanging Chapel, Langport

Wedmore Church from the east

Satirical bench-ends in Brent Knoll Church depicting the fox dressed as a bishop *left*, the fox with his hindlegs fettered in the top panel and in the stocks below *below left*, and finally the fox being hung *below right*

ated with the playing of 'God Save the Queen'. At the same time the newly minted hexameter would form before his incredulous gaze. And when in due course he wearied of this marvel there was an 'illustrative lecture'.

John Clark spent thirteen years in making and perfecting his machine, which led one critic to remark that a boy could be made into a verse-making machine in shorter time than that. On the other hand, no boy could compose hexameters at the rate of 10,000 a week, which was the machine's non-stop output. As to its usefulness, John Clark concluded his pamphlet on the general history and description of the machine, which was published in Bridgwater in 1848, with these words: 'Every new thing is an intellectual accession, and every accession may, possibly, be of important use.' I wonder if pure research has ever been justified in terms more simple and dignified than that.

The worth of the verses composed by *The Eureka* is, of course, negligible. They follow monotonously the nebulous oracular style of a surrealist Old Moore, on the lines of 'Gloomy clouds swiftly foretell fierce combats', and the general tendency is towards a vague ambiguity which allows the translator plenty of freedom. When I watched the machine in operation it produced this line, 'Turpia facta cito progignunt proelia fusca.' My companion, a good Latin scholar with a nice sense of humour, construed this as: 'Engagements after dark swiftly produce disgraceful deeds.'

But the quality of the verses in unimportant. John Clark's interest in making the machine was to perfect mechanically an ingenious form of verbal kaleidoscope. For his purpose he used — in his own words — 'about eighty-six wheels, giving motion to cylinders, cranks, spirals, pulleys, levers, springs, ratchets, quadrants, tractors, snails, worm and fly, heart-wheels, eccentric wheels, and star-wheels — all of which are in essential and effective motion, with various degrees of velocity, each performing its part in proper time and place'. However, in spite of that grandiloquent inventory the interior of *The Eureka* looks disarmingly simple. Its main ingredients are some clockwork mechanism; 6 revolving wooden drums, bristled like porcupines with wire 'fingers'; and 48 strips of wood, each of which displays all the letters of the alphabet.

When a line of verse 'decomposes', the lettered strips are drawn up to their highest extent; when the machine begins to compose a fresh line, the strips commence to descend, and the windows in front display a row of alphabets moving past. One by one the letters halt, as the wire 'fingers' check the descending strips, until each of the 6 words is formed. The disposition of the wires predetermines the words that can be formed, and the total number of possible words can be calculated. The machine was in fact designed to form the appropriate combinations for 105 words, so distributed among the 'wire-finger' drums that each drum has one word more than its predecessor: the 1st drum can produce 15 words, the 6th can produce 20. And the maximum number of different sentences that the machine could display is in the neighbourhood of 28 million — which is surely enough to satisfy the most unbridled passion for hexameters.

Has it any value, this 'intellectual accession' of John Clark's? Not much, I suppose; and even its ingenious novelty is dimmed by the computers and electronic 'brains' of the present day. Nevertheless it is no bad thing that this little masterpiece of sheer fantasy should still after a century flourish in the very citadel of practical utility. It is excellent to be well shod and businesslike; but good also to be reminded that what may be of value is never quite certain and not always obvious.

CHAPTER SEVENTEEN

THE POLDEN VILLAGES

Through Street the main road from Glastonbury bears up to the Polden ridge, rising gently past Walton to disclose the wide landscapes of Avalon and of Sedgemoor on either side. The Polden villages, for the most part, nestle among the more gradual slopes that unfold on to the peat moors, and the traveller on the main road passes them by with scarcely a recognition of their existence. Only an occasional signpost reveals the nearby presence of these pleasant stone built villages, bowered with elm and chestnut, softly veiled with their canopies of foliage which give a pleasing contrast to the openness of the moors. The whole length of the ridge has a modestly sylvan atmosphere of occasional woods and copses and open parkland, with rooks flinging off into the wind and riding out over the marshland. Insignificant as it may appear on the map, this little fold of low hills has a well defined character of its own.

Although the brick and tile works of Bridgwater were so near, the local stone of the Poldens — the blue lias — resisted any alien challenge. Barns and cottages and garden walls blend the stone in finely graded tones of colour from the colder greys and blues to an almost golden honey; added graciousness comes with the kindly dappling of lichens. The airy treetops add a pliant and whimsical contrast to the sturdy buildings. And the voice one notices here is a woodland voice — the nuthatch's jaunty whistle, like a boy whistling to a puppy. In spring this merry sound breaks in on all sides.

Until quite recently the villages on the Avalon side of the Poldens were specially esteemed for the waters of their holy wells. The principal wells were at Edington, Chilton Polden and Shapwick; and it has also been argued that Pedwell, near Ashcott, is a corrupt form of 'St Peter's Well', and refers to a well which has long since disappeared. These wells spring from the clays of the Lower Lias, a source of medicinal salts and sometimes of sulphuretted hydrogen. As late as 1928 a local vicar reported that the wells were still used by some of the inhabitants and continued to attract visitors from the neighbourhood and from Bridgwater. Some came with bottles in order to take a supply home with them.

The most celebrated of these holy wells was one at Shapwick. About 1830 the well-water was diverted into a small building 'having a pump room and an enclosed bath for the accommodation of patients resorting to it'. Dr Beddoes of Bristol analysed the water that was offered to the patients and found that it resembled Harrogate water. Dom Ethelbert Horne, who made a study of the holy wells of Somerset, saw the building in 1914 and described it as 'a poor-looking affair'. It is still referred to locally as 'the bath-house', although it has long since disintegrated into a heap of rubble, and the spring has been diverted as a result of drainage work.

More fortunate is the holy well of Edington. Describing it at the end of the eighteenth century, Collinson wrote: 'A little below the church there is a perpetual spring, which contains sulphur and steel and stains silver yellow in two hours. Against the change of weather it smells like the foul barrel of a gun. It is very cold, leaves a white crust on the bodies it passes over and has been found efficacious in scorbutick cases.' The well was restored in 1937, in memory of Margaret Charlotte Fownes Luttrell, and is easy to find. It stands beside a road and gives off a smell so strong, and indeed so like 'the foul barrel of a gun', that nobody could overlook it. The taste of the water confirms every expectation aroused by its smell. Only the hardiest of visitors sips a second time.

The humblest and most elusive of the three wells is the one at Chilton Polden. It has missed both the pumproom fashion and the piety of modern restoration. During his investigations in the district, Horne failed to find it: to me that was a challenge not to be refused, so I set out to search for it. And I discovered it, some thirty years ago, in a field, situated incongruously by two bridges on the Somerset & Dorset railway. Yet it was perhaps not so incongruous, for the two bridge roads may perhaps have perpetuated old rights of way from Chilton Polden and Cossington to the well. The well itself was unimpressive and I passed close by it several times before I recognised it. A little cluster of bushes gathered about it and hid from view the opening, which was still further obscured by having a large block of stone wedged in it, presumably for safety's sake. The masonry inside the rim of the well was crumbling into decay, and there were the rotting remains of a wooden cover and a surrounding fence. In the natural course of things, all trace of the well has probably disappeared under the tangle of briar and brushwood in the years that have passed since I found it.

The opposite flank of the Poldens — overlooking Sedgemoor — is considerably steeper and its human settlements are fewer and smaller. Particularly at the eastern end, the clear-cut escarpment in the vicinity of Ivy Thorn and Marshall's Elm gives a quite majestic sense of height to the open prospect across the moor to Dundon Hill and High Ham, with the Quantocks and Brendon Hills in the distance. Ivy Thorn Hill is a National Trust property. The view from Marshall's Elm is commemorated in one of Thomas Hardy's narrative ballads, 'A Trampwoman's Tragedy'.

Thus Poldon top at last we won,
   At last we won,
And gained the inn at sink of sun
   Far-famed as "Marshal's Elm"
Beneath us figured tor and lea,
   From Mendip to the western sea —
I doubt if finer sight there be
   Within this royal realm.

At about the middle of Polden's southern flank Greinton and Moorlinch gather about the Greylake Fosse which made the first link across Sedgemoor from the 'Sowy' villages. Further westward Bawdrip draws attention to its church, by strategic signposts on the main road, and it is worth a visit for its tower and for a curious exposed stone staircase to the belfry. An inscribed tablet behind the altar supports a not very convincing claim to the Mistletoe Bough legend of Lovell's bride. Edward Lovell was rector here for fourteen years in the seventeenth century, and six years after his death in 1675 his surviving daughter, Eleanor, died at the very time of her marriage celebrations. The tablet was erected by her husband, on the north side of the sanctuary, and was moved in 1866 during the restoration of the church — to which presumably is also due the incongruous red-tiled roof.

Bawdrip seems to have suffered from the Black Death: there is a gap in the roll of rectors between 1333 and 1402. Another outbreak of plague came near in 1665, but on this occasion Bawdrip was spared although there were many deaths at Bridgwater. Freedom of communication between the village and the stricken town was forbidden, and a 'frontier' for necessary trade was established at the tree known as the Watch Elm.

The neighbouring village of Stawell was at one time the hiding-place of the Robin Hood of the Poldens, a highwayman named Pocock, who enjoyed considerable local celebrity. Stradling, who lived only a quarter of a mile away, recorded a ballad about Pocock which he heard sung at a Harvest Home:

Run, my boys, run, the moon shines bright,
Pocock's in his cave, his purse is light;
But, when the night is murky and dark,
He's off with his steed, blithe as a lark.

Like most successful highwaymen, Pocock was credited with great ingenuity; his horse's shoes were said to turn on a pivot, so as to deceive his pursuers, who presumably could never tell whether Pocock was coming or going. The cave mentioned in the song was at the end of a long and deep gully, through which ran the stream that supplied Ford Mill. I explored this gully in part, but in some places it was heavily overgrown and all but impenetrable, and I was unable to identify Pocock's cavern; the best I could find seemed to offer very inadequate shelter. Nor can I find any local singer who recalls the song that Stradling heard. As for Pocock himself, there is no reference to him in Alexander Smith's *History of the Lives of the Highwaymen*; this may perhaps mean that he flourished after 1720. What little we do know about him is due to the enthusiasm of Stradling, who built a grotto in memory of the highwayman and named it Pocock's Cell.

Stradling's own memorial is on the main road above Stawell — the self-consciously archaic building on Cock Hill known as Chilton Priory. The Priory combines Stradling's eccentric tastes with his genuine antiquarian zeal. In 1839 he published a description of the place, saying that he had erected it 'as a Repository for many curiosities which would otherwise have been destroyed'. His design included a nave, an oratory at the east end, a south porch and an embattled tower at the west, under which is a crypt. Into the fabric went so many discarded fragments from older illustrious buildings that Stradling's 'Repository' became the architectural equivalent of a Lost Dogs' Home. In his account of the Priory's three pinnacles Stradling wrote:

> They were for several centuries on Langport Tower, and though likely to last for as many more, were degraded from their proud and lofty situation, in order to make room for new ones. They, with their companion now on my lawn, were thrown about for some years in a stonemason's yard, but are now placed in such a situation as to enable them to look down with contempt on their tawdry usurpers, and on the taste of the repairers and beautifiers of the venerable Edifice they so long decorated.

In his one-man rearguard action against nineteenth-century restoration Stradling gave sanctuary to a host of refugee objects from the surrounding churches and ancient homes — a corbel from one, a door, a finial and a window frame from another, tiles from Glastonbury Abbey, communion rails from North Petherton: they all went into the ark that Stradling built to save them. And when the Priory was completed, he filled it with an astonishing collection of objects, including a large stone ball shot into Bridgwater during the siege in the Civil War, a Roman basin, a head of a New Zealand chief, British weapons and tools found in the nearby peat, coins, furniture, stained glass, part of a brass drum taken at the battle of Copenhagen, a tomahawk, a large ammonite, a mandarin hat and a pair of chopsticks, and the red waistbelt of a Fiji chieftain.

One of the virtues of William Stradling was the assiduity with which he pounced on any fragment of antiquity that came to light in the turbary. His collection included part of a canoe-paddle and an intact Romano-British jug, salvaged from the peat; and also the Late Bronze Age hoard of palstaves and sickles and bracelets, now preserved in Taunton Museum, which was put into a wooden box at Edington Burtle by some marshland farmer, perhaps, about 3,000 years ago.

Some two miles from Chilton Priory is Loxley Wood, which again reinforces one's impression of the complete difference of the Polden scene from the surrounding moorland. Loxley is noted for its varieties of wild orchid, and in winter it is a favoured haunt of woodcock. Four stones in the wood, near the main road, call to mind one of the most striking of the many stories of Monmouth's Rebellion that are still green in local memory. The stones commemorate a man named Swayne, a native of nearby Shapwick, who saved his life by using his wits and his phenomenal skill in jumping. Captured by the King's soldiers, and with a reasonable expectation of being shortly put to death, Swayne pleaded for a chance to give a last display of his ability as a jumper, on the pretext that 'his children might keep him in remembrance'. This odd request must have aroused the soldiers' curiosity, for they released him; and as they watched, Swayne made a succession of three enormous leaps and disappeared into the wood. If the measurements between the stones are to be believed, he sprang 14ft 9in, 12ft 6½in and 13ft 6in in successive bounds, so it is hardly surprising that he was not recaptured.

The comedy of Swayne's Leaps has a grim companion in another story of an athletic challenge, which is not so well known. After the battle of Sedgemoor a young ensign was offered his freedom if he could run a race, naked, with a marsh-colt. A halter was put round his neck and tied to the colt, and the two ran for three-quarters of a mile — at which point the colt fell exhausted. The young man claimed his liberty, but his tormentors seized him and immediately executed him.

But unhappy memories of that kind seem remote as you stand on Cock Hill and look across the wide expanse of Sedgemoor. In spite of its low elevation the Polden ridge commands wonderful views on both flanks. The far-reaching moors present an open scene in which each detail has a detached significance — a line of pollard willows, an occasional elm, the darker groove of a rhine. The eye picks them out, one by one, from the general background of level green, and they interrupt the stillness of the moors like occasional laconic phrases in a pervasive silence.

To the north and east the Poldens look across to the Mendip Hills, which rear up dramatically beyond the Vale of Avalon like a mountain-chain, gaunt and dark and final. This is a wonderful spectacle when rain clouds scud across from the west: the Mendips are engulfed and then struggle free again like tidal rocks, and changing lights play up and down the length of the hills. For a while they vanish completely, before the pale sunlit patches begin to show among the black curtains of rain. In other contexts these inconsiderable hills would be unimpressive, but as a background to the peat moors the Mendips have an unexpected grandeur; they swell and tower up on the horizon, seemingly impassable and imprisoning.

The Polden villages, with their pleasant churches and an occasional fine house of architectural worth, are typical of the general tendency here to colonise the higher ground. The low levels that skirt the Poldens are strikingly empty; they are worked from above, from the hills that look down on them. And not only by men. Watch the herons and you will see that their lives are organised in the same way. The bird that spent the day fishing down on Shapwick Heath returns in the evening to the copse on the slope below the village, where it borders the moor.

Icehouse Copse contained a substantial heronry for many years, although it has more recently been depleted by the felling of timber. And the icehouse itself serves to underline the general stragegy which the birds so nicely illustrate. A solid structure of about 20ft in depth, of which two-thirds is underground, this ample forerunner of the refrigerator speaks of high living and points to the presence of a substantial mansion in the neighbourhood. Shapwick has indeed two such, each with its own dove-house, a fact which gives the village an unusual distinction. These columbaria would have held several hundred birds and were so designed that only the older birds — the ones kept for breeding — could get out. The plump youngsters were systematically culled by the fowler for the needs of the kitchen. The older of the two, at Shapwick House, is thought to be a Norman building and argues a long tradition of refined and prosperous living.

No doubt the superior civilisation of the Polden villages, particularly on the Avalon side of the ridge, is largely due to their connection with Glastonbury. Shapwick was a pilgrim station on the way to the Abbey, and seven of the other villages were known as the 'Seven Sisters' of the Poldens because they were the only churches in the neighbourhood which the Glastonbury monks personally supplied. These sister parishes were Chilton, Catcott, Edington, Greinton, Sutton Mallet, Stawell and Moorlinch, and they had an unfortunate quarrel as to which of them should be 'mother'. The quarrel for precedence centred on the legacy of a fine set of bells, and the Lord Abbot had to be called in to adjudicate.

Having heard the claims of each he ruled that the bells should go to the first parish to have three births and three deaths. Stawell got off to an early lead, with three births and two deaths, and the parishioners began building a suitable tower to hold the bells, which they felt sure must come to them. But with such stirring events afoot everybody in Stawell was reluctant to die, and meanwhile Moorlinch crept up with a second birth and then a third, and romped home dramatically with three sudden deaths. Perhaps the excitement became too tense. Anyway, Moorlinch won the bells, and work on Stawell's church tower stopped abruptly.

Beyond Woolavington and Puriton the Poldens fall away to the lush pastures of Pawlett beside the Parret estuary, as it winds into Bridgwater Bay. Northward is the pleasure coast of Burnham and Berrow and Brean Down, with Weston-super-Mare in the background behind the beaky promontory of Brean: westward are the desolate Steart Flats, embracing one of the most deserted stretches of coastline in the West Country.

CHAPTER EIGHTEEN

THE SEA COAST

Bridgwater Bay does not offer the conventionally beautiful scenery that one expects of a West Country bay. Where other bays have a framework of rocky headlands and a sense of containment, the Somerset coast from Brean to Stolford stretches out in an undisciplined sprawl. What makes it attractive indeed is its very spaciousness, the open expanses of its foreshore and the far receding levels of sandbank and mud laced with shallow channels that catch the light of sun and sky. It is a scene which can be desolate and tinged with melancholy at one moment; and yet at another moment its vast glistening amplitude can be charged with the magical illuminations that have made the Bay famous for its Turneresque sunsets. With its great rise and fall the Bristol Channel ebbs back to expose an immense half-world, owing allegiance neither to land nor sea. Only the eye and the imagination can range freely over it. To the landsman, and more particularly to the townsman, the wide freedom of the scene generates a keen exhilaration. The whole mood of the place is bold, open, breezy; inviting movement. A winter's walk along the shore from Burnham to Berrow with half a gale blowing is one of the sharp and tonic pleasures of life.

The shallow levels of the Bay are the Steart Flats to the south and the Berrow Flats to the north, with the seagoing channel of the Parret separating them as it curves past Burnham and broadens to a westerly course beside the ridge of the Gore Sands. Steart Point, a narrow strip of land between the Parret estuary and the sea, is about as precarious as any part of England's coastline — a low shingle ridge with spartina grass on the seaward side and estuarine saltings embanking the river. Steart takes its name from an Anglo-Saxon word meaning a stalk or a tail. And its tail was docked in 1783 when Steart Island was separated from the mainland. Since that time the island has had an unstable existence, fighting for survival in the swirling, scouring tides that beat round it so that one part of it is eroded and washed away while another part is built up and extended with fresh deposits of mud and sand. In the early years of this century Steart Island had fifty acres of grass and was let for grazing. Today it is mainly shingle, sand and mud. Its fate seems to hang on its ability to join up again with the mainland by means of new deposits before it is completely bitten away and overwhelmed.

From Steart to Stolford is a cowering, crouched landscape, exposed to the vehemence of wind and tide, in which any vestige of shelter is a thing to be prized by man and beast. Offshore the great waste of soft oozy mud at low tide denies any foothold and the fishermen of Stolford use a sort of upright sledge, a cradle on wooden runners, to bear their weight and carry them about their business. Unable to stand erect without sinking into the mud, they lean forward on these 'mud-horses' and push themselves along with their feet. Attempts to mechanise the traditional mud-horse in recent years, on the lines of the motorised sledges used in polar exploration, have not really overcome the peculiar conditions of the Stolford foreshore. Salt water and fine particles of sand can play havoc with machinery not designed to withstand them.

Beyond Stolford is Hinkley Point, a location of total obscurity until the end of the 1950s when its name was given to the first of two atomic power-stations.

Another innovation of the fifties was the creation in 1954 of the Bridgwater Bay Nature Reserve. It covers over 6,000 acres, mainly of foreshore where large numbers of wildfowl congregate and where the shifting, changing nature of the Bristol Channel coast can be studied. In particular it offers a well-documented story of intertidal reclamation on the mudflats between Steart and Stolford. In an attempt to improve coastal defences against erosion an experiment was made here in 1928 with the planting of a hybrid cord-grass *(Spartina townsendii)*. This cord-grass, discovered about 100 years ago in Southampton Water by Francis Townsend, had subsequently colonised Poole Harbour and spread rapidly there. A couple of truck-loads of the grass were brought from Poole to Bridgwater Bay, where the plant soon established itself and began to trap the silt and build up the level of the foreshore. Measurements were taken regularly and by 1965 there were areas which, thanks to the cord-grass, were 6ft higher than they were in 1928. The extent of the grass by then was two miles long by a quarter of a mile wide. By the fifties other plants were able to establish themselves in the wake of the cord-grass.

The Steart Flats, which form the main part of the Reserve, are too bleak and forbidding in autumn and wintertime to arouse any enthusiasm in the generality of visitors, but for the naturalist they have a powerful attraction. Wildfowl and waders gather here in great flocks — mallard, teal and wigeon, pintail and shoveller, dunlin and ringed plover, curlew and lapwing, a great concourse of birds of many kinds, riding the high winds and pitching in groups on the shore as the tide ebbs back. Snipe rise from the reeds and an occasional merlin may patrol the land's edge. And as the light fades in the evening, at slack water, the piping cries of invisible curlew far out over the flats make an indescribably eerie sound, like ghosts passing in the gathering shadows of the night sky. Forbidding and inhuman this coast may be on an icy January day, but for the bird-lover it can be charged with a wild magic that makes kindlier shores seem insipid.

The Parret estuary is an attractive wintering area for knot, which concentrate here in such strength that their numbers may exceed 1,000. In the last thirty years it has become increasingly attractive to the black-tailed godwits on their spring and autumn passages and some now stay during the winter. Whitefront geese are another impressive addition to the winter scene: their biggest numbers are to be found higher up the Severn estuary, at Slimbridge in the vicinity of the Wildfowl Trust grounds, but 4–500 may come down the Bristol Channel after Christmas to the vicinity of the Parret's lower reaches. The golden plover is another species which appears in really big flocks along the coast. But, for the ornithologist, the bird which has the most specific and singular association with Bridgwater Bay is the shelduck, that large and handsome pied duck with the chestnut stomacher.

About 1950 two surprising discoveries were made about this remarkable bird. R. H. Coombes, studying shelduck in Morecambe Bay, discovered that they flew *eastwards* after breeding: they crossed the Pennines and headed away to the south eastern corner of the North Sea. There, in the vicinity of the Heligoland Bight and the mouth of the Elbe, they joined great numbers of shelduck from other places and took part in a communal moult. The consequence of Coombes's discovery was the realisation that this great concentration of flightless birds in German waters included at various times not only the shelduck from Morecambe Bay but virtually the whole British population of this species.

And then, as if this strange rule of the shelduck's migration to a special moulting area hundreds of miles away were not sufficiently surprising, a Bridgwater man — Douglas Perrett — began to uncover, with the help of one or two colleagues, the first and so far the only exception to the rule. Along the Somerset coast the local population of shelduck in springtime is about 1,000 and there seems to be no reason to doubt that they conform to the orthodox pattern and depart in July to the North Sea to moult. But throughout the period of high summer and early autumn large numbers of non-local shelduck gather in Bridgwater Bay and moult. Keeping well out to sea — up to two miles from the shore — they are protected at low tide by the big expanses of soft mud between Steart and Hinkley Point, which is the area most favoured by them. Their numbers vary greatly from year to year but totals of 5,000 have been claimed.

There seem also to be identifiable peaks at different stages in each year, which suggest that non-breeders arrive first, successful breeders supply the next wave, and birds whose breeding has been delayed for some reason make up the final peak. Probably they come from further west — including Irish birds therefore — and it is tempting to think that, en route to the North Sea, they break their journey at Bridgwater Bay and find there the conditions they need, particularly security from predators when their inability to fly leaves them defenceless. Whatever the explanation the moulting shelduck of summer have given Bridgwater Bay a unique and fascinating distinction.

North of the Parret the coast is fringed with sand dunes, curiously sculptured by the wind. In places the belt of dunes is as much as three quarters of a mile wide and new saltings are constantly in process of formation as the sea deposits fresh mud. To protect the dunes, which were mainly covered with marram grass before 1900, sea-buckthorn was introduced and has become quite rampant in places, creating rough thickets in which willow, alder and sallow can develop. The plump golden berries and spear-like thorns of the sea-buckthorn are an unexpected sight here on the Somerset coast. It is a plant of east and south-east England and was a decidedly alien innovation when it first appeared in Burnham in 1890. Its colonisation of the coastline northward has been so successful that it is a dominant feature of the landscape.

Burnham is the only seaside resort worthy of the name between Weston-super-Mare and Minehead. That in itself is an instructive comment on the nature of the coast. And Burnham has hardly been a roaring success. It retains the well-mannered atmosphere of a late Victorian watering-place, brought discreetly up to date. Going to Burnham is like visiting an intelligent, sympathetic but slightly puzzled aunt. The old dream of fortunes to be made in a maritime link with Wales have long been forgotten, sublimated perhaps in the modern achievement of the GPO radio station which links Burnham with shipping on the trade-routes of the world.

Berrow and Brean were a favourite 'anchorage' in the early years after the war for touring caravanners, but those first moments of easygoing rapture have inevitably given place to a more permanent and developed commercialisation, with caravans yielding to chalets and chalets to bungalows. The coast road seems to settle into an interminable triviality when suddenly it ends against the abrupt flank of Brean Down, that last splinter of Mendip which thrusts into the Bristol Channel towards the islands of Steepholm and Flatholm, and seals off the left bank of the Axe at Uphill. One of the rectors of Uphill was the father of the poet, William Lisle Bowles, who thus recalled the scene 'where once a child I wandered':

> *There* is the Church,
> Crowning the high hill-top, which overlooks
> Brean Down, where in its lovelier amplitude
> Stretches into grey mist the Severn Sea.
> *There*, mingled with the clouds, old Cambria draws
> Her line of mountains, fading far away;
> *There* sit the sister Holms, in the mid-tide
> Secure and smiling.

When those lines were first published the Somerset Sea-Bathing Infirmary had just been established at Uphill 'for the purpose of extending the advantage of sea-bathing to the poor, who suffer from scrofulous diseases'. The cult of sea-bathing was simultaneously having an astonishing effect on Uphill's neighbour, Weston-super-Mare, which before 1800 was an unimportant fishing village and even in 1811 had a population of only 163. In 1819 Mrs Piozzi visited Weston and wrote 'the breezes here are most salubrious; no land nearer than North America when we look down the Channel'. Weston's first hotel had opened in 1812 and by 1821 the population was up to 738. In the next seven years it doubled and 2,000 visitors responded to its offered attraction of 'health, not dissipation'. Success was clearly in sight for this new health resort. John Rutter might observe tartly in 1829 that 'the shore is so nearly level, that at ebb tide a stranger would suppose that the sea had abandoned the place', but there were many who credited all those acres of mud with the ability to exhale health-giving vapours.

In the forties Brean Down was a bird sanctuary and its warden could claim that its breeding species included a pair of peregrines. After the death of the warden access to the Down was no longer restricted. It is a National Trust property. In recent years it has suffered from a decline in the population of rabbits which maintained a short sward of downland turf and kept down the scrub which can otherwise establish itself all too readily. This is one of the sites where volunteers belonging to the Somerset Trust for Nature Conservation have exerted a valuable control, by checking areas of bramble and scrub growth and cutting fire-breaks. Botanically Brean Down is important as the main British location of the white rock-rose; Honewort is another rarity that may still survive there. A plant much prized in earlier days was samphire, for which Brean was famous. Large quantities were gathered for pickling by the local people, who then sent it away to be sold in the towns inland. The task of gathering it seems to have been a hazardous job:

> Nor untrembling canst thou see,
> How from a scraggy Rock, whose prominence
> Half overshades the Ocean, hardy Men,
> Fearless of rending Winds, and dashing Waves,
> Cut Samphire, to excite the squeamish Gust
> Of pamper'd Luxury.

For sea-birds this is a perilous coast when strong westerly gales are blowing up the narrowing funnel of the Bristol Channel. Once they are trapped on a lee shore large numbers of exhausted birds may be driven down to die along the coast. In the autumn of 1950 there was a 'wreck' of little auks in such circumstances. In 1952 a similar but greater disaster overtook a species of petrel, Leach's forked-tail petrel. In 1954, 1955 and 1957 it was the turn of the kittiwakes: in the gales of February 1957 122 dead kittiwakes were reported. And this is sadly a continuing and inevitable story.

CHAPTER NINETEEN

THE SEDGEMOOR COUNTRY

Inland from Bridgwater Bay the Quantocks fold down to the left bank of the Parret, holding the town of Bridgwater in a narrow neck of low land, with the Poldens on the other side. The moors begin to broaden out behind Bridgwater, in the vicinity of the 'zoy' villages — Chedzoy, Westonzoyland and Middlezoy. These villages stand in a trim and well-kept setting, quite unlike the deep moorland country. There are no birch trees, no peat, no withies, no untidy pastures ragged with reeds and wild iris. And here, among neat meadows bordered with closely pollarded willow, the magnificent tower of Westonzoyland church rears up, a landmark for miles around.

The tower was built by Abbot Bere of Glastonbury, for Westonzoyland was a part of the Glastonbury manor referred to in 1384 as 'Sowy', and it is yet another reminder of the debt this countryside owes to the Abbey builders. The interior of the church is no less fine than its outward appearance. One's first sight of the elaborately carved wooden roof is a breath-taking moment, even in this county which has so much to show of the carver's art. Surely Westonzoyland roof must rank with those of Somerton and Martock as being among the most marvellous examples of this kind of craftmanship that Somerset, and indeed the whole West Country, has to show. It would be worth anyone's while to visit the village to see it, even if there were no other reason for going to Westonzoyland.

And of course there is another reason, displayed succinctly on a signpost in the village street. 'To the Battlefield', it reads; and there can hardly be any other signpost in England with such an odd inscription. The battlefield, of course, is that of Sedgemoor where, in 1685, the Protestant rebellion led by the Duke of Monmouth was defeated and broken by the soldiers of James II. If you follow the direction of the signpost you will come to a field at the end of a drove, where a modern memorial stands flanked with four 'staddles' on which are recorded inconsequentially some famous battles in the four centuries from 1600.

It is an uneasy place, this last battlefield in England, for the victory was as empty as the defeat was ignominious. The throne of James II soon afterwards began to topple, and the 'glorious revolution' of 1688 made Sedgemoor irrelevant, except for those who on either side had given their lives for what they conceived to be their duty. Monmouth was evidently misled by a belief that he would meet no serious resistance, and was unable to arm those who were prepared to fight for him. When he failed to enter Bristol his chances were already fading, and there must have been mixed feelings in Bridgwater — still scarred from the Civil War — when 'King' Monmouth withdrew into the town and set up his headquarters there.

As the King's troops advanced past the Poldens, under the leadership of the Earl of Faversham and with the future Duke of Marlborough as second-in-command, Monmouth watched their approach from the steeple of St Mary's, Bridgwater, with the aid of a spy-glass. With no alternative but to fight while he still held the line of the Parret, Monmouth attempted to do what Washington did at Trenton: he launched a surprise attack across the river under cover of darkness, hoping to outflank the enemy who was thought to be ill-guarded and probably drunk. The surprise nearly succeeded, until a chance shot betrayed the plan; and then the proper training and superior arms of the military settled the issue.

The parish register of Westonzoyland contains an interesting account of what happened in the village at the time of the battle. It was probably written by one of the churchwardens, Richard Alford, whose cousin was mayor of Lyme Regis when Monmouth landed there. I have modernised the spelling.

> The engagement began between one and two of the clock in the morning. It continued near one hour and a half. There was killed upon the spot, of the King's soldiers, sixteen: five of them buried in the church: the rest in the churchyard; and they had all Christian burial. One hundred or more of the King's soldiers wounded, of which wounds many died: of which we have no certain account. There was killed of the rebels upon the spot, about 300: hanged with us, 22 — of which 4 were hanged in gemmaces (ie chains): about 500 prisoners brought into our church, of which there was 79 wounded, and 5 of them died of their wounds in our church.

Certain expenses were incurred as a consequence of the battle, and these were entered in the church accounts. The bellringers had to be paid for ringing in thanksgiving for the victory and for the capture of the Duke of Monmouth; one may wonder what the ringers said among themselves as they performed their duty. And there were payments to Ben Page for mending a seat, mending the clock and doing something about the key of the north door. And there was a bill for frankincense and resin and other things that were burnt in the church to sweeten it 'after ye prissoners was gon out'.

There was one prisoner, by the name of Scott, who made an unofficial and hurried exit from the church. Scott, who was a horse-dealer, had realised that Monmouth was probably the best customer for horses he was ever likely to see, so off he had gone to Taunton to trade with the Duke. And after him went a prudent Quaker friend, John Whiting, who was engaged to a sister of Scott's wife and had the task of trying to persuade Scott to think more of his safety and less of his horse-dealing. But business came first with Scott, and in due course he found himself under guard in Westonzoyland church. His plight and subsequent escape were later described by Whiting, who wrote:

> He was wonderfully preserved, being taken and put into Weston Steeple-house, with many more, the night after the fight, in order to be hanged next day, as many were, but he got out at the little north door, while the watch was asleep, and so escaped with his life: lying in cornfields by day, and going by night till he got home, and so lay about till after the general pardon.

Brother Scott was lucky. Before the general pardon came to set men's minds at ease again, there was the Bloody Assize; and he did well to 'lie about' until that was over. Whiting writes with passionate indignation of the hanging of naked men in chains, 'to the terror and shame of the country'. He was himself a witness of some of the executions, for his religious views brought him into Ilchester Gaol, and from his cell there he saw a horrible scene. 'There were eight executed, quartered and their bowels burnt on the market place before our prison window.' Righteously he condemns this 'forcing poor men to hale about men's quarters, like horse-flesh or carrion, to boil and hang them up as monuments of their cruelty and inhumanity'.

Of those who escaped hanging, many were transported. There was indeed a shameful traffic in the transportation of rebels, and not even the most exalted personages felt it to be beneath them. The Queen asked to be given 100 rebels, after sentence, and made herself a profit of 1,000 guineas by transporting them. It is small wonder that the people of Somerset nursed their bitter memories for so long; small wonder that the Countess of Pomfret found it unsafe to travel from Bristol to Bridgwater, simply because she was a great-grand-daughter of Judge Jeffreys. To this day the word 'transported' has a forceful place in the vocabulary of the moors. I know transportation was a general punishment for long after 1685, but it is now archaic and I suspect that the word's power of survival locally owes more than a little to the searing impressions of the Bloody Assize. I once heard a labourer, speaking of some wrongdoers in his village, recall a stern magistrate of his younger days and remark, 'If the old 'un 'ad bin alive, 'e'd'a' transported 'n.'

Such was Westonzoyland's hour of unhappy fame. The village ought also to be able to capture one's attention with the Devil's uping stock, an ancient stone from which the Prince of Darkness mounted his horse. Tradition asserted that the stone was immovable, but tradition was wrong, alas: a Mr Hitchings of Bridgwater, caring nothing for the Devil, bought the stone and had it cut into chimney-pieces. And if the Devil ever rides into Westonzoyland these days, he will have to scramble up and down as best he can.

Beyond the 'zoy' villages is Burrow Bridge, which might be described as the modern gateway to the heart of Sedgemoor. Here is the only public road-bridge over the Parret between Bridgwater and Langport; here the Tone joins the Parret, and beds of withies begin to appear. Burrow Bridge was the last toll-bridge in Somerset; it was not 'freed' until 1946. Prior to that the annual toll charges were put up for auction, and bidding continued during the running of an hour-glass until sometimes a figure in excess of £2,000 was reached.

South of the Parret, the moors are divided by a narrow ridge. Here, as with the Poldens, the villages cluster on the higher ground and the open levels of West Sedgemoor are virtually uninhabited. Stoke St Gregory and North Curry were important local centres in the heyday of the withy trade, and both had their annual withy auctions. Both also have impressive churches, with a central polygonal tower in the earlier Somerset style. Stoke St Gregory takes a special pride in its Jacobean carved pulpit; while North Curry, in a more comprehensive way, claims for itself the title of 'the Cathedral of the Moors'. North Curry was a royal manor until about 1300, when Richard I gave it to the Dean and Chapter of Wells, who built the church. An ancient elm chest with a curious lock, which now stands in the church, may perhaps have come from Athelney Abbey. North Curry church, like the village, has a neat and prosperous air, tactfully blending modern workmanship with ancient. It is beautifully set among lofty horsechestnut trees which, like the more conventional yews, seem to be associated with churches hereabouts.

North Curry for long kept up its annual custom of a Reeve's Feast, during which those present were free to drink as much ale as they pleased while a couple of one-pound candles were burning. This form of time limit seems to have been much practised in the area. I have mentioned the hour-glass auction at Burrow Bridge, and there is a similar custom at Chedzoy. Here, every twenty-one years, a piece of land is auctioned to provide funds for church repairs, and bidding takes places while half an inch of candle burns. The last few bids, as the candle begins to gutter, are made in an atmosphere of tense excitement. In 1946 the top bid was £125; in 1967 it rose to £204.

The Reeve's Feast was instituted in the reign of King John and survived until 1868. A marble slab in the church vestry sets out the procedure that was followed: the tenants were to provide wheat, and the reeve had to put three fat heifers in the manor pound, in readiness, on the Sunday before Christmas. He also had to provide a medley of other things, including half a pig, some beef, onions and bread. When the party entered the reeve's house they had to sing a traditional rhyme, and toasts were drunk to King John, the real Jack of Knapp, and the real Jack of Slough. Knapp is a little hamlet nearby, and Slough is the name of a local farm.

The parish registers of North Curry, Stoke St Gregory and West Hatch have been closely studied and made available in a book by H. P. Olivey, which provides many interesting little pictures of life here in earlier days; it also demonstrates what can be accomplished by a bold originality in the matter of spelling. How much more interesting a hedgehog become when it is called a 'hogdoge'. What fresh charm an affidavit acquires when it is named 'affy davy' or 'after daved', or — in 1807 — 'after David'.

Money was 'disbursted' for many reasons. Itch ointment cost 3s 6d in 1733. Vestments had to be laundered for special occasions, and an entry during the reign of James II reads: 'Procklymacion, washen of ye surplus, Prince of Walls.' The ejection of tramps could be costly, and one glorious entry in the eighteenth century reports the expenditure of 12s 4d for 'removing fragrants out of ye parish'. One can imagine how fragrant those vagrants may have been. Then there was compensation to a travelling man — presumably a drover — whose cattle were drowned in 1745 when the sea broke in to the moors. All he got was 3s 6d. There were frequent charges for putting local paupers to a trade: numerous spinning-wheels were bought, and in 1817 Mary Curry was taught the craft of gloving at a cost of 10s.

The killing of 'hogdoges' was a steady charge here as in other parishes. Our ancestors attacked wild animals of every kind with great vigour and at varying prices. For example, West Hatch would pay 4d for a hedgehog, but North Curry stuck at 2d regardless of which way it was spelt. For an otter 1s was paid in 1793; and in 1763 the astonishingly large sum of 6s 8d was paid for catching a badger. One would almost expect a dragon for that.

Those who kept the register were not always very good naturalists. It is hard to believe that the 2d expended in 1782 was really in respect of a 'porcupine'. Alas, it was just a highbrow version of 'hogdoge'. Perhaps there was wisdom in the more cautious man who made a comprehensive entry for the killing of 'all sorts of varmints'.

Occasionally a tragic little story comes through the bare record. Inquests and burials had to be paid for: in 1715 16s were paid for 'the crownen of too peopell', and in 1704 the burial of Rachel Curry was recorded at a cost of half a crown, with a further note that makes a grim postscript to her story — 'Paid for taking her out of the Well, 1s.' Poor Rachel! Like Mary, who was taught the glover's trade, she bore the name of the parish — perhaps the seeds of her tragedy lay there. Tragedy, too, of another kind is revealed in the entry of a small payment — only 1s 6d — to five men and three women who were shipwrecked on their way to Boston. They had probably sailed from Bridgwater, which was a favourite port for emigrants to America.

West Sedgemoor is almost enclosed by the pincer of higher land on which the Curry villages stand. North Curry, with Stoke St Gregory, is on the narrower north-western arm. To the south and west are Curry Mallet and Curry Rivel, above the sudden escarpment where the land first begins to rise away finally from the marshland. To see Sedgemoor, there is no better vantage point than Redhill; there the road climbs sharply off the moor in the direction of Curry Rivel, and below you lies a magnificent level expanse in varying tones of green — the silvery green of willows, the darker olive-green of withy-beds, the infinitely changing greens of meadow grasses as the wind ruffles them. And then, in sharp detail, you notice the black-and-white and the warm reds of the cattle, and the rectangular borders of the rhines, which cut the moor into squares as precise as those of a chessboard. With summer cloud moving above, it is a rare and lovely sight.

A short distance along the ridge is a tall stone column which seems to have escaped from Trafalgar Square. This is the Burton Pynsent Monument —

known locally as 'Burton Steeple'. It preserves the memory of Sir William Pynsent, an admirer of William Pitt, Earl of Chatham, who bequeathed the adjoining estate of Burton Pynsent to Pitt. In gratitude for this windfall the great statesman had this monument erected, at a cost of £2,000, bearing the words 'Sacred to the memory of Sir William Pynsent' — but it has not proved to be very sacred, so far as the horrid race of initial-cutters are concerned. One of them even took an odd pride in recording the fact that he was a schoolmaster.

The column looks impressive against the sky, at the end of an avenue of trees; and the view from the top of the monument must have been magnificent, but the doorway is now bricked up. There is a reason for this apparently gratuitous obstruction, and a very strange reason it is. Apparently on more than one occasion an inquisitive cow entered the doorway and climbed the spiral stairs — 175 of them — to the top of the monument. The sight of a cow on the top of Burton Steeple must have put a great strain on those who liked their cider in the daytime, and it certainly caused anxiety to the owner of the cow. So there was nothing for it but to brick up the entrance.

Inland, behind the Curry villages, is the valley of the Isle, which flows down to join the river Parret in the marshes about Muchelney. The valley bottom is low lying, but the quality of the landscape is quite different from the true moorland area. Mixed farming flourishes in the 'teazle' villages of Isle Abbots and Isle Brewers and Fivehead, and the countryside is better wooded. The gentle seclusion of Isle Abbots is irradiated by the gem-like loveliness of its church, which is considered by many to be the perfect expression of the characteristic Somerset style.

The delicately wrought church towers of the area, usually of blue lias dressed with golden Ham Hill stone, make a poetry of height in this flat landscape; time and again as you move among the moorland villages your gaze is caught upwards in a sudden dramatic exultation of exquisite tracery and finely drawn pinnacles, so graceful and airy and supple that they seem to mount and unfold, detail by detail, with some inner organic life of their own. They belong to the period of recovery after the Black Death until the Reformation, which put an end to the settled context in which such building was possible. Never again was England to see such a copious and lyrical dedication of native genius to the building and adornment of her churches as was spent in raising the superb towers of Somerset. And of them all, the church of Isle Abbots may most fittingly serve as the prime example, modestly withdrawn in a remote village in a little-frequented valley in the moors.

By contrast, the neighbouring church of Isle Brewers is a very odd building indeed. It was rebuilt in 1861 by Dr Joseph Wolff, and Dr Wolff was a very odd man. Born the son of a Jewish rabbi in Bavaria in 1795, he became a Christian and was the first modern missionary to preach to the Jews in Jerusalem. He also travelled extensively in the East in search of the Lost Tribes, and on one occasion arrived in Kabul after walking 600 miles without clothes or money. He was accustomed to sign himself 'Apostle of Our Lord Jesus Christ for Palestine, Persia, Bokhara and Balkh'. I do not know what the people of Isle

Brewers made of Dr Wolff, but at least the village was not entirely unaccustomed to eccentric arrivals: in May 1681, Siamese twins were born there.

Muchelney stands on a very slight swell in the marshy area south of Langport where the river Yeo or Ivel joins the Parret. It must have been a naturally isolated stronghold, like Athelney, protected by the rivers and the surrounding bogs. It was an ideal site for a small religious community. There is a tradition that the first Benedictine monks were settled here by King Ine early in the eighth century. Their presence is noted in a charter of 762 but the invading Danes probably put an end to this chapter in Muchelney's history. In the middle of the tenth century the Abbey was refounded by Athelstan as an act of repentence for having executed his brother, Edwin, on the groundless suspicion that Edwin was plotting to murder him.

Muchelney has always been overshadowed by Glastonbury, but in some ways it has more to show. Two of its monastic buildings are in relatively good condition, the abbot's house and the priest's house, and a Saxon church has been discovered under the Norman chancel. The monastic buildings contain what must be one of the largest surviving fireplaces in the country; it measures 17ft.

At the time of the Domesday survey Muchelney had an acre of vineyard and two fisheries which yielded 6,000 eels a year. Before the Dissolution the Abbey revenues increased greatly from £97 in 1444 to £447 in 1534. Little is known of the monks who served here down the centuries, but a diverting tale of one of them is worth mentioning for the sake of the gleam of humour which extenuates his reprehensible career. He was a local man, from Cathanger, which is near Fivehead. His name was John Walshe and he became a monk in the reign of Henry VII until he was degraded from his order and dismissed from the Abbey for an act of rape; whereupon the injured lady married dear John, and the naughty couple named their child — Lucrece!

Henry VIII disposed of the Abbey by giving it to the Earl of Hertford. By 1630 it had passed to a family named Banbury, and from 1735 to 1839 it was in the hands of the Stuckey family, prominent bankers in Langport. Prior to 1900 the occupier was a farmer named Westlake, and the buildings had fallen to meaner uses as labourer's cottages and cider store before the Office of Works took charge of them. The spoliation of four centuries has left its mark on a number of buildings in the vicinity; for example, on a fine old barn at Kingsbury Episcopi I came across three lions' heads and the mask of a man which had come originally from the ruins of Muchelney.

It was 1930 when the Office of Works took possession. The cloisters were then in use as a cider house, and the great casks — 'the largest casks in the country'— had to be sawn up before they could be got out. Muchelney church, which adjoins the Abbey grounds, adds a charming postscript to the majestic ruins. Its altar steps are tiled with thirteenth-century tiles salvaged from the Abbey when it was excavated in 1873, and it has the most gaily painted roof I have ever seen. Every inch is covered with billowing clouds, blue skies, deliciously feminine angels and gilded stars stuck on like beauty patches. The whole thing might have been commissioned by a Jacobean cabaret impresario: the angels with their heynonny costumes and carefree bosoms look like saucy maids of honour playing charades.

Langport, which lies a couple of miles to the north of Muchelney, is surely entitled to be called the capital of Sedgemoor. Bridgwater has always looked to the seaward; its horizon is wider. In Langport you are conscious of little else beside the Parret and the moors. Modern transport has undoubtedly stripped it of some of its ancient functions and transferred them to Bridgwater, to Taunton, even to Bristol, but the little town still has an air of dignity and a self-contained life of its own. This is not the common insipid urban generalisation that so many towns have become. Langport retains much of the traditional flavour of the moors, of moorland speech and customs and crops. If you look up the length of Langport's main thoroughfare, Bow Street, you may notice that the buildings tend to lean slightly backwards. Bow Street is built on brick arches which support the fronts of the buildings, but in the rear they settle into the softer ground. The street has a mellow appearance, with pleasant old houses of weathered brick, some colour-washed cream or white; occasionally there is a front of lias stone and here and there a mullioned window in the stone of Ham Hill, softly golden or — as Thomas Hardy described it — 'snuff-coloured'. Most of the buildings seem to have been built in the period of Langport's prosperity between 1750 and 1850.

Before the Parret was deepened in 1840 it could be forded at Langport, and the strategic value of this river crossing presumably accounts for the early settlement of a town here. Langport was already a place of consequence in Saxon times and included a royal mint among its amenities. Coins minted at Langport have been found dating from the reigns of Athelstan, Canute, Hardi-canute and Edward the Confessor. The town was a royal borough until Henry II gave it to Sir Richard Rivel, a Sheriff of Devon and Cornwall, who died between 1211 and 1213 and was subsequently buried at Muchelney. About a century later Langport acquired its famous Great Bow, a bridge of nine stone arches which survived until 1840 when it had to yield to the navigation company that at the same time deepened the river to accommodate Langport's growing waterborne trade.

The town of Langport was strictly the area inside the old wall or stockade. The wall has now vanished, but the old east gate survives in the form of the unusual 'Hanging Chapel' which was built on top of the gate in 1353. The common belief that the chapel derives its name in some way from the executions of the Bloody Assize is quite false. The hanging chapel is so called for the dazzlingly simple reason that it hangs in the air instead of standing upon the ground. Originally it was a Merchant Guild chapel, after the Reformation it became the Town Hall, and it is now a Masonic Lodge.

In course of time Langport has spilled over its walls into the parish of Huish Episcopi, which is a sort of Langport Without. The two parishes seem to be inextricably mixed and there is a local saying that you cannot get out of Langport without passing through Huish. The proximity of the two parish churches led to a dangerous moment when the Reformation commissioners ruled that 'one of these two churches may well be spared and taken down for they stand within a bird-bolt shot together'. All Saints, Langport, is not a very exciting building, it is true, but it holds one of the county's art treasures in the superb glass of its Perpendicular east window. Incidentally the window displays some unusual figures, including St Joseph of Arimathea, carrying the two famous cruets, and two female Saxon saints, Etheldreda and Osyth or Sitha. Huish Episcopi church is rightly esteemed as one of the finest in the characteristic county style, with its beautifully proportioned and decorated west tower. It is a wonderfully satisfying experience to stand outside the church and let your attention move slowly up the tower to the topmost pinnacle. And to avoid the disappointment of a shattering anticlimax, it is as well to stay outside, except for the purpose of devotion and worship.

Fortunately neither church had to be spared, probably because no one made a good enough bid for the stone of the fabric, and they remain 'within a bird-bolt shot' of each other. There must have been other moments of anxiety, though, during the troubled years of the seventeenth century. In 1645 Langport was a key-point in Goring's attempt to stand on a line from Bridgwater to Sherborne; but the Royalist defence of Langport, under the command of Sir Francis Mackworth, was a confused and irresolute affair and the best the Cavaliers could do was to set fire to the town as they fled from the Roundheads. The coming of the Protectorate brought fresh worries to the local vicar — who bore, incidentally, the resounding name of Cananuel Bernard. He was turned out of Langport and went to Pitney, where he showed his spirit by defiantly holding services there. With a bland disregard of Puritan authority, Cananuel married and baptised people from eighty-five parishes, who journeyed to Pitney for the purpose. The fact that the baptised included the twentieth child that Cananuel had had the satisfaction of fathering confirms one's impression that this was a redoubtable man.

But the most illustrious name in Langport history is that of Walter Bagehot, doubly distinguished as an economist and as a man of letters. If we try to find his like in our own century we must perhaps describe Bagehot as the Maynard Keynes of the Victorian Age. He was born at Langport in 1826 and attended Langport Grammar School. Some verses he wrote when he was fourteen have been preserved; they refer to the school's Shrove Tuesday custom of egg-shackling. Each boy wrote his name on an egg, and the eggs were then shaken in a sieve until only one remained uncracked. The owner of that one was crowned and chaired as the winner. The rest had to write some appropriate verses in order to gain a half-holiday. Young Bagehot's egg must have smashed, for he set to and composed these lines:

> Shrove Tuesday is a happy day
> For all the boys to go and play.
> By ancient custom good,
> We shackled eggs and broke them too;

Each face with sparkling eyes then smiled,
In hope of proving Fortune's child:
And when the victor's name was known,
Around his brow we placed his crown;
And far abroad we spread his fame,
With long loud shouts his joy proclaim.

The Bagehots in alliance with the Stuckeys dominated the trade of Langport for a century and a half, from the middle of the eighteenth century. Their prosperity was founded on waterborne trade and later developed in the field of banking. In 1866 the firm had £100,000 invested in shipping, and owned two dozen East Indiamen and nineteen river barges. Before the coming of the railway a score of ships' captains lived in Langport. These are indeed facts to ponder when you see the rotting remnants of the wharves and quays of this now derelict port.

After completing his education at London University and being called to the Bar, Bagehot returned to Langport and entered the family business; but in 1858 he married the daughter of the founder of *The Economist* and two years later he became its editor, a post which he held until his death. To forsake the family counting-house must have seemed an adventurous decision at the time; but it is *The Economist* which survives, while Stuckey's Bank disappeared in an amalgamation with Parr's in 1909, and nobody in Somerset now looks scornfully at a Bank of England note and says — as they used to do — 'Gi'e I a Stuckey instead.'

CHAPTER TWENTY

WEDMORE AND THE VALE OF AVALON

The pleasures and amusement of Someset folk in the last century were in some ways very different from those of today. One popular country sport which has quite disappeared is recalled in an advertisement which appeared originally in 1768:

> On June 16 a purse of two guineas will be played for at sword and dagger, and on June 17 will be backsword play for one guinea, and in the afternoon play with sword and dagger for one guinea more. Suitable encouragement will be given to compleat gamesters. Dinner on the table one o'clock each day. At the White Horse, Langport.

The backsword was of wood, and the contest was decided as soon as blood was drawn. I have talked with old men who can just recall backsword contests at village revels, so the sport must have survived until the eighties of last century. Two of Somerset's greatest exponents were brothers, by the name of Wall, who were natives of Wedmore. Victory seems to have been a custom with them: at any rate they built a house with their winnings. And when the backsword went out of vogue the Walls of Wedmore continued to distinguish themselves in a way more familiar to us; they fielded a complete cricket team of members of the Wall family.

Wedmore stands on its own 'island', close to the southern border of Mendip. This wavering ridge of higher land is cut off from the hills west of Wookey by the Panborough Gap, and its other extremity looks towards a union with the Mendip Hills near Axbridge but is held off by the river Axe and its tributary Yeo. Thus surrounded on all sides by the moors, Wedmore is the capital centre of the little group of villages and hamlets which cluster about it. It must early have gained an importance as a centre of communication for traffic passing north of the peat moors along the line of Mark Causeway, but the town itself is a reticent and elusive place, as secret as a maze, hidden among trees and winding roads. I call it a town where I should perhaps say a village; but Wedmore is one of those ambiguous places which seem too big to be the one and not quite big enough to be the other.

Wedmore church, with its compact and sturdy central tower, has a four-square masculine presence — like Winchester Cathedral reduced to a parochial scale. It is altogether more severe and massive than the later Perpendicular west towers of the county with their lighter and more genial mood, the softer graces of their embellishments and the more sanguine warmth that the Ham Hill stone brought to its marriage with the blue lias. From its comparatively lofty situation Wedmore seems to issue a challenge to North Curry for the title of 'Cathedral of the Moors'. Without denying the loveliness of North Curry, I think Wedmore would bear the title more fittingly. It has the pervasive air of dignity, unsoftened by any homely touch, which one expects in a cathedral; and in a poorer countryside, which lacked a Wells and had never seen a Glastonbury, it would be treated as such.

An unusual feature of the church is a mural of St Christopher above the pulpit; there seem to be at least three different versions of this mural, painted one on top of the other. In addition to the central figures of the saint and the infant Jesus there are three ships, a mermaid and groups of fish at the foot of the design. The mermaid has in one hand what might be a tambourine and in the other what appears to be some other kind of musical instrument. Behind the present painting you may see a second head of Jesus and the ghostly forms of two larger fish. And then in one corner is an elderly man in a building, holding out with both hands something which might be a lantern.

What it all means, and how and when the different versions were laid on each other, is a problem — but it is a striking and fascinating sight to see, and its air of mystery heightens its charm. Fish, mermaid and ships combine to stir in one's mind the recollection that the church stands on what is still called the Isle of Wedmore. In the centuries since it was built the parishioners of Wedmore have watched the sea flow past their island, inundating the low moors as far as Glastonbury, and many a local traveller must have offered a more than perfunctory prayer to St Christopher. Even within living memory the marooned inhabitants of the moors have taken to their boats and rowed to Wedmore's temporary shore to collect their groceries.

The mural was discovered in 1880, when the church was restored, and the vicar of the time estimated that the third and latest version was painted in about 1520 and that the second was sixty years older. This vicar, S. H. A. Hervey, who was a son of the Bishop of Wells, published for a time a remarkable work called *The Wedmore Chronicle* into which he poured his many enthusiasms. He made a collection of local field names and found such treasures as Whore Acre, Tumbledown Dick's, Lousy Bush, Flaxland, Bove Scrubbett and Cutdown Bacon. And he celebrated the millennium of King Alfred's Peace of Wedmore by excavating the traditional site of Alfred's Palace, which is about halfway up Mudgeley Hill in a field called, significantly, Court Garden. Finds of pottery and foundations indicated, not a Saxon palace, but a medieval building, which he dated at about 1100. Mudgeley had belonged in the past to the Bishop of Wells, and a will dated 1340 had been proved at Mudgeley in 1342 'in the house of the Lord Dean of Wells'. Presumably it was this house which Mr Hervey's digging had uncovered.

But here is the interesting point. An old man told Mr Hervey that the 'great house' had belonged to a man who was 'not a king but just like a king'. Who could that be — Cromwell perhaps? No, we must look earlier than Cromwell to another 'protector': to be precise, we must look back to 1547, when Mudgeley passed from the care of Wells to the Duke of Somerset. Could there be a better description of Protector Somerset than these words uttered more than three centuries later? 'Not a king but just like a king.' No wonder they say memories are long here.

A present-day reader of *The Wedmore Chronicle* can hardly fail to warm to Mr Hervey, for he typifies so much that English rural life owes to the best of its clergy. Besides performing his priestly duties he not only cherished the history and antiquities of his parish but succeeded in heading the village batting averages and also fought for political tolerance in a notoriously Tory strong-hold where — if rumour is to be believed — one Liberal voter was upended in a barrel and drowned. Mr Hervey published his view that 'if the Liberal agent comes into Wedmore, he is liable to be insulted and assaulted': after which, not to be daunted, he made it his practice to accompany nervous Liberals to the polling-booth, establishing their right to vote and deterring any interference by conspicuously carrying a brace of pistols. He was also a keen defender of the racy vigour of local speech. The Inspector who visited Wedmore's three Board schools must have been astonished by the comments on his report that Mr Hervey published:

> One very satisfactory part of the Report says, — 'The higher standards were again very weak in parsing and analysis.' I read that with great joy. Considering how short is the time that children spend at school, and how many interesting and useful things there are to be learnt, I marvel how anyone can order several hours to be spent every week in learning such a thing as Grammar. Grammar does not need to be taught. It will come. As much as is wanted will come. Let children use the words that they hear their fathers use (except the bad ones), and put them in the way that they hear their fathers put them in, and that will do. When they have got anything to say, let them put it short, and put it plain, and put it true, and then the grammar will be right enough.

Education had earlier been a thorny subject in Wedmore. A free school was established there at some time before 1707, but darkness had again descended when Hannah More began her famous mission to north Somerset. The school she opened in Wedmore excited local opposition, and the Vestry appealed to the Dean of Wells to close it 'as having in our opinion the doubtful, if not dangerous, tendency to Innovation'. This was in 1799, and the Vestry's mistrust of Innovation was still flourishing when Sir Robert Peel founded the police force. In 1839 Wedmore resolved bluntly that 'no police are wanted for this parish'. After all, there were other and more satisfactory ways of dealing with intruding Liberal agents.

At the top of Mudgeley Hill, on the edge of the Isle of Wedmore, you are about 200ft up , and as you come over that crest the whole moorland scene opens dramatically before you. Down below lies another world. One Wedmore man put it in these words: 'Out on the black dirt there's what the Book says, creeping things innumerable.' And that is in its way true of this all but amphibious scene where all forms of life keep close to the earth. Your eye is held at ground level more than in any other sort of country. If you are unaccustomed to this kind of scene you will keep making exciting discoveries of your own. Water-violets (or Featherfoil) lift their leafless stalks from the water of the rhines and unfold clusters of pale mauve and white flowers with a golden star in the centre. Beneath the water they have a great mass of herbage like sodden feathers, and this is somehow typical of the beauty of the moors — this rank, abundant underwater life of the plant, and then the pale, delicately virginal uplifted flower rising from the water. In a variety of ways the water-logged, sullen blackness of the moor throws up sudden piercing touches of exquisite colour.

The rhines in particular are unfailingly exciting to explore, especially when they bear the gay colours of amphibious buck-wheat or flowering rush or arrow-heads, which the moor people call adders' tongues. Incidentally some of the local names are nicely expressive. Round-leafed pond weed, for example, is 'shillings and sixpences'. The great tit, which commonly bears the nickname of 'knife-grinder', is here called 'saw-whetter'. One or two other bird names are perhaps worth mentioning: a redwing is a 'windle', a mistlethrush is a 'squab-t'rush', and a woodpigeon is a ''ood-quist'.

A comparatively rare plant that is fairly abundant on the peat is bog myrtle. This little shrub has a variety of other names — Sweet Gale and Dutch Myrtle and, pleasantest of all, Candleberry Myrtle. The cone-like berries are indeed well described as tiny red candles. Possibly another reason for the name, and a more practical one, is that the catkin, when boiled in water, throws up a waxy scum from which candles can be made — or so Collinson says. Bog myrtle was also used for dyeing wool yellow, for tanning calfskins and as a fodder for horses and goats. It would be a most estimable plant even if its uses ended there, but William Turner writes in his Herbal of 1568 that it is good to be put in beer (as a substitute for hops), 'both by me and by diverse other in Summersetshyre'. And a perfume has been prepared from it by an industrial research chemist of my acquaintance, who has also found 152 plants of medicinal value on the moors of Avalon.

Certain areas have an outstanding botanical interest and are protected where possibly by the Nature Conservancy or the Somerset Trust for Nature Conservation. Catcott Heath, Westhay Moor and Shapwick Heath are important in this way. Brown beak sedge, saprophytic liverwort, great sundew and marsh pea are among the rarities for which some degree of protection is necessary. The Nature Conservancy reserve on Shapwick Heath is also a valuable breeding ground for such birds as nightingale, willow-tit, grasshopper-warbler and nightjar. In a larger sense the peat moors have a European importance as one of the 'wetlands' designated by the International Union for the Conservation of Nature — a distinction that would have appealed to William Diaper who celebrated the wetness of Brent Marsh in a poem published in 1727.

> Tho' Venice boast, Brent is as famed a seat,
> For here we live in seas, and sail thro' every street;
> And this great priviledge we farther gain,
> We never are oblig'd to pray for rain.

Diaper was born in Bridgwater in 1685, ordained at Wells in 1709 and for a time served as a curate at Brent. Dean Swift thought well of Diaper's poetry and tried to help him. In the course of the poem entitled *Brent* Diaper makes an interesting reference to the great break-in by the sea in 1703:

> Not only rain from bounteous heaven descends,
> But th' Ocean with an after-flood befriends;
> For nature this as a reliefe designs
> To salt the stinking water of the rines;
> As when of late enraged Neptune sware
> Brent was his own, part of his lawfull share;
> He said, and held his trident o're the plain,
> And soon the waves assert their antient claim,
> They scorn the shore, and o're the marshes sound,
> And mudwall cotts are levell'd with the ground.

The fact that Diaper rhymes 'rines' with 'designs' seems to bear on the familiar argument about the correct pronunciation of the word. But the balance is swiftly redressed by a note in the 1754 edition which explains that rines are 'Wide Ditches of Water, which separate the Fields or Moors from each other, and are called Rheens'. In the eighteenth century as in the twentieth both pronunciations were commonly used. The reference to 'mudwall cotts' is a reminder of the hard and primitive conditions of the poorer moorland families. Writing in the 1830s Stradling observed that 'it is not uncommon at the present day to see walls of decent cottages in the moor built of brocks of turf plastered with clay, with the assistance of a framework of wood'. And I recall a peat-cutter at Catcott who described the dwellings of 'the old people' (presumably in his parents' or grandparents' time, therefore) as single-storey mud houses, with walls of mud and reeds.

The savage hardships that could accompany such conditions are illustrated vividly in Richard Warner's account of a native of Huntspill, Johanna Martin, whom he encountered by chance in 1799. She was travelling in a cart drawn by a small pony 'not much larger than a stout Newfoundland dog' and she told Warner that she was an illegitimate child, born and bred in the village workhouse and sent into domestic service at the age of twelve. She married a labourer and, in her own phrase, 'took terribly to breeding', having seven children in seven years. Her husband then died and as no parish relief was forthcoming she determined to support the family by her own efforts. She described how she had 'risen daily at two o'clock in the morning, done what was needful for the children, gone eight and ten miles on foot to a market with a large basket of pottery-ware on my head, sold it, and returned again with the profits before noon'.

By this means she accumulated savings of a guinea and a half and, as she was compelled to quit her cottage, she decided to build one and engaged a local man to help her. Inevitably, while she was at market, the man took her savings and decamped with some of the timber as well. In the face of this misfortune Johanna decided to work harder than ever and finish the building herself. 'To be sure,' she said, 'the children and I were obliged to sleep for several weeks in the shell of the Tenement, with no other covering [for it was not roofed] than a dew-board; but 'twas summertime, and for the matter of that, we were warm enough, for all six slept in one bed.'

CHAPTER TWENTY-ONE

TODAY AND TOMORROW

The quarter of a century of social and industrial change that I have tried to describe has in some ways settled into the stability of new forms, but the impetus is certainly not spent. The transforming forces that bear on Avalon and Sedgemoor are much the same as those that operate elsewhere in England. Motorways, nuclear power-stations, multiple-stores and light industry are not local phenomena but the increasingly familiar features of a generalised way of life that requires no organic relationship with the natural endowment of a particular stretch of country. That kind of pressure towards conformity and standardisation shows no sign of relaxing and it must menace everything that is distinctive, idiosyncratic, specific. If the 'spirit of place' has a value is has never more sorely needed defenders.

To prophesy is to court ridicule but one can at least recognise some of the major physical factors that will influence the end of the last century of this second millenium. The long struggle to control the floodwaters will have overcome the perils and discomforts and inconveniences of the past, and they will gradually fade into distant memories. The M5 will open up the rural areas in the same way that the canals and the railways did in their day. The exhaustion of the peat deposits will present a challenge in landscape planning. Conventional methods of agriculture, no longer hampered by flooding, will find it easier to enter the traditional centres of specialised crops like withies. Mechanisation, bringing a welcome relief from the hardest forms of labour, will also drive its own bargain with such familiar sights as the rows of willows that line the rhines — and in so doing obstruct the operation of the mechanical excavator. Some things that we cherish will undoubtedly disappear. But so many changes and alterations have already marked and moulded this scene that we can take some comfort from the knowledge that opportunities often come as the companions of change.

There is at least one such opportunity already being canvassed. As the extraction of peat is completed the owners are prepared to offer the derelict land to the River Authority for a nominal sum. One such sale, of 117 acres at £10 per acre, has already been negotiated and it inaugurates what is known as the Kelting Plan for the Avalon Lakes. The ultimate intention is to have a group of ten lakes covering 2,000 acres in the Vale of Avalon, thereby converting the abandoned peat-workings into wildlife habitats and amenity areas for sailing and fishing. The lakes would also have a practical value for the River Authority in terms of water-storage and irrigation. It is an imaginative but realistic scheme which will perpetuate the traditional role of this area as an important European 'wetland' within the framework of wildlife conservation. The old railway from Edington to Sharpham has also been bought by the River Authority to provide eight miles of footpath and bridle-path in the projected lake-complex. It may be too much to hope for a return, after 2,000 years, of the pelicans the lake villagers knew; but the Kelting Plan certainly offers a valuable extra insurance for the species we have today.

This kind of ingenuity in reshaping the land and controlling and deploying water points to a continuity that links the Avalon Lakes with the Huntspill river, the King's Sedgemoor Drain and the Pillrow Cut. It is a continuity that promotes the hope of a Somerset countryside in which the traditional values may be transformed but not lost. In looking for evidence of that continuity it may not be entirely fanciful to suppose that when Alfred's men built their causeway from Athelney to Burrow Mump, and when the engineers of the ecclesiastical landlords constructed the Greylake Fosse, they were adventuring into the same technological problems that today engage the motorway builders. The soft yielding subsoil makes a timeless challenge to all comers, whether the subject for construction is a road, a railway, a canal or a motorway.

For the builders of the M5, easing their burden on to 90ft of silt, the problem was to estimate and allow for the extent of subsidence under the weight of their material. In general a sinking of 3ft in the course of fifty years had to be envisaged. The way of dealing with this problem was to overload temporarily with a 'surcharge' of as much as 10ft of additional material so as to achieve most of the subsidence during the period of construction, leaving a safe margin of about 6in during the first fifty years of the motorway's life. Trial embankments were constructed at Clevedon and East Brent and experiments showed the need for a light-weight material to form the base of the motorway. A ribbon of black coal-ash threading its way across the moors was the outcome, a pulverised waste from the Aberthaw Power Station with a weight only one-third that of quarry waste. To transport the ash from Wales meant building special sidings for the railway to handle it. After it was unloaded and compacted it was covered with a layer of top-soil and sown with grass which helped to stabilise it.

The M5 is merging into the landscape, like the Huntspill river over which it strides, and the story of its making will be forgotten. Down its highway will come a growing multitude of visitors — many of them hurrying through Avalon and Sedgemoor without seeing more than the motorway verges. But others will turn aside to explore the historic scenes, the legendary places and the serene beauty of the moors. I hope they will be as richly rewarded in their generations as I have been in mine.

BIBLIOGRAPHY

History and Antiquity
Alcock, Leslie. *Arthur's Britain*
Ashe, G. (ed.). *The Quest for Arthur's Britain*
Ashe, G. *From Caesar to Arthur*
Avery, Michael. *Excavations at Mere East*, 1966 (Proc Som Arch)
Bazell, C. *The Edington Campaign, AD 878*
Bulleid, A. *Ancient Trackway in Meare Heath* (Proc Som Arch)
Chadwick, J. M. *About Athelney and Burrow Bridge*
Chambers, E. K. *Arthur of Britain*
Clark, Grahame. *Prehistoric England*
Collinson, John. *History of Somerset*
Cornish, Vaughan. *Historic Thorn Trees*
Darby, H. C. and Finn, R. W. (eds). *Domesday Geography of S.W. England*
Dickinson, W. Howslip. *King Arthur in Cornwall*
Dilks, T. Bruce. *The Story of St Mary's Church, Bridgwater*
Dobson, D. P. *The Archaeology of Somerset*
Earle, John. *The Alfred Jewel*
Finberg, H. P. R. *Lucerna*
Giles, J. (ed). *Gildas: Liber de Excidio et Conquestu Britanniae*
Godwin, H. *Studies of the Post-Glacial History of British Vegetation* (Phil Trans Roy Soc)
Gray, H. St George. *Excavations at Burrow Mump* (Proc Som Arch)
Greswell, W. H. P. *Chapters on the Early History of Glastonbury Abbey*
Greswell, W. H. P. *Dumnonia and the Valley of the Parret*
Harford, Charles Joseph. *Antiquities in Somersetshire*
Hayward, F. H. *Alfred the Great*
Hill, O'Dell Travers. *English Monasticism*
Hole, Christina. *English Folk Heroes*
Jarman, S. G. *History of Bridgwater*

Jeboult, E. *History of West Somerset*
Little, Bryan. *The Monmouth Episode.*
Major, Albany. *Early Wars of Wessex*
Olivey, H. P. *Notes on North Curry, Stoke St Gregory and West Hatch*
Phelps, W. *History of Somerset*
Powell, Arthur H. *Bridgwater in the Later Days*
Radford, C. A. R. *Glastonbury Abbey*
Robinson, J. Armitage. *Two Glastonbury Legends*
Ross, D. M. *Langport and Its Church*
Stenton, F. M. *Anglo-Saxon England*
Stevenson, W. H. (ed). *Asser's Life of King Alfred*
Stokes, H. F. Scott. *Glastonbury Abbey before the Conquest*
Stokes, H. F. Scott. *Glastonbury Abbey during the Crusades*
Stradling, William. *The Priory of Chilton Polden*
Tratman, E. K. *The Glastonbury Lake Village; A Reconsideration* (Proc Univ
    Bristol Spelaeological Soc)
Wedmore Council School. *Wedmore through the Ages*
Williams, Patrie. *Alfred of Wessex*
Willis, R. *Architectural History of Glastonbury Abbey*

Flora and Fauna
Palmer, E. M. and Ballance, D. K. *The Birds of Somerset*
White, J. W. *The Bristol Flora*
Somerset Trust for Nature Conservation *Newsletters and Reports*

Topography and Travels
Beaumont, George and Disney, Capt Henry. *A New Tour Thro' England,
    perform'd in the Summers of 1765/6/7*
Cartwright, J. J. (ed). *The Travels through England of Dr Richard Pococke*
Cole, Sandford D. *The Sea Walls of the Severn*
Defoe, Daniel. *Tour of England and Wales*
Harris, L. E. *Vermuyden and the Fens*
Horne, Dom Ethelbert. *Someset Holy Wells*
Knight, F. A. *Seaboard of Mendip*
Legg, L. G. W. (ed). *A Relation of a Short Survey of the Western Counties, by
    Lieutenant Hammond*
Morris, Christopher (ed). *The Journeys of Celia Fiennes*
Phelps, W. *On the Formation of Peat Bogs from the Bristol Channel into
    Somerset* (Proc Som Arch)
Richardson, L. *The Wells and Springs of Somerset*
Rutter, John. *Delineations of the North Western Division of the County of
    Somerset*
Shaw, S. *A Tour to the West of England in 1788*
Skrine, Henry. *The Rivers of Note in Great Britain*
Steers, J. A. *The Coastline of England and Wales*

Warner, Richard. *A Walk through some of the Western Counties of England*
Williams, Michael. *The Draining of the Somerset Levels*

Agriculture, Trade and Transport
Atthill, Robin. *The Somerset and Dorset Railway*
Billingsley, John. *A General View of the Agriculture of the County of Somerset*
Cheke, Val. *The Story of Cheesemaking in Britain*
Dale, R. W. *Peat in Central Somerset*: a planning study
Hadfield, Charles. *British Canals*
Hadfield, Charles. *Canals of South-West England*
Hudson, Kenneth. *Towards Precision Shoemaking*
Porter, Edmund. *Bridgwater Industries, Past and Present*
Smith, R. Trow. *A History of British Livestock Husbandry up to 1700*
Thomas, David St John. *Regional History of the Railways of Great Britain*
Twamley, J. *Dairying Exemplified, or the Business of Cheesemaking*

General
Allen, Frank. *The Great Church Towers of Somerset*
Aubrey, John. *The Natural History of Wiltshire*
Barrett, C. R. B. *Somersetshire*
Diaper, William. *The Complete Works*
Foord, Edward. *Wells, Glastonbury and Cleeve*
Fraser, Maxwell. *Companion into Somerset*
Fuller, Thomas. *The Worthies of England*
Hervey, S. H. A. *The Wedmore Chronicle*
Lawrence, Berta. *A Somerset Journal*
Pevsner, Nikolaus. *The Buildings of England: South and West Somerset*
Phillips, John. *Collected Poems*
Smith, E. H. *Happy Memories of West Somerset*
Wade, G. W. and J. W. *Somerset*
Warner, Sylvia Townsend. *Vision of England: Somerset*
Wickham, A. K. *Churches of Somerset*
Wolff, Joseph. *Travels and Adventures*

INDEX